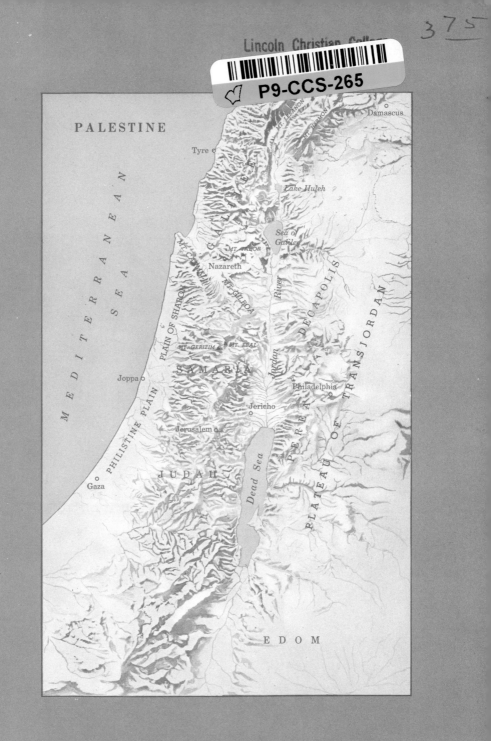

PALESTINE

Damascus

MT. LEBANON
MT. HERMON

Tyre

Lake Huleh

GALILEE

Sea of
Galilee

MT. TABOR

Nazareth

MT. CARMEL

MT. GILBOA

River

DECAPOLIS

Jordan

PLAIN OF SHARON

MT. GERIZIM   MT. EBAL

SAMARIA

Joppa

Jordan

Philadelphia

PEREA

PLATEAU OF TRANSJORDAN

MEDITERRANEAN SEA

Jericho

PHILISTINE PLAIN

Jerusalem

Dead Sea

JUDAH

Gaza

EDOM

A Historical Approach
to the
New Testament

Harper & Brothers, Publishers, New York

A Historical Approach
to the
New Testament

Frederic R. Crownfield

PROFESSOR OF BIBLICAL LITERATURE AND RELIGION

GUILFORD COLLEGE

A HISTORICAL APPROACH TO THE NEW TESTAMENT
Copyright © 1960 by Frederic R. Crownfield

L-K

Library of Congress catalog card number: 60–15344

Contents

vi   *Contents*

Illustrations

Maps

Maps, except for the cross section at Jerusalem, are based on the *Westminster Historical Atlas,* Revised Edition, edited by G. E. Wright and F. V. Filson, Westminster Press, 1956. The cross section is re-drawn from G. A. Smith, *Historical Geography of the Holy Land,* 20th edition, Hodder and Stoughton, n.d.

Preface

THIS BOOK has developed out of a required course in the New Testament given to undergraduates. That has determined its nature and scope. It does not presuppose the intellectual maturity or the type of interest which can reasonably be assumed in courses which are part of the technical education of the minister. It attempts to acquaint the college student with the methods by which the New Testament is studied by scholars, some of the problems which challenge them, and a body of conclusions which would be widely accepted, though the fact must not be concealed that on any specific point it will be possible to find influential dissenters even among those committed to the historical approach. Considerable attention has been given to the background in thought and culture. But the main emphasis is intended to be on what the authors of the various parts of the New Testament were trying to say.

The book is not, of course, intended as a substitute for reading the New Testament itself. But as Dr. Johnson is said to have remarked, the New Testament is a very difficult book, and to set the student to reading it without guidance may be edifying, but it is almost certain to produce more darkness than light.

The translation of the Bible is generally from the Revised Standard Version. The use of other translations has been indicated.

The "Suggestions for Reading" are offered in the belief that the books mentioned will be useful to those who wish to pursue a subject further or get a different view. They do not provide a systematic bibliography, nor are they to be taken as a list of works consulted, if for no other reason than that the list has been deliberately limited to books in English.

One of the happy conventions with regard to prefaces is that they afford an opportunity for an author to express his gratitude and appreciation for the help of those without whose interest he would not have been able to complete his task.

First, I would thank the members of the library staff of Guilford College: Treva Mathis, Mildred Farrow, Gay Spivey, and Eleanor Bailey, for their continued concern and assistance. To my colleagues, Dr. E. Daryl Kent and Dr. J. Floyd Moore, I am grateful for encouragement and suggestions as they have tried out earlier versions on their classes. I am also indebted to Dr. Moore for assistance with the proofreading and for making, with the help of Abigail Moore, the index.

The large debt I already owe Henry J. Cadbury, not only as a scholar but as a friend and Friend, has been greatly increased by his willingness to read and criticise my manuscript. Of course, he is not to blame for the shortcomings which remain.

My wife Margaret, by her skill with the typewriter and her watchful eye, and especially by her constant interest and encouragement, has played an indispensable role in the production of this book.

FREDERIC R. CROWNFIELD

Guilford College
August 9, 1960

PART I

Introduction

CHAPTER 1

What Is the New Testament?

THE NEW TESTAMENT consists of twenty-seven short books written in Greek between about A.D. 50 and A.D. 150 by the followers of Jesus of Nazareth, who was crucified about A.D. 30.

They consist of four *Gospels* which tell what Jesus meant to his followers; an account of the process by which these followers spread this message to the very heart of the Roman Empire, and of how in the process the center shifted from Jews to Gentiles; a series of letters by a gifted leader, Paul, to churches which he had founded, with one brief note to an individual; a number of more general treatises, sometimes in the form of letters; and a Revelation intended to strengthen resistance of the growing Church to persecution by the government. These books contain statements of faith; admonition and exhortation; matters of theology, moral conduct, worship, and the government of the Church.

In the early days the followers of Jesus did not depend on books for their knowledge of him. They did appeal to the Old Testament in justification of their belief that Jesus was the expected Messiah and in explanation of his unexpected death; but the leaders themselves had been with him during his life, and had been instructed by him and were the witnesses of his res-

3

urrection. Teaching and the guidance of the community were recognized as being under the immediate direction of the Holy Spirit. Jesus' return was expected at any moment. There was no need for new writings.

But as the movement grew beyond the possibility of personal contact with the companions of Jesus and the witnesses of his Resurrection, as enthusiasm cooled with the passage of time and the rise of a second generation, as new questions and problems arose and as, with delay, the expectation of the imminent return of Jesus became less vivid, books began to be written. When they were, it was not with any thought that they would eventually become part of Scripture, in supplement to the ancient Scriptures which Christians now call the Old Testament. It was only later, in response to further needs and problems, that they came to be recognized as a separate, definitely limited collection in addition to the Old Testament.

The designation of this collection of books as the *New Testament* or, as the Greek expression might better be translated, the *New Covenant*, reflects the belief that God had now fulfilled the prophecy found in Jeremiah: "Behold, the days are coming, says the Lord, when I will make a new covenant with the house of Israel and the house of Judah, not like the covenant which I made with their fathers when I took them by the hand to bring them out of the land of Egypt." (Jer. 31:31–32.) The term thus has a twofold significance. It reflects a sense of the continuity between Christianity and Judaism; and, at the same time, the conviction that in the life and teaching of Jesus of Nazareth and the events associated therewith, God had fulfilled his ancient promises and that, as a result, a new relation between man and God had become possible.

The purpose of the collection was thus not that of a modern scholar who might edit and publish a collection of sources for the history of an ancient religion—though it is true that the modern scholar who wants to investigate the history of the origins of Christianity will have to use these writings as his sources, and he will have to make use of the appropriate techniques in so doing. Those who made this selection of books from a number of others, some still preserved in whole or in part, did so not because they believed these were authentic records while other books were not, but because they believed that in a unique way these particular books were a definitive statement of their faith. Neither was this collection a symposium, arranged by some now-forgotten editor to contain contributions from all the prominent leaders of the Christian movement, with due care that all sides be fairly represented. How and why it came into being is the problem before us.

The writings which compose the New Testament were, from the first, highly valued by those to whom they were addressed; but as has been said, the belief that they together formed a single whole, equal in authority to the Jewish Scriptures which had been the Bible of Jesus and his earliest followers, came later. Actually, the recognition of just these books as representing a closed, sacred collection, of equal authority with the Old Testament, was reached about the end of the second century (even later in some places). The Latin writer Tertullian (about A.D. 200) was the first to use the expression *New Testament.*

We need now to distinguish two quite different things: the development of the concept of some set of writings as being the New Testament, and the process of selection by which it was determined just what writings belonged in the set.

THE CONCEPT OF A CANON

The technical word for the collection of books which was recognized as possessing unique value and authority is *canon.* Books in the collection are said to be *canonical.* Books excluded are *uncanonical.* Thus, as we shall see, there were a number of uncanonical Gospels. The process by which a specific book came to be recognized as belonging to the canon is called *canonization*. Without using this word for it, the earliest Christians had a canon of Scripture—which later they came to call the *Old Testament*. This was God's revelation to men. Christians approached these Scriptures from quite a different point of view from that of the Jews; but the basic notion, already reached in Judaism, that God had spoken to men through a set of writings which carried in some sense or other the full authority of God himself, was taken over with the books.

There were a number of reasons why eventually a second collection of sacred writings came to be recognized, to which an authority equal to that of the first was ascribed. Indeed, while it was never asserted in orthodox circles that the New Testament was superior in authority to the Old, in practice the Old Testament came to be interpreted regularly in the light of the New. This was made necessary by the belief that, although the Old Testament was not to be abandoned, the Law in some sense had been abolished. This made it necessary to have a supplement which made plain in what sense the older Scriptures were to be taken. Then, from the first, Jesus' words were considered to be of equal authority with the Jewish Scriptures. The earliest Christian writings—those of Paul—appeal occasionally to what Jesus said as authoritative. This, it must be remembered, was before any of our Gospels were written. When books containing the teachings of Jesus were composed, then those books were bound to be held in the highest regard. Equally important was the fact that they contained an account of his mighty works and the story of his death and Resurrection.

The case of the letters of Paul is somewhat different. These were written to different churches; and some unknown person, at some unknown date (perhaps about the year A.D. 100?) must have gathered them up and issued them as a whole, thus giving them a wider circulation. In this form they came to be referred to by various writers, not long after the beginning of the second century, as *Scripture*, although they do not seem at first to have been put quite on a par with the Gospels or the Old Testament. Eventually, they also, with other early books which were valued by the Church, came to enjoy the same authority as the original Old Testament Scriptures. In all such books the events they recounted were believed to have occurred as told, their injunctions were binding, and the promises they contained were believed to be God's own word to his people. They provided the Church with its message and with the weapons to combat opponents.

One important factor in the development of the concept of a canon was the practice of reading from some of the Church writings as a part of the service of worship. When and how this began we do not certainly know; but by the middle of the second century, the writer Justin, later martyred, writes in his "Apology": "On the day called Sunday there is a meeting in one place of those who live in cities or in the country, and the memoirs of the apostles or the writings of the prophets are read as long as time permits."[1] The "memoirs of the apostles" are certainly the Gospels, and the significant thing is that they are mentioned as though they were interchangeable with parts of the Old Testament. The books which were finally accepted as canonical are books which had made a place for themselves in the worship of the Church.

THE PROCESS OF SELECTION

The first person to put out a list of books intended to be recognized officially as Christian Scripture was a heretic named Marcion, who came to Rome about A.D. 140. Marcion was struck by the contrast between the loving God preached by Jesus and the God of the Old Testament. The latter appeared to Marcion as a cruel and arbitrary tyrant. So Marcion declared that Chris-

---

[1] Justin, "First Apology," E. R. Hardy (trans.), in *Early Christian Fathers*, Library of Christian Classics, Westminster Press, 1953, vol. I, p. 287.

tianity had nothing to do with the Old Testament. This was to be rejected completely. In place of it Marcion set up a list of writings to be recognized as Scripture by his followers. It contained a form of the Gospel of Luke and letters of Paul. He did not include Hebrews or the pastoral Epistles, and did not list Ephesians; but he did list a letter to the Laodiceans. Those listed and those alone, he thought, were the Scriptures which Christians should recognize in place of the Old Testament. The Church could not accept his rejection of the Old Testament, but it was forced to follow his example and define more carefully the list of books which it recognized as Scripture.

Another important influence in the development of the conception of the canon was the conflict in the latter part of the second century with a group of heretics known from the name of their leader, Montanus, as Montanists. In the early Christian congregations, as has been said, the Spirit had been accorded a central role. Leadership in the Church was by persons in whom the Spirit of God was manifested, rather than by elected or appointed officials. Worship as pictured in Paul's letter to Corinth was not according to a set liturgy, but under control of the Spirit to determine the order of events and the content of the messages. But as time passed, the vivid sense of dependence on the Spirit faded—no doubt in part because such a procedure was open to abuses which were soon only too obvious. When the Montanists attempted to revive this ancient attitude and claimed the inspiration of the Spirit for various extravagant assertions, the Church countered with assertions of the authority of the Christian Scriptures, which thus took on added prestige and, at the same time, came to be more sharply defined in such a way as to exclude any claims that the Spirit was still speaking directly to men.

A decisive element in this development of the New Testament canon was the combat during the second century with another party which had quite a different conception of the meaning of

Christianity from that which finally prevailed. Those who held this position were known as *Gnostics*.

The name *Gnostic* indicates that they claimed to have special *knowledge* of what Jesus really taught. Their views will be considered in some detail later. What made their position difficult to combat was the fact that they admitted that the ordinary Christian teaching was what Jesus and his disciples had taught publicly, some such doctrine being necessary to keep the common herd in order; but they asserted that their version of Christianity was what he really taught his close associates in private. Such claims were hard to refute, improbable as they may seem.

To combat them, the Church developed a threefold appeal to the standards set by the apostles. It was argued that if Jesus had given any private teaching it would have been to these apostles, and they in turn would have passed it on to those whom they left as successors in the great churches. Second, the creed held by these churches and the doctrines held by their leaders would show whether Jesus really taught what the Gnostics claimed. The third point in their appeal was to the writings of the apostles (or, in certain cases, such as the Gospels of Mark and Luke, to their close companions). This argument operated in such a fashion as to exclude from the list of accepted books any which could not thus claim apostolic authorship or association with the apostles.

It must be understood that the issue between the Church and the Gnostics was not simply a dispute over rival lists of books, each side rejecting *in toto* what the other claimed. The Gnostics also appealed to apostolic writings. What the Church did was to lay claim to all writings bearing apostolic names that it could use, and deny the claim of apostolic authorship to the rest. In some cases, probably, a process of "research" led to the conclusion that various books that were in common and valued use in the Church, without any attention previously having been paid to their authorship, were actually by apostles or "apostolic men." Books such as Clement's *Epistle* or Hermas' *Shepherd,* whose authors were well known as not belonging to the first generation, were rejected, although they were entirely orthodox in content and, at least in some sections of the Church, in general use. In addition to Paul's letters, including Hebrews and the pastoral Epistles which were ascribed to him, letters believed to be by Peter, James, Jude, and John were eventually recognized, as was the Revelation of John. Also recognized was the Acts of the Apostles, or, as it was frequently but hardly accurately called, "The Acts of *All* the Apostles." By this means the Church was able to assert against the heretics that it represented the consensus of apostolic teaching rather than a one-sided development of it.

From these circumstances under which the content of the canon was determined, certain important results for the conception of the nature of Scripture followed. Despite the diversity of the various writings, it was necessary to hold that they were completely in harmony with one another. This was possible only when the writings were looked on as a collection of independent statements, without regard to context or general background. It was necessarily assumed that the authority thus set up was adequate to deal with all problems which might arise. Since a great many points were not explicitly covered, it was necessary to develop methods for finding answers when they were not obvious. Here two devices were of great help. The first was unlimited combination of passages from the most diverse sources. This depended on the treatment of statements from various places as independent of context. Statements about faith from Hebrews could be combined with statements about faith in Galatians without the necessity of inquiring as to whether the word *faith* meant the same thing in the two cases. (Actually, it does not.) The most flexible device, however, for finding in Scripture whatever one wanted was allegory. In allegory the written words are taken as symbols of spiritual realities. Since there is no standard for matching words with their spiritual counterparts, anyone using the method is free to invent his own equivalents to suit his convenience. By the exercise of sufficient ingenuity, contradictions and absurdities can easily be removed. Meanings not present in Scripture may easily be read in. Tempting as this procedure is, there is no way of being assured that it gives anything but someone's fancy. Consequently, it is worthless as a means of discovering the meaning of Scripture, though some of the things which have been read in by this method have been interesting and valuable in their own right.

The first list which has come down to us, published under Church auspices, is a fragment from about A.D. 200, known as the Canon of Muratori, from the scholar who discovered it. It begins with a broken sentence which seems to refer to Mark, and goes on to mention Luke and John. Then come Acts and Paul's Epistles, with those of Jude and John. In addition to the Revelation of John, a "Revelation of Peter" is mentioned, though the author indicates that there is some hesitation, at least, about including the latter. Neither the Epistle of James, the Epistles of Peter, nor Hebrews is mentioned. These latter books were questioned in various sections of the Church for some time.

The first list identical with the list in present-day copies of the New Testament is found in a letter issued at Easter 367 by the great bishop Athanasius of Alexandria. After listing them he says: "These are the springs of salvation, so that he that is thirsty can fill himself with the [divine] responses in them; in these alone is the good news of the teaching of true religion proclaimed."[2] It does not follow that because the process of selection had resulted at Alexandria, by A.D. 367, in the list eventually accepted universally, that the same result was attained everywhere at the same time. In some places it may have been earlier. In others it was certainly later.

[2] Athanasius, "Festal Letter XXXIX," in A. Souter, *Text and Canon of the New Testament*, Scribner's, 1925, p. 215.

But however slow the process may have been in arriving at a uniform list acceptable to all everywhere, the main principle of selection, and the framework and nucleus of the actual final list, were arrived at by the end of the second century. Justin Martyr, about A.D. 150, puts only the Lord's words on a par with the Old Testament. Irenaeus, about A.D. 190, and Tertullian, A.D. 200, have the new conception of a closed canon, a New Testament alongside the Old, containing the widest possible selection of apostolic writers, all of equal authority and all equal in authority to what has now come to be called the Old Testament. By the end of the fourth century, the details of inclusion and exclusion were practically settled in final form.

****

CHAPTER 2

The Historical Approach to the New Testament

To ADOPT the historical approach to the New Testament is to use the methods historians commonly use in studying ancient documents in order to determine the meaning of the writers and the truth of reports as to what happened and what was said.

The general use of this method in New Testament study is less than a hundred years old, though its origins go back to the eighteenth century. There were two reasons for its adoption. In the first place, there was the desire to find some objective basis for settling the claims of different groups, each professing to represent the true teaching of the New Testament although the various interpretations were mutually exclusive. The proposal to study such matters historically is the proposal to deal with them by trying to discover the original context in which they arose. Can we find out, for example, what the letters of Paul meant to those who read them—not by inspired guesses which gain acceptance because they appeal to a particular temperament or some pet prejudice, but by research into the thought forms and mental habits of the age in which they were written? To the extent that historical research can find this, we have a basis for conclusions which can command the assent of all who would rather know the truth than hold on to preconceived ideas. It is true that there are many unsolved historical problems and that historians have prejudices too. But even with these limitations, historical study offers us our only chance of reaching results which have some claim to objective validity.

There is a tendency in some quarters today to darken counsel by attacking the quest for objectivity. By twisting the meaning of *objectivity* into an equivalent for *neutrality*, it is easy to show that no study is pursued without interest and therefore one cannot be neutral. But the search for objectivity is not a search without interest, but a search for what is there for everyone. A real chair is an object; and anyone who refuses to recognize its presence may get hurt, not to mention the fact that he is deprived of the comfort of sitting in it. There are historical facts which are simply there for everybody, whether they like them or not. Historical method is the process of determining what these are.

The second reason for making use of this approach is the conviction that matters of fact must be decided on the basis of evidence. If the evidence—and this means evidence which is there for everyone to see—does not substantiate an assertion, then we have no right to make it. The kind of "evidence" that appeals only to those who have already accepted the conclusion which it is supposed to support is not evidence.

This issue is only confused by an appeal to faith. Religion without faith is impossible, but religious faith is not a substitute for evidence when it comes to establishing matters of fact. Faith is a commitment of one's life based on a vision of the meaning of facts, but it cannot produce the facts out of itself.

SOURCES

Any account of past events is based on what the historian calls *sources*. If we are to know what went on in the past, we must establish some links between then and now. If the events are in the recent past, our own memories may provide the link. If they are farther away, there may be others older than we who still carry the events in their memories. But for happenings in the more remote past, we are dependent on records which testify as to what went on. Someone who saw and heard must have written what he thus knew, or have told someone who wrote, or passed it on by word of mouth until it reached someone who did write. For some purposes, material remains are an important source. Thus, the discovery of the ruins of a buried city, burned at a determinable date, would be an important source of information. A dated inscription may provide a fixed point on which a whole chronology depends. These by no means exhaust the possible sources, but in all cases what we need is a link with the past.

In the study of a given period, the historian's first problem is to assemble his sources. Sometimes he is so fortunate as to discover hitherto unknown materials. In the case of the events associated with the beginning of Christianity, the assembly of sources is a fairly simple task, since the sources are rather limited, being largely confined to the New Testament itself. A historian who undertook to write a history of World War II or some phase of it would have a very different task.

THE ESTABLISHMENT OF THE TEXT

Once the historian knows what his documentary sources are, he faces the problem of learning just what was originally written. Even modern printed materials contain misprints. Sometimes these can easily be corrected. In other cases one may suspect a misprint, or be sure that there was one, without being sure just how to emend it. In the case of materials coming down to us from the ancient world, like the Gospels, the difficulties are greatly increased because the original writings have perished and we are dependent on copies of copies of copies, with all the errors that this may involve. The process of forming a reasoned judgment, based on evidence, as to what the original author wrote is known as textual criticism.

THE PROBLEM OF INTERPRETATION

When we have determined what our authorities wrote, we have the problem of determining what they mean. If the documents are not in the historian's native language, this involves, first of all, translation. It seems to be taken for granted by beginners in the study of foreign languages that dictionary and grammar possess an absolute authority, quite as high as they would enjoy if given by divine inspiration. The student never stops to ask how the dictionary maker knows what to put down as the meaning of a word. The fact is that such things are learned in the same way we learn our native tongues—by observing how words are used in a meaningful context. The point is that linguistic knowledge is a growing knowledge, and the historian whose materials are written in an ancient language must keep abreast of linguistic studies. Thus the discovery of masses of papyrus fragments in the ancient dump heaps of Egypt toward the end of the last century has thrown a flood of light on the vocabulary and grammar of the New Testament. The first full-scale English lexicon of New Testament Greek which makes adequate use of this material was not published until 1957.

But the problem of interpretation is not simply a problem of translation. Even in a language we know, we often misunderstand or are misunderstood. It is easy to translate the Greek phrase, *basileia tōn ouranōn*, as *kingdom of Heaven*, but just what these words mean in the Gospels requires, as we shall see, arduous study. *Sōter*, translated *savior*, was widely used as a designation for the divinities of religions known as *Mysteries*. Did the New Testament writers who used the term use it with the connotations it had in the Mystery religions? The problem of determining the meaning of our sources is often a difficult one, but it cannot be avoided. It involves, eventually, a thorough knowledge of the physical, historical, cultural, and intellectual background out of which our documents come. This does not mean that the authors are limited to saying what everyone else was saying, but it does mean that what they said must be relevant to what was being said and intelligible to those who heard it. It is inexcusable provincialism to suppose that people in the ancient world saw everything just as we see it. If we would understand ancient documents, we must learn to see things through the eyes of the ancients. This is as true of the New Testament as of anything else.

THE EVALUATION OF THE SOURCES

After we have discovered our sources, and learned to translate and interpret them, there is still the problem of evaluating their testimony. First, we need to know as precisely as possible the relation of the author to the events or teaching he is telling us about. Who wrote the book? When? The testimony of an eyewitness, written immediately after he has seen and heard something, is more valuable than if he only writes it down a year or ten years or fifty years later. Where was the book written? What was the author's purpose and how did that influence his account?

We need to ask next whether the witness is able to tell the truth. Was he in direct contact with the situation he reports? If he was, was he really competent to form an opinion? Here again, we may often find that our test is too stringent for much of our material to pass with a high grade, so that all we can do is to state a conclusion and attach the appropriate degree of probability to it. If the result is disappointing, we will simply have to make the best of it.

We have also to ask whether our witness is willing to tell the truth. Does he have an ax to grind which leads him to present his material so as to favor his case? Does he keep anything back because it might throw doubt on what he believes or because it violates the expectations or conventions of others? Does he embroider a story to make it plainer (i.e., more obviously supporting his point) or more interesting? Does he fill in from his imagination what he believes ought to have happened? In greater or less degree, every reporter warps his report in some such way. Unfortunately, even sanctity is no guarantee of adequacy as a reporter. Of that adequacy we must judge as best we can on the basis of whatever information we can gather. With respect to anyone in the ancient world, we shall have to form a judgment largely on the basis of his self-revelation in his work.

In many cases we have no firsthand testimony; and if we are to form any conclusions we shall have to make the best of secondary witnesses, who simply repeat what they have been told, either orally or by earlier written sources now lost. Here we need to know, if possible, where the author got his information and how careful he has been in transmitting it. In the case of a New Testament author like Luke, for example, it turns out that we have one of his sources in independent form in Mark's Gospel, so that by comparing Luke's account with Mark's we can learn exactly how he deals with his material and can draw inferences as to how he has proceeded in cases where we no longer have his source in independent form. Luke comes off well from this examination, but it must be realized that care in using what material he had throws no light on the intrinsic value of that material. Such considerations are often very inconvenient, but they must be raised and faced if one is to claim any objectivity for his results.

With even the best witnesses we must be aware of the fallibility of human testimony. The problem is illustrated by the following story. The essential points can be duplicated in any court where, for example, an automobile accident case is being tried.

The professor had spoken about a book. One of the older students suddenly shouts, "I want to throw light on the matter from the standpoint of Christian morality!" Another student interjects, "I cannot stand that!" The first starts up exclaiming, "You have insulted me!" The second clenches his fist and cries, "If you say another word . . ." The first draws a revolver. The second rushes madly upon him. The professor steps between them and, as he grasps the man's arm, the revolver goes off. General uproar.

At that moment Professor Liszt secures order and asks a part of the students to write an exact account of all that has happened. The whole had been a comedy, carefully planned and rehearsed for the purpose of studying the exactitude of observation and recollection. Those who did not write the report at once were, part of them, asked to write it the next day, or a week later; and others had to testify as to their observations under cross examination. The whole objective performance was cut up into fourteen little parts which referred partly to actions, partly to words. As mistakes were counted omissions, wrong additions, and alterations. The smallest number of mistakes gave twenty-six percent of erroneous statements; the largest was eighty percent. The reports with reference to the second half of the performance, which was more strongly emotional, gave an average of fifteen percent more mistakes than those of the first half. Words were put into the mouths of the men who had been silent spectators during the whole short episode; actions were attributed to the chief participants of which not the slightest trace existed; and essential parts of the tragi-comedy were completely eliminated from the memory of a number of witnesses.[1]

There is therefore one further question which must be asked about our sources. We are never on firm ground if we have only

[1] Hugo Münsterberg, *On the Witness Stand*, pp. 49–51. Quoted in Allen Johnson, *The Historian and Historical Evidence*, Scribner's, 1930, pp. 35–36. The account is obviously translated from the German and I have ventured to improve the translation at one or two points without having the original: e.g., substitution of *interject* for *throw in* (doubtless *einwerfen*) and *testify* for *depose* (*bezeugen*), and omission of some unidiomatic definite articles.

one account of an event; and even when we have several accounts we need to be sure that they are independent. Three people telling exactly the same thing are of no more value than one if it turns out that two of them are simply repeating what the first one told them. This unfortunately is the case in regard to the material common to Matthew, Mark, and Luke. As will appear, Matthew and Luke derived this material from Mark, so that their repetition does not provide any independent confirmation of it.

In the determination of the historian's data, the highest degree of objectivity must be sought. When from the data he attempts to draw a finished picture, subjective factors inevitably enter. He must form his own judgment of the relative importance of his materials and how they fit together. In this process of evaluation he is inevitably guided by factors which are not part of the data. Actually, the data are never certainties; and his estimate of probabilities and importance is necessarily affected by his whole philosophy. The kind of connection he will tend to find between events may depend, for example, on whether he believes history as a whole has any meaning or exhibits any general trends.

All this means that the historian's reconstruction of the past can, in general, never claim certainty, but at best only a considerable degree of probability. Likewise, his objectivity is never complete. This does not excuse him, however, from being satisfied with anything less than the highest degree of probability and the greatest possible objectivity. Because the truth is hard to come by, we are not thereby authorized to believe whatever fancy —or tradition—dictates.

MIRACLES

A particularly thorny problem for the historian who undertakes to apply his established techniques to the New Testament is the presence of reports of miracles.

The problem begins with the meaning of the term. Traditionally, a miracle has meant an event in the physical world which cannot be accounted for by the known laws of nature, and which is therefore attributed to a superhuman agency that brought it about as a manifestation of power. There are various watered-down modern definitions which concentrate on the marvelous or inexplicable character of the occurrence, and would leave out this factor of display of supernatural power; but this is to empty the concept of meaning, and then, of course, there is no problem. Cosmic rays have most unusual properties, and up to now their origin is without a generally accepted explanation; but there would be no gain either for science or religion in calling their origin a miracle.

Another attempted escape from the problem is by rationalization. The rationalizer accepts the report of the occurrence as fact but offers a nonsupernatural explanation. Thus, the report that Jesus on a certain occasion walked on the surface of the Lake of Galilee has been "explained" by saying that he was really walking along the shore, which was shrouded in mist. The disciples in the boat were much closer to the shore than they realized (a common plight of navigators in foggy weather), and when Jesus waded out a few feet and got into the boat with them they thought he had come walking over the water! Such efforts at saving the veracity of the reporters at the expense of their judgment have nothing to commend them except the general recognition that all experience involves an interpretation of given data and that the same data can support various interpretations. We have all seen coins taken out of ears, objects disappear, rabbits pulled out of hats, and beautiful girls sawed in two. We see these things under conditions which predispose us to believe that they are the result of some trick, even though we cannot explain how it is done. But suppose we came on such a happening without warning. We might take it at its face value; or, on the basis of our experience at magic shows, we might still infer that our eyes had deceived us. If we lived in an atmosphere where real miracles were expected, we would be much less critical.

The upshot of these remarks is simply that it is difficult to be sure that a reported occurrence is really a miracle. Inability to provide an explanation is no proof of supernatural activity, nor is the possibility of inventing an explanation disproof of supernatural activity. But if the supernatural element cannot be clearly shown, then the concept of miracle as a display of supernatural power becomes useless. We never can be sure we really have a miracle, however inexplicable an occurrence may be.

Even supposing that these difficulties can be overcome, there is another equally formidable. That is the question as to whether we have sufficient evidence that the thing occurred at all. One point can be disposed of at the outset. It is sometimes said that science proves that miracles are impossible. This is nonsense. Science has to take the world the way it finds it. It can say that there is no explanation for a given phenomenon within the limits of its vision; but if it were to say that nothing beyond the limits of its present vision could occur, it would cut its own throat. The progress of physics in the twentieth century has been based on the discovery of things which Newton's mechanics declared impossible. Our knowledge of nature is not exhaustive; and even if it were, it would not follow therefore that God was limited to action within the ordinary course of nature.

We come back then to the demand for evidence. It is often forgotten that evidence that is sufficient to establish a common happening is not sufficient to establish an uncommon one. If I come from outdoors into a room with no windows and report that it is raining I will probably be believed, especially if I am wet. I may be lying and have sprinkled myself to back up my story. But if a second person comes in with the same report, everyone will be practically certain that it is so. If, however, I were to report that on a July day, with the temperature ninety degrees in the shade, I had seen the college lake covered with a sheet of ice, no one would believe me. If three other people came in and told the same story, it still would not be believed. I would not believe it if I saw it with my own eyes. I would conclude that I must be dreaming or subject to a hallucination. If such a thing really occurred it could doubtless eventually be established, at least with a high degree of probability; but it could not possibly be established by the testimony of a few well-intentioned people who simply said they saw it.

To put it bluntly, if we ask for adequate evidence that most of the Gospel miracles (the healings, as will be seen, are in a different class) occurred, it is simply not forthcoming. What is offered as evidence is only acceptable to those who are already convinced of the conclusion.

At this point the discussion frequently becomes involved in confusion. These reports, we are told, are not ordinary reports. They are in the Bible, and that vouches for them. When the seeker for evidence asks why he should put reports in the Bible on a different plane from other reports, he is offered either a theory about the Bible or an argument in a circle. He is told that God's Word is certainly infallible. But granted that God reveals himself to men in the Scriptures, is it not presumptuous to try to lay down the rules by which he must proceed in revealing himself? Offhand, it is hard to see why the analogy of an important executive dictating to his stenographer is any more appropriate as a picture of revelation than the analogy of a parent or teacher leading his children through a process of trial and error, growth and discovery, and taking responsibility for errors and learning from them. Which of these ways (or some other) God chooses in revealing himself should be determined by looking at what he really did—not by approaching the subject with a ready-made answer and forcing the facts to fit it. As for arguing in a circle, that is what happens when we are asked to accept the Bible as a supernatural book because it tells of supernatural occurrences, and then we are assured that these occurrences really took place because they are testified to by the Bible. If this is the kind of trap we are in, it is nonsense to talk about studying the Bible from the point of view of the historian. Objectivity vanishes, and only those can be saved who are so fortunate as to be unable to think clearly.

CHAPTER 3

The Text and Translation
of the New Testament

In the attempt to recover the story of the past from the sources, the historian's first problem is to make sure the documents which he has are either the originals or faithful copies of them. In dealing with recent history this is usually a relatively simple matter. The original documents are accessible and may be studied in exact photographic copies. Unfortunately, none of the sources for a knowledge of the beginnings of Christianity has survived in its original form. If we want to know what the authors of the Gospels, for example, wrote, we are dependent on copies, indeed on copies of copies of copies. Since the books of the New Testament were written some fourteen hundred years before the invention of printing in the West, these copies had to be made by hand. Hand copying always introduces errors, so that no two copies are exactly alike. The problem of the student of the New Testament is to determine from the various copies what the original words must have been. Not everyone made the same errors, and if all the differences are studied it may be possible to infer what the original text was.

For the study of the New Testament text, there are abundant materials—so abundant, indeed, that the actual handling of them presents a difficult and complex problem. There are hundreds of Greek manuscripts alone, and the number of variations among them runs into the hundreds of thousands. To deal with so much material is obviously a complicated matter. But just because there are so many copies we have a better possibility of discovering the best reading in any given case. Actually, we can know much more exactly what the authors of the New Testament books wrote than we can what any other ancient author wrote, whether Greek or Latin—Plato, Aristotle, Caesar, Cicero, or anyone else.

GREEK MANUSCRIPTS

The material in Greek is in various forms. The oldest are some papyrus fragments which have survived in the dry climate of Egypt from the second century. A very important find is known as the Chester Beatty papyri. These consist of thirty leaves of a Gospel manuscript, eighty-six out of one hundred and four leaves of a manuscript of the Pauline Epistles, and ten leaves of the book of Revelation.

Very important are the great manuscripts written by professional copyists on vellum, in large letters. These manuscripts are called *uncials*. The oldest of them is from the fourth century and is found now in the Vatican Library. From a century later is the famous manuscript found by the German scholar Tischendorf in a monastery at the foot of Mt. Sinai. He persuaded the monks to give it to the Russian Czar, who gave the monks a present of money in return. Finally, the Soviet government sold the manuscript to the British Museum for about half a million dollars. Another important uncial is the Codex Alexandrinus from the fifth century, once in Alexandria, now also in the British Mu-

A page of the Washington Codex of the Gospels. An uncial manuscript on parchment, dating from the fourth or fifth century. The text is the opening of Mark's Gospel, with heading, and Mark 1:1–7. The manuscript is on display at the Freer Gallery. (Courtesy of the Smithsonian Institution, Freer Gallery of Art, Washington, D.C.)

The leaves of the Washington Codex were held between two painted wooden covers. The front cover, poorly preserved, had the figures of Matthew and John. This back cover shows Luke and Mark. (Courtesy of the Smithsonian Institution, Freer Gallery of Art, Washington, D.C.)

seum. The Codex Bezae is an uncial manuscript from perhaps the fifth century which is most unusual in being bilingual, with Greek on one page and Latin facing it. The Latin is not a translation of the Greek, so this is really two partly independent manuscripts.

The Koridethi Gospels, though later, are important because they led to the recognition of a new type of ancient text. In our own country, in the Freer collection, is the Washington manuscript from the fourth or fifth century. There are a number of other uncial manuscripts, but they are in general less important than those which have been mentioned.

Most Greek manuscripts are written in a running or cursive hand. They differ from the uncials as script differs from hand printing. Some of these are of considerable importance for the support they give to certain readings in which one or more of the uncials differ from the majority of the cursives, but they can hardly be described usefully without going into technical matters out of place here.

THE CHURCH FATHERS AND THE LECTIONARIES

Another important source of information is found in the writings of the early controversialists and theologians, commonly called the Church Fathers. In their writings they frequently quoted Scripture, and thus give information as to what was in manuscripts which have otherwise perished. They also make it possible to date certain forms of text and to show the locality in which these variations were current.

There is one more source of information about the Greek text, the *lectionaries*. These are books of selections of "lessons for the day" for reading in public worship. The text is often modified slightly for the purpose; but these modifications are usually obvious and, when allowed for, the lectionaries make a valuable contribution to our knowledge of the original text.

ANCIENT TRANSLATIONS

Also of importance are the ancient translations or *versions*.
In cases where the Greek manuscripts differ from one another,
it is usually possible to tell from the translation which of the
Greek alternatives was in the manuscript which the translator
had before him.

Of these ancient translations the Latin is of particular importance. There is an Old Latin in several forms which is very early,
and also Jerome's revision of this which we know as the Vulgate.
This became the Bible of the medieval church. Here again, we
have the problem of determining what the original form of these
versions was. For this we have abundant materials in the thousands of Latin manuscripts of the New Testament that have
come down to us.

Other translations were made into Syriac, the language of the
Syrian church; into Coptic for the church in Egypt; Ethiopian,
Armenian, and Georgian. Each contributes to a sound judgment
as to what was the original form of the New Testament writings.

THE ORIGIN OF VARIATIONS

The source of the variations is plain to anyone who has tried to
copy out in writing an extensive extract from an article or a
reference book. Words are omitted; words are duplicated; one
reads different words from those actually in the text before him,
perhaps because he needs glasses (ancient scribes had none);
and, reading rapidly, he "sees" what he expects to find. That this
can happen is only too evident to one who, brought up on the
Authorized Version, tries to read publicly such a familiar story
as the story of the Wise Men from, say, the Revised Standard
Version. Again and again he becomes aware that he has said the
familiar words and not those before his eyes. He also suspects
that he has done the same thing many times when he did not

A page from an illuminated eleventh-century Byzantine lectionary, written in a cursive hand. It contains Matthew 18:10, 11. The seated figure is the apostle Matthew. (Courtesy of the Pierpont Morgan Library) catch himself. If he were copying instead of reading aloud, he would have assimilated the text before him to the familiar one.

Another source of error in New Testament manuscripts arose from the effort to make many copies at the same time. A number of scribes would be assembled at desks in a large room, and one would sit at the front and dictate from a manuscript. Instead of errors of seeing, this produced errors of hearing, some of them caused—like the errors of seeing—by lapse of attention, hearing what was expected, etc.; but there are also errors peculiar to this method. An especially common source here was what is called *itacism,* the habit which grew up in Hellenistic times of pronouncing a number of quite different vowel sounds all as if they were *i.*

Beside these accidental errors, there were also deliberate changes. Some of these would be the result of previous errors. If words were left out or misspelled, the result might be nonsense. In copying such a wording the next scribe would have to guess what the original must have been. Sometimes he would guess correctly and sometimes he might be far off. To take a modern example in English, I once wrote the phrase, *where severe compression.* In the typed copy which went to the printer the last *e* was accidentally omitted from *severe,* giving *where sever compression,* which was nonsense. In an effort to make sense, the printer's proofreader inferred that an *o* had been omitted and changed it to *wheresoever,* which made sense of the phrase, but was not what was originally written or meant.

Other deliberate changes were made for other reasons. In some cases, rough spots in the writer's style were smoothed, or explanations of unfamiliar terms or allusions were added. In a few cases, changes were made for doctrinal reasons. A famous example concerns the words in I John 5:7, "There are three that bear record in heaven, the Father, the Word, and the Holy Ghost." These words are found in no Greek manuscript earlier than the sixteenth century, though they are found in Latin manuscripts. When Erasmus published the first printed Greek New Testament, he omitted them. There was a great protest from the theologians, who accused him of undermining the doctrine of the Trinity. He replied that, to the best of his knowledge, the words occurred in no Greek manuscript; but that if they were to be found in Greek, he would put them in his next edition. Soon he was shown a Greek manuscript which included them, and he kept his promise. But it is clear now that the manuscript with the words inserted was produced for the purpose.

Another source of deliberate change arose in the attempt to harmonize variations. To people who worked with manuscripts all the time, it was no secret that errors arose in copying. If a church had more than one copy of the Scriptures, this would be obvious as soon as they were compared. In the attempt to remedy this, two courses were open: to decide between the variants or to compromise and try to include them both. The latter was the more common procedure, and this is reflected by the medieval Greek texts.

Some Examples of Variations

The operation of these factors can be illustrated by a few simple examples from the Revised Standard Version, which gives some selected alternative readings in footnotes. In the first place, many variants consist of added words. These generally result from the attempt to harmonize different texts. Often in the Gospels the addition consists of words found in a parallel passage in another Gospel. Thus Matthew 7:9 reads, "What man of you, if his son asks him for a loaf, will give him a stone? Or if he asks for a fish, will give him a serpent?" The best manuscripts of Luke 11:11 say, "What father among you, if his son asks for a fish, will instead of a fish give him a serpent?" Other manuscripts of Luke have the additional words about the bread and the stone, which have been added from Matthew.

At Mark 11:19 some texts read "They went out of the city";

others have "he went out of the city." In the manuscripts the two readings would look something like EXEPOREUETO and EXE-POREUONTO. Prior to this word, *he* had been the subject; and this seems to have originated as a simple case of misreading something which looked similar under the influence of what was in the scribe's mind. In I Thessalonians 2:7, some texts read "we were gentle" (EGENĒTHEMENEPIOI), others have "we were babes" (EGENĒTHEMENNEPIOI), where the scribe presumably read the last N twice, first as the final letter of the preceding word, and then perhaps, as he looked back, as the first letter of the next word. This sort of error was easier because the ancient texts were written, as shown, without breaks between words.

Probably scribes, then as now, did not really read all the syllables of a long word; and this may account for the two readings in Acts 13:18: ETROPOPHORĒSENAUTOUS, "he bore with them," and ETROPHOPHORĒSENAUTOUS, "he cared for them."

In Luke 2:14 the difference between "good will to men" and "among men with whom he is pleased" is only the difference between EUDOKIA and EUDOKIAS, with the latter having the strongest support in the manuscripts.

One of the commonest types of variation is between *we* and *you*. Thus, in I Corinthians 7:15 we have "God has called us," KEKLEKENĒMASOTHEOS, for "God has called you," KEKLE-KENUMASOTHEOS. These look rather similar, but this is probably a case of itacism, E and U being pronounced alike. Here, the first reading is to be preferred. A similar case (there are many others) is II Corinthians 3:2: "written on your (UMŌN) hearts" or "written on our (ĒMŌN) hearts." Here the confusion seems to be in the other direction.

Mark 1:2 seems to offer a case of deliberate alteration correcting the original. Mark seems, according to the clear weight of manuscript evidence, to have written, "As it is written in Isaiah the prophet." The quotation which follows is actually part from

Malachi and then from Isaiah, so scribes corrected "Isaiah the prophet" to "in the prophets."

These simple examples are only a few out of the hundreds of thousands which occur. Many, of course, are obviously wrong, like that produced by a sleepy scribe who found a marginal note in the manuscript he was copying, which indicated that the reading of this manuscript had support elsewhere. When he absentmindedly took this for a correction and copied it into the middle of the text the result was something like, "to receive us *in many copies it is found thus* and not as we hope." (II Cor. 8:4–5.) Unfortunately, not all cases are so simple; and the preparation of a Greek text based on careful weighing of the manuscript evidence is not an easy task.

DECIDING BETWEEN READINGS

Probably the first proposal which comes to mind is to count the manuscripts and let the majority rule, but this would be satisfactory only if all our copies were made directly from the original. Let us construct an imaginary genealogy of manuscripts, where the vertical lines show what manuscript a given one was copied from:

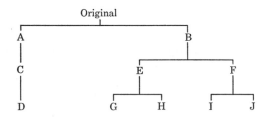

Suppose the scribe of B made a mistake not made by A or those who followed him. B's mistake would be copied by those dependent on him. If the original is lost but all copies survive, there will be seven with the mistake and three without. Clearly the majority will be wrong. If, as someone has said, "Democracy is the best form ever devised for giving the mass of people the kind of government they deserve," it still has no application to textual criticism.

The diagram also reveals the fallacy of supposing that an older manuscript is always better than a more recent one. Suppose now that the only copies which survive are B and D, B being made in the second century and D in the fourth. Although B is the older, D will be the one which is correct. We must try some other approach.

If we examine a manuscript carefully, it soon appears that in general it is "good" or "bad." It will have few or many obvious mistakes. Where a good and a bad manuscript offer equally plausible variations, there is a presumption that the good one is right. But this presumption is by no means a certainty, for even the best scribes have their off moments.

The next step, then, is the recognition that manuscripts tend to form groups. There is a pattern to the occurrence of variations. Again and again the same set of manuscripts will agree in supporting one form of text, while an alternative form will be supported by another recurring group. Furthermore, there are good groups and poor groups. Thus the reading "Isaiah the prophet" in Mark 1:2 is supported by the Vatican and Sinaitic manuscripts and a number of others which regularly form a good group. The other reading is supported by Codex Bezae, the Koridethi and Washington manuscripts, and the great mass of medieval cursives. This is a weaker group when it is opposed to the other one. However, the group test is not infallible either.

A great advance in this field was made by the British scholars B. F. Westcott and A. J. F. Hort. They recognized that there were certain very old text types from which all our manuscripts were derived. These basic types go back to the second century. Except for a few fragments, our manuscripts are later than this and actually show various degrees of mixture of the different types. The mixture arose as manuscripts were compared and "corrected" by a manuscript of another type, or where a scribe had before him a variety of manuscripts and chose readings from one or the other as it seemed best to him.

Westcott and Hort recognized four types of text. The first, which they called *Neutral,* is found in the Vatican manuscript and in a number of others which habitually agree with it. Closely related is a type called *Alexandrian.* They also recognized a *Western* type, found in Codex Bezae and the Old Latin. The text found in the great mass of medieval manuscripts they called *Syrian.* They showed clearly that most of the Syrian variations had no claim to be part of the original text. They made what they called the Neutral the basis for their printed edition.

Since their day, further advances have been made. The distinction between Neutral and Alexandrian has broken down, while a new type, the Caesarean, has been recognized. The value of Western variations is still debated. But despite these facts, and despite criticism of some of Westcott and Hort's theories, their printed edition is still very close to what any scholar would recognize as the best text.

For the future, much is expected from the International Greek New Testament Project. This is an effort to assemble the evidence of the variations of the manuscripts with a thoroughness and accuracy never before achieved. When this is completed, it will be possible to make a new approach to the problem of selecting the best reading from the mass of variations.

In this discussion, attention has been focussed on the variations. They run, as has been said, into the hundreds of thousands. But it would be a mistake to conclude that our knowledge of the true text is correspondingly uncertain. With such a great number of witnesses, we are the more able to determine the truth. In the words of Westcott and Hort: "If comparative trivialities, such as changes of order, the insertion or omission of the article with proper names, and the like, are set aside, the words in our opinion still subject to doubt can hardly amount to more than a thousandth part of the whole New Testament."[1] In Westcott and Hort's own edition, with 528 pages containing text, and approximately 275 words per page, this amounts to about one word in nearly four pages, a degree of accuracy far higher than we can attain for any other ancient book.

TRANSLATIONS

Most of us are dependent on a translation if we want to read and study the New Testament.

The earliest translation of the entire New Testament into English that has come down to us was completed by John Wyclif in 1380. His translation was made, however, not from Greek but from the Latin Bible which was in universal use in the medieval Church. Wyclif was a sharp critic of various aspects of the Church of his day, believing that it had departed from the true pattern as found in the Scriptures. He believed that if men generally could read the Bible, the abuses would have to be corrected. Determined efforts were made to suppress his Bibles and the movement which he started. These seemed to be effective, but Wyclif's influence continued to flow through subterranean channels until the Reformation.

Wyclif's Bibles had to be copied by hand. The first printed New Testament was the work of William Tyndale. Following the example of Martin Luther, who translated the Bible into German, Tyndale undertook to make an English translation. The English Reformation had not begun, and Tyndale was forced to flee to the Continent. Even here his way was far from smooth. He had to flee from one city to another; and his Testaments had to be smuggled into England, where all that could be

[1] B. F. Westcott and A. J. F. Hort, *The New Testament in Greek,* Macmillan, 1928, p. 565.

crõmes/which fall from there masters table.Then Jesus an=
swered and sayde vnto her.O woman greate is thy fayth / be
hit to the/even as thou desyrest.And her doughter was ma=
de whole even at that same tyme.

¶Then Jesus went awaye from thence / and cam nye vnto
the see of galyle/and went vppe in to a mountayne/and sat do=
une there. And moche people cam vnto hym havynge with
them/halt/blynde/dõm/maymed/ and other many: and cast
them doune at Jesus fete. And he healed them / in so moche
that the people wondred / to se the dõm speake /the maymed
whole / and the halt to go / the blynde to se/and gloryfyed the
god of israhel.

*Mar. ¶Jhesus called his disciples to him and sayde: I have com=
viij. passion on the people/be cause they have contynued with me
nowe iij.dayes/and have nothinge to eate:and I wyll not let
them departe fastinge leste they peryshe in the waye.And his
disciples said vnto him:whece shuld we get so moche breed in
the wyldernes as shulde suffyse so greate a multitude:and Je=
sus saidē vntothē: howe many loves have ye ? and they seyde:
sevē and a feawe fysshes.And he cõmaunded the people to syt
doune onthe grounde.and toke the sevē loves/and the fysshes
and gave thankf/ and brake them/and gave to hys disciples/
and hys disciples gave thēto the people. And they all ate/and
were suffysed.and they toke vppe of the brokē meate that was
lefte vij.basketf full.They that ate were iiij. M. men/ besyde
weimen and chyldren.And he sent awaye the people/and toke
shyppe and cam in to the parties of magdala:

The xvi.Chapter.

Mar. viij.
Luc.ix.

Then cam to him the pharises
with the saduces also /and dyd tēpte him /desyr=
inge that he wolde shewe thē some sygne frõ he=
ven. He answered and saide vnto them: At even
ye saye/we shall have fayre wedder.and that be cause the skye
ys reed:ri the mornige:ye saye/todaye shalbe foule wedder/z
Luc.xij. that because the skye is trõbelous and reed. O ye ypocryt/ye
G ij.

*A page from Tyndale's New Testament, printed in 1525 at Co-
logne because the publication was forbidden in England. Even
abroad the printing had to be done secretly and Tyndale's efforts
eventually cost him his life.* (The Bettman Archive)

rounded up were burned. But Tyndale persisted. He constantly revised his translation of the New Testament and worked out a translation of part of the Old Testament. In 1515, still an exile, he was betrayed to the ecclesiastical authorities, tried for heresy, and given over to the secular government for execution. On October 6, 1536, he was strangled and then burned. His last words were, "Lord, open the King of England's eyes."

Tyndale's work was based on careful scholarship and the ability to write effective English. It is the direct ancestor of the Authorized Version and even of the Revised Standard Version of today. "You cannot serve God and mammon," "Consider the lilies of the field how they grow," "Where two or three are gathered together in my name, there am I in the midst of them" are still, in the most recent revision, expressed as Tyndale expressed them.

Tyndale did not live to enjoy the change which came over the English scene after the Act of Supremacy of 1534 that marked the break of Henry VIII with the Pope. It was Miles Coverdale who brought out, in 1535, a few months after Tyndale's arrest, the first complete English Bible, with the encouragement of the ecclesiastical authorities and with a dedication to the King. Coverdale was not the scholar Tyndale was; and his version, where not dependent on Tyndale, was translated from the Latin and German, not from Greek and Hebrew.

Meanwhile, John Rogers had produced a Bible based largely on Tyndale's translation. When this and Coverdale's revised work both appeared in 1537 under royal license, the divergences between them led to a new edition to replace them both, which appeared in 1539. Coverdale edited this Great Bible, as it is called, and made large use of his predecessor's work.

Another important ancestor of the King James Version of the Bible was the Geneva Bible, produced by exiles from England during the Catholic restoration under Queen Mary. It was a careful piece of work, with verse divisions, marginal notes, maps, and other helps. The Geneva Bible was a very popular Bible, especially, as might be expected, where Calvinism was strong. Thus it was the cherished Bible of Scotland, and of the Pilgrims who came to New England. From it come such expressions as "in all these things we are more than conquerors through him who loved us," "We have the mind of Christ," "so great a cloud of witnesses."

This Calvinistic Bible seriously affected the popularity of the official version, the Great Bible of 1539. The bishops of the Church of England therefore undertook a revision of the Great Bible, which appeared in 1568 and came to be called the Bishops' Bible. Different sections were done by different scholars and the resulting version was very uneven. It was never successful as a competitor of the Geneva Bible, but has contributed to the Authorized Version and its successors such expressions as "persecuted for righteousness' sake," and "overcome evil with good."

The climax of nearly a century of Bible translation was the appearance in 1611, under the auspices of King James I of England, of what has come to be known as the Authorized Version. The translators, who were the best scholars of their day, went back to the original Greek and Hebrew; but they also took account of previous English versions. With the knowledge available at that time, it was as accurate a translation as could be made. In addition to being clear, the language was sonorous and rhythmical. At first it had to struggle against opposition, as every new Bible translation has had to do. But gradually it forged to the front; and for two hundred and fifty years it had its critics but no serious rival.

The English Revised Version of the New Testament, when it appeared in 1881, opened a new era in Bible translation. This was followed in 1901 by a variant version embodying the preferences of the American members of the committee which had produced the English Revised Version. This is known as the American Standard Version. In a sense, however, these versions were premature; and the most recent translation which is in some sense an "authorized" version is the Revised Standard Version, of which the New Testament portion was published in 1946.

Meanwhile, there had been several private versions, of which the best known are those of James Moffatt and E. J. Goodspeed. Others are the Twentieth Century New Testament, the Weymouth New Testament, and the Riverside New Testament, and most recently the rather free translation by J. B. Phillips.

The reasons for the appearance of all these translations are three. In the first place, the English language has developed during the three hundred years since the King James Version was made. No doubt some of the archaisms of language add a mysterious and hence "holy" atmosphere to this version, but presumably the first requirement of a translation is that it convey to the reader the sense of the original. If it does not do that, any literary beauty it may possess is a snare and a delusion. An extreme example of how English has changed is afforded by Psalm 119:147: "I prevented the dawning of the morning." If God were speaking this might make sense even today, but it is not God but the Psalmist who says this about himself. How many are familiar enough with Elizabethan English to know that *prevent* was then used in the sense of "to be beforehand"? What the writer means is not that he kept the dawn from happening but that he got up before daylight. A New Testament example is the use of *charity* in Paul's well-known I Corinthians 13. Paul is simply not talking about giving to the poor, as the word now suggests. What he means is much better expressed by *love*. Those who according to Mark 1:34 were sick of *divers* diseases did not have "the bends." The list can be extended indefinitely. The demand for "modern English" is not a demand for slang or "pep" or the diction of advertising copywriters, but for clear, simple English which conveys directly to the intelligent present-day reader what the original author tried to convey to his readers.

The second reason for a new translation is that we now know

more nearly than did the translators of the Authorized Version just what the original writers put down on papyrus. The fifteen hundred years between the writing of the books and the late medieval manuscripts which were the basis for the early printed Greek Testaments had produced an accumulation of errors of the kind which have been described above. Now, as a result of the discoveries of many manuscripts, some much older than those available when the King James Version was made, and as a result of improved methods of making use of the great mass of evidence we possess, we are able to arrive at a text much more nearly what the original authors wrote than anyone could have done three hundred years ago.

Finally, new translations are needed because we now know more about the Greek in which the New Testament was written. This knowledge has come mostly during the present century, and is one of the main reasons for the rapid obsolescence of the English Revised Version of 1881 and the American Standard Version of 1901.

It has long been obvious to students of Greek that the Greek of the New Testament differs from the language of the writers of the Golden Age of Greek literature. Some grammatical forms are different; other classical forms are almost or quite eliminated. The meaning of words as given in classical dictionaries sometimes does not make sense in New Testament contexts, while a number of words found in the New Testament do not appear in the classical dictionaries at all. The problems thus raised were brilliantly illuminated toward the end of the nineteenth century by the discovery in Egypt of vast quantities of papyrus sheets from later Greek, much of it contemporary with the New Testament. These fragments included receipts, letters, magic spells, advertisements, petitions to government officials, and many other types of composition as well. Study of these materials has thrown a flood of light on the grammar and vocabulary of New Testament Greek and revealed the fact that this Greek was simply the common Greek of the day. In the four hundred years between the great Greek dramatists and the New Testament, Greek had undergone changes similar to the changes which English has undergone between Shakespeare's day and ours.

In another respect, too, these discoveries are important: they show that the literary standard of the New Testament writers was not in general very high. The chief reason why translations like those of Moffatt and Goodspeed are made into colloquial English is that such English is comparable to the kind of Greek in which the books were originally written. But even where there is no deliberate effort to imitate the colloquial style of the New Testament Greek, modern translations done by competent scholars are much more accurate than anyone could have made in the seventeenth century. No translation is perfect, and there is still much to be learned; but our modern translations take us much nearer than ever before to what the New Testament authors originally wrote.

PART II

Jesus

CHAPTER 4

𒁉𒁉𒁉𒁉𒁉𒁉𒁉𒁉𒁉𒁉𒁉𒁉𒁉𒁉𒁉𒁉𒁉𒁉

Sources for the Life and Teaching of Jesus

THE ADOPTION of the historical approach to the study of the New Testament commits us to the procedure of basing our statements on sources, going back ultimately to persons or things directly involved in the events we are interested in. This is as true for the life and teaching of Jesus as for anything or anyone else in the past. Faith can interpret the facts, but it cannot supply them. What, then, are our sources for a knowledge of Jesus?

Since Jesus was a controversial figure, both in his life and after his death, the historian would like to have accounts derived not only from his friends but also from his opponents. There is no presumption that a picture derived from Jesus' opponents would be more accurate than one supplied by his friends; but if we could see how he appeared to those who opposed him, we might better understand what his partisans say of him and secure confirmation of at least some points which might otherwise be explained away as due to wishful thinking. Unfortunately, we have very little such material; and what we have does not come from a period very close in time to the events. What there is must now be examined.

JEWISH SOURCES

What do Jewish sources tell us about Jesus? Nearest to him in time are the works of Josephus, the Jewish historian who wrote at the end of the first century of our era. Unfortunately, his works have been transmitted to us only in copies made by Christians, and there is clear evidence that at some points Christian copyists have made Josephus say what they believed was true and what therefore he ought to have said. Thus, the first of the two references in Josephus is:

> Now about this time arises Jesus, a wise man, if indeed he should be called a man. For he was a doer of marvellous deeds, a teacher of men who receive the truth with pleasure, and won over to himself many of the Jews and many also of the Greek [nation]. He was the Christ. And when on the indictment of the principal men among us, Pilate had sentenced him to the cross, those that loved him at the first did not cease, for he appeared to them the third day alive again, the divine prophets having [fore]told these and ten thousand other wonderful things concerning him; and even now the tribe of Christians, named after him, is not extinct.[1]

It is obvious that this could not have been written in this form by anyone who continued to be a Jew, for anyone who recognized Jesus as the Messiah (*Christ* in Greek) and believed that he had risen from the grave on the third day would be by definition a Christian. That Josephus ever became a Christian, no one —Jew or Christian—has ever maintained. Indeed, the scholar Origen, in the third century, explicitly states that Josephus did not acknowledge Jesus as Messiah or Christ. Either the whole passage is a Christian insertion, or it has been worked over by Christian copyists. If the latter is true, it is not possible to know

[1] Josephus, *Antiquities*, xviii, §§ 63–64, in H. St. J. Thackeray, *Josephus, the Man and the Historian*, Jewish Institute of Religion Press, 1929, pp. 136–137.

just what Josephus did write originally. That he had said something about Jesus seems implied by the second passage: "[Ananus the high priest] summoned the court of the sanhedrin, brought before it the brother of Jesus, who was called Christ, (James was his name) and certain others, and after accusing them of transgressing the law, delivered them up to be stoned."[2] This seems to presuppose a previous reference to Jesus and an explanation of why he was called *Christ*. The most, however, that we can possibly extract from Josephus is the information that Jesus had been acknowledged by some as Messiah and had been crucified by Pilate.

Josephus published his books in Greek, at Rome; and while he wrote to defend Judaism, there were many who regarded him as a traitor to it. We must now inquire whether the classical sources of Judaism have anything to tell us. Here the material falls into two classes. Some of it comes from the period after Christians had come into control in the Roman empire and had begun to persecute Jews. These stories, as is understandable, have a strong bias against Jesus. Scandalous stories about his birth are typical. These are held by Jewish scholars of the present day[3] to be of no historical value.

There are, however, traditions from an earlier period, some perhaps as old as some of the Gospels. Their content can be summarized in these words of Klausner: "There are reliable statements to the effect that his name was Yeshu'a (Yeshu) of Nazareth, that he 'practiced sorcery' (i.e., performed miracles, as was usual in those days) and beguiled and led Israel astray; that he expounded Scripture in the same manner as the Pharisees; that he had five disciples; that he said he was not come to take aught away from the Law or to add to it; that he was hanged (crucified) as a false teacher and beguiler on the eve of the Pass-

2 *Ibid.*, p. 134, quoting *Antiquities*, xx, §§ 197–203.
3 See, for example, J. Klausner, *Jesus of Nazareth*, Macmillan, 1946, pp. 47–54; and M. Goldstein, *Jesus in the Jewish Tradition*, Macmillan, 1950, see index.

over which happened on a Sabbath; and that his disciples healed the sick in his name."[4]

ROMAN SOURCES

Roman sources are, if anything, even less productive. We have no official Roman records of the trial of Jesus, or of anything else about him. The so-called *Acts of Pilate* are late and entirely fictitious, a Christian's imaginative account of what he thought Pilate should have reported. The only accounts which need to be considered at all are found in the Roman historians Tacitus and Suetonius.

Tacitus, in his *Annals*, completed about A.D. 115, describes the reigns of the various emperors. Telling of Nero, he speaks of the great fire which raged in Rome in A.D. 64. A number of suspicious circumstances pointed to the emperor as having had the fire set. "But all human efforts, all the lavish gifts of the emperor, and the propitiations of the gods did not banish the sinister belief that the conflagration was the result of an order. Consequently, to get rid of the report, Nero fastened the guilt and inflicted the most exquisite tortures on a class hated for their abominations, called Christians by the populace. Christus, from whom the name had its origin, suffered the extreme penalty during the reign of Tiberius at the hands of one of our procurators, Pontius Pilate, and a most mischievous superstition, thus checked for the moment, again broke out not only in Judaea, the first source of the evil, but even in Rome, where all things hideous and shameful from every part of the world find their center and become popular."[5]

This at best does not give us much information; and it has been argued that even such as there is, is derived indirectly from Christians or from the Gospels (or their sources) and therefore

[4] Klausner, *op. cit.*, p. 46. (Parentheses are his.)
[5] Tacitus, *Annals*, xv, 44, J. Jackson (trans.), Loeb Classical Library, Harvard University Press, 1937, vol. IV, p. 283.

is not the independent witness we are looking for. It is to be noted, however, that the idea that the movement had been suppressed, only to break out again in Rome shortly before the fire, is not the Christian version of what happened; and, unless it is simply an inference from the execution, it seems to indicate some other source of information. That such a source was not Jewish seems to follow from the use of the title *Christ*. Jews would have called him Jesus. Tacitus therefore may provide independent confirmation of the existence of Jesus, the approximate date of his activity, and his execution by Pilate.

Suetonius' reference is even more dubious. He tells us, "Since the Jews constantly made disturbances at the instigation of Chrestus, [Claudius] expelled them from Rome."[6] *Christus* and *Chrestus* are different words; but *Chrestus* was a familiar name, while *Christus* was unknown. In addition, the two would have been pronounced alike in the Greek of the time, so that it is an attractive conjecture that what Suetonius reports as riots instigated by Chrestus were really riots among Jews caused by preaching about Christ. But even if this interpretation is right, it tells us nothing about Jesus except the fact that within twenty years of his death his followers were carrying on vigorous propaganda in the Roman synagogues.

Our survey of non-Christian sources, Jewish and Roman, for the life and teaching of Jesus has not turned up any new information about him; but it has furnished confirmation of his existence and the broad general outline of the picture which the New Testament gives.

CHRISTIAN SOURCES OUTSIDE THE NEW TESTAMENT

The important materials dealing with Jesus are in the New Testament, but there are other possible sources of information which should be briefly examined.

[6] Suetonius, "Life of Claudius," xxv, 4, in *Suetonius*, J. C. Rolfe (trans.), Loeb Classical Library, Harvard University Press, 1939, vol. II, p. 53. Claudius' expulsion of the Jews is probably to be dated about A.D. 50.

The first of these are the apocryphal Gospels. Some of these writings, composed after the middle of the second century, tell especially of the childhood and infancy of Jesus, where information would be very welcome if it were available. But when these books tell us how Jesus and his playmates made mudpies in the shape of birds and how he waved his hand and made them fly away; or when they tell us that as the children played, one boy accidentally bumped into Jesus, who picked himself up and said to the boy, "You'll not get where you're going," whereupon the child dropped dead—then we simply cannot take them seriously.

Ancient scholars such as Origen (third century) and Jerome (fifth century) refer to other gospels besides the familiar ones, such as the Gospel of the Hebrews, the Gospel of Peter, and the Gospel of the Egyptians. These are chiefly names, although we have a few brief quotations from some of them; and there are several papyrus fragments which are portions of some such works. For example, a portion of the Gospel of Peter was discovered in a tomb at Akhmim in Egypt in 1884. In 1935 several fragments, also found in Egypt, of an otherwise unknown Gospel were published.

The most extensive portion so far discovered of a noncanonical gospel is the Gospel of Thomas, found in 1945 as a part of a Gnostic library of thirteen volumes at Nag Hammadi (ancient Chenoboskion) in Upper Egypt. The material is written in the Coptic language, but most if not all of the books are translations or adaptations of Greek originals. The Gospel of Thomas is a collection of sayings, many preceded by a question or bit of dialogue. There are no new incidents. The sayings include all those found in the papyri discovered at the end of the nineteenth century in Egypt at Oxyrhynchus, with the same introductory paragraph and with the sayings in the same order. There are also links between the Gospel of Thomas and some of the other apocryphal Gospels.

There are also to be found outside the Gospels and the New

Testament a number of other sayings which are attributed to Jesus. Some are found in early Christian writers, some even in Mohammedan sources. These books add nothing to our knowledge, and there is little reason to suppose that they would do so even if we had them all in complete form. Many of the sayings are interesting, but few have any claim to be genuine. Those that may be genuine are the ones which conform to the familiar sayings, so that these materials are also of little help to us. There are some scholars, however, who believe that the Gospel of Thomas represents in spots an ancient tradition going back ultimately to an Aramaic source.

THE NEW TESTAMENT

When we turn to the New Testament it must be borne in mind that the earliest books are not the Gospels but the Pauline Epistles. I Corinthians, written not long after A.D. 50, provides us with the earliest account of the Lord's Supper (11:23–26) and the earliest testimony to the Resurrection (15:3–8). Paul also quotes a few sayings of Jesus known to us otherwise in the Gospels. But when all is said and done, Paul gives us surprisingly little about Jesus. Nor does the rest of the New Testament contribute anything significant to our knowledge of Jesus' life and teachings.

We are forced back, then, to the Gospels as our chief sources of information about Jesus. We cannot begin by assuming anything about date, authorship, or literary relationship. The first thing that strikes us, however, is that the Gospels fall into two clearly marked groups: Matthew, Mark, and Luke on the one hand, and John on the other. The first three can be usefully printed side by side in parallel columns for comparative study. Since the eye can thus take in at a glance their mutual relationships, they are commonly called the Synoptic Gospels. If the attempt is made to include John in this scheme, it turns out to be of little value. John's column will usually be blank where the others have something, while there is usually nothing in the others to parallel what is in John.

Other striking differences are noticeable. John mentions three celebrations of the annual feast of the Passover, the Synoptic Gospels have only one; John tells of Jesus cleansing the Temple at the beginning of his ministry, while the Synoptic Gospels tell of such an act only in the last week of his life. The Fourth Gospel tells much of activities in and around Jerusalem; the Synoptics only indicate activity there during the closing days of his career. The driving out of evil spirits characteristic of the Synoptic accounts is entirely missing in John. The miracles reported by John are not done as the Synoptic accounts report, in response to and on condition of faith; but they are done for the very purpose of producing faith where it did not previously exist. Most significant, however, is the different picture given of the content of Jesus' teaching.

In the Synoptics we find practical precepts adapted to concrete situations. Jesus deals with life's great moral problems, the relation of man to God and to his fellows; he speaks little of the mystery of his Person and of his relation to the Father. His teaching deals almost exclusively with the question, What must one do to enter the Kingdom of God? In the Fourth Gospel, on the other hand, we find set discourses, abstract rather than practical in character, abounding in enigmatic allusions and the elucidation of misunderstandings, which often in themselves are not a little artificial, and bearing constantly on such subjects as Christ's own divinity, his relation to the Father, or on mysteries of faith such as the indwelling of the Spirit or the efficacy of the sacraments. But nowhere is the contrast greater than in the demands which Jesus makes upon his followers. In the Synoptics, indeed, Jesus requires faith, but there "faith" is rather an act of moral "trust." In our Gospel his demand is for belief in the divinity of his own Person. "What he asks of people is not, as in the Synoptics, moral conduct, but acceptance as true of his assurance that he has come from heaven."[7]

THE SYNOPTIC PROBLEM

The question of the significance of these differences between John and the Synoptic Gospels must be postponed until the relation between the Synoptic Gospels themselves has been considered. Here we have a twofold problem arising out of the striking resemblances between these three Gospels on the one hand, and their differences on the other. A general similarity of content and outline might be expected, since they all relate to the same events (though the divergence of John shows that this is certainly not a necessity). But it is not by any means to be expected that resemblances should extend to the use of identical language in detail. Even though two students have heard the same lectures and studied the same textbooks it is not to be expected that they will answer the examination questions in precisely the same words. If they do, then the teacher will be sure that one has copied from the other. In the case of the Gospels, there is no moral question involved; and it is usual to state the principle in the form: "Identity of language involves literary dependence on one side or the other."

This is a basic principle in the solution of what is called "the Synoptic Problem." Before applying it in detail, we need to have a general view of the situation. The illustration on page 56 (where X indicates occurrence of a given saying or incident in the Gospel at the head of the column) shows the various situations which may occur for any incident or saying.

Thus Matthew, Mark, and Luke may have an incident, or it may appear only in Matthew and Mark, or Mark and Luke, etc.

[7] G. H. Macgregor, *John,* Moffatt New Testament Commentary, Harper, n.d., p. xvii. The concluding quotation is from P. W. Schmiedel, *The Johannine Writings,* p. 42.

Some material is peculiar to one Gospel, but it is to be noted that there is practically no material which appears in Mark alone. Over 95 percent of Mark's material appears in either Matthew or Luke, over 90 percent in Matthew and over 75 percent in

Matthew	Mark	Luke
X	X	X
X	X	
	X	X
X		X
X		
		X

Luke. The material which Matthew and Luke have in common with no parallel in Mark is about one-fifth of each Gospel.

When one turns to consider the order of the various sections in the three Gospels, there is a tantalizing impression of general sameness, with numerous variations which seem to have some pattern, but one which is hard to make out. Careful examination shows that if the order of events in the other two Gospels is compared with that of Mark, it turns out that while both Matthew and Luke vary from the Markan order from time to time, they never happen to agree on a difference in order. Where Matthew has a variation, Luke has the same order as Mark; where Luke varies from Mark's order, Matthew always agrees with Mark.

PRIMACY OF MARK

These facts of content and order suggest the hypothesis that Mark was written first, and that copies of Mark were in the hands of both Matthew and Luke when they wrote their Gospels. Both accepted its order as basic, but each varied from it occasionally for reasons (often fairly obvious) which seemed good to them. Each made some omissions. The very few cases where both made the same omission are easy to explain—Mark's title, parenthetical explanations, matter somewhat similar to that found elsewhere in these Gospels, miracles whose performance is less impressive than usual (Mark 7:32–37; 8:22–26), etc. Other omissions are intelligible in terms of the author's purpose, which was different in each case. Another factor which doubtless played a role here, as well as elsewhere, was the limitation on the available space set by the normal length of a papyrus roll, which was in turn set by the physical necessities of ease of handling, just as the size of modern books is primarily determined by the same sort of considerations. This may help to account for the different proportions of Markan matter used by Matthew and Luke, since each deals with the problem of space in a different way—Matthew, as will be seen, by compression; Luke by selection.

Clearly the hypothesis of the use of one Gospel by the writers of the other two will account in general for the evidence of literary dependence. Comparison shows not only the fact of literary dependence but also that the Markan hypothesis can explain both the occurrence of identities in language and also the existence of differences. A typical illustration is found in Mark 1:29–31 and its parallels, Matthew 8:14–15 and Luke 4:38–39. In the chart on page 58, words common to all three are in capital letters. Note how these words form the backbone of all three selections. Words common to Matthew and Mark are underscored with a broken line; words common to Mark and Luke only are underscored with a full line.

The following observations can be easily verified:

1. All three accounts are basically the same and imply literary dependence. All three give the same information in much the same words.

MATTHEW 8:14–15	MARK 1:29–31	LUKE 4:38–39
AND when Jesus ENTERED Peter's HOUSE,	AND immediately he left the synagogue, and ENTERED the HOUSE of Simon and Andrew, with James and John. Now Simon's MOTHER-IN-LAW lay sick WITH A FEVER, and immediately they told him of her. AND HE came and took her by the hand and lifted her up, AND THE FEVER LEFT HER; AND SHE SERVED them.	AND he arose and left the synagogue, and ENTERED Simon's HOUSE.
he saw his MOTHER-IN-LAW lying sick WITH A FEVER; AND HE touched her hand,		Now Simon's MOTHER-IN-LAW was ill WITH A high FEVER, and they besought him for her, AND HE stood over her AND rebuked THE FEVER, AND it LEFT HER; AND immediately SHE rose AND SERVED them.
AND THE FEVER LEFT HER, AND SHE rose AND SERVED him.		

2. Matthew's account is a stripped-down version of Mark's. Almost all his words are found in Mark. He has to supply *Jesus* as the subject of *entered* because of what immediately precedes this in his Gospel. He substitutes *Peter* for *Simon*, probably because this apostle was better known to Greek readers by his Greek name. To say that "she *rose* and served them" is less awkward than Mark's bald statement. In any case, it serves to emphasize the cure. Luke makes the same obvious addition.

3. Luke's version is about the same length as Mark's and uses more of Mark's words than Matthew does. In general, Luke is much the best writer among the authors of the Gospels; and here, as elsewhere, while he follows Mark closely in content if he uses him at all, he smooths out the style and introduces more variety of expression. He is able to make more use of the great possibilities of Greek for effective writing. He also avoids many of the expressions and usages that had crept into the common Greek of the time. If he had been writing English, he would probably have avoided expressions like "finalize" and "to contact." Matthew and Mark would have had no scruples about them.

Thus, if we assume Mark to have been available to Matthew and Luke, we can easily account for the variation in wording among them in parallel accounts. But if we were to assume that one of the others was the primitive version, it would be impossible to find any simple way of accounting for the differences. Augustine's theory that Mark abbreviated Matthew is clearly wrong. Though Mark as a whole is shorter, where they have parallel passages it is Matthew who is the abbreviator. Mark is sometimes ungrammatical in Greek, and then both Matthew and Luke correct him. Experience (with student term papers, for example) shows that when a writer is following a well-written source, he approximates to the standards of his source even though his own standards are very much lower. Sometimes Mark has a sentence which does not finish, where Matthew's and Luke's versions have complete sentences. Sentences which do not come out anywhere are common in poor writers composing freely, but poor writers are not likely to introduce unfinished sentences into material which is correctly written.

To sum up, the hypothesis that Matthew and Luke knew and used Mark accounts simply and adequately for the facts of content, order, and wording where the three Gospels have parallel material.

Q

Besides the passages where Matthew, Mark, and Luke run parallel, there is a group of passages where Matthew and Luke have the same material, with nothing comparable in Mark. As has been said, this accounts for about one-fifth of each Gospel. In some cases, the resemblance is especially striking, as appears in the following passage in which this time *variations* are in italics.

MATTHEW 11:4–9	LUKE 7:22–26
And Jesus answered them, "Go and tell John what you hear and see: the blind receive their sight, *and* the lame walk, lepers are cleansed and the deaf hear, *and* the dead are raised up *and* the poor have good news preached to them. And blessed is he who takes no offense at me." *As they went away, Jesus* began to speak to the crowds concerning	And *he* answered them, "Go and tell John what you have seen and heard: the blind receive their sight, the lame walk, lepers are cleansed, and the deaf hear, the dead are raised up, the poor have good news preached to them. And blessed is he who takes no offense at me." *When the messengers of John had gone, he* began to speak to the crowds concerning

John: "What did you go out
into the wilderness to behold?
A reed shaken by the wind?
Why then did you go out?
To see a man clothed in
soft raiment? Behold, those who
wear soft raiment are in

kings' *houses.*
Why then did you go out?
To see a prophet?
Yes, I tell you, and
more than a prophet."

John: "What did you go out
into the wilderness to behold?
A reed shaken by the wind?
What then did you go out to see?
A man clothed in
soft raiment? Behold those who
are *gorgeously appareled and live
in luxury* are in
kings' *courts. What*
then did you go out
to see? A prophet?
Yes, I tell you, and
more than a prophet."

In other cases the differences are much greater, as in the following, where again differences are in italics.

MATTHEW 6:9–13

Our Father *who art in heaven,*
Hallowed be thy name.
Thy kingdom come,
Thy will be done,
  On earth as it is in heaven.
Give us *this* day our daily bread;
And forgive us our *debts*
  As we *also have* forgiven
    our debtors
And lead us not into temptation,
But deliver us from evil.

LUKE 11:2–4

Father,
Hallowed be thy name.
Thy kingdom come.

Give us *each* day our daily bread;
And forgive us our *sins,*
As we *ourselves* forgive *every one
who is in*debted *to us;*
and lead us not into temptation.

Such variety presents a problem, but in general we can apply the principle we have already used: that common language implies a common source. In the case of the matter common to Matthew and Luke but absent from Mark there are three possibilities: Matthew used Luke, Luke used Matthew, or both used some other source which has since disappeared. The third possibility seems to be the correct one. In the first place, if either Matthew used Luke or Luke used Matthew, it is hard to see why either would have made some of the omissions of material that they must have made on this hypothesis. Why would Matthew omit the parable of the Prodigal Son? Or why would Luke omit the parable of the Sheep and the Goats? But even if we suppose they had reasons satisfactory to them which we cannot conjecture (after all, mind-reading across a gap of two thousand years is a little difficult), there is a decisive reason for rejecting the idea that either Matthew or Luke drew material from the other. It has already been seen that the order of Mark's Gospel is basic to the other two. If now we inquire as to where in the Markan outline Matthew and Luke insert this other material, it turns out that with one or two obvious exceptions they never insert a given piece of non-Markan material at the same point in Mark's outline. Suppose, then, that Luke used Matthew's Gospel. Then Luke must have taken Matthew, compared it with Mark, removed each non-Markan section from its context in Matthew and inserted it at some other point in Mark, even when its context as given in Matthew was very appropriate. This is, to say the least, highly unlikely. Moreover, though the argument has been stated in terms of the possible use of Matthew by Luke, it holds just as well if we were to suppose Matthew used Luke. It eliminates both possibilities and leaves us with the third: that both Matthew and Luke used a source now lost. It is the custom of Biblical scholars to call this lost source *Q*, doubtless because this is the initial of the German word *Quelle*, which means "source." (The reason for taking the initial of a German word is simply that the theory was first worked out by German scholars.)

When we try to be specific about the nature and content of *Q* as an independent source, some things are clear, but others seem to be forever shrouded in obscurity. In the first place, the material so designated consists almost exclusively of sayings of Jesus. It appears first in connection with John the Baptist, and ceases just before the story of the final week in Jesus' life. It thus contains no account of the Crucifixion or the Resurrection and cannot therefore have been a Gospel. It contains the Temptation story, much of the Sermon on the Mount, instructions to the disciples, some parables of the kingdom (leaven, lost sheep), woes on the Pharisees, and predictions of the coming of the Son of man.

As has been said, the order of this material is quite different in Matthew and Luke; and since Jesus' sayings as given by Matthew are in five large blocks which are determined by Matthew's specific purpose and plan, it seems likely that his order is artificial. It is assumed therefore that Luke's order is more like the original order of the sayings in Q.

It has already been pointed out that in some cases the parallelism between Matthew and Luke is extremely close, in others rather loose; and this poses a problem. We can easily discover from the way these two authors treat Mark what their habits were when they used a source. They may abbreviate or rewrite, but we are quite unprepared for such radical changes as would be necessary by one or both authors if the Lord's Prayer, for example, were derived by both Matthew and Luke from a source which was identical in both cases. Perhaps the best solution is to recognize that Q was not a single fixed document, but a collection of the teachings of Jesus, which was to some extent fluid and which varied in content and wording in different localities. It is also possible that Matthew and Luke derived parallel but widely varying versions of some stories from entirely independent sources.

With these uncertainties about the exact form and content of Q, it is not possible to arrive at any very definite date for Q. It is generally supposed to be somewhat earlier than Mark. This would be certain if, as some scholars think, Mark made some slight use of Q; but it is by no means clear that this is a necessary hypothesis. In any case, Q in some form or other may be as early as the decade from A.D. 50 to A.D. 60.

The bulk of the material in Matthew and Luke is accounted for by their use of Mark and Q. Yet each has important material which is unique. This includes the stories of the Wise Men in Matthew; of the appearance of the angels to the shepherds in Luke; such parables as the Good Samaritan and the Prodigal Son in Luke; the Wise and the Foolish Virgins in Matthew; to take only a few striking examples. Where they got this material, whether from oral tradition or from otherwise unknown written documents, we simply cannot say.

We may sum up the account of the literary relationships between the Synoptic Gospels by an illustration in which rectangles stand for existing books, circles for assumed sources, and arrows point to sources. M and L stand for the unknown sources of unique material in Matthew and Luke respectively.

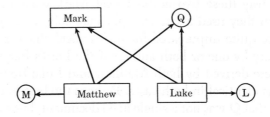

CHAPTER 5

The Evaluation of the Sources

THE HISTORICAL approach not only commits us to an appeal to the most ancient sources as a basis for any assertions we make about Jesus and his teachings; it also commits us to an evaluation of those sources. As the first step in such an evaluation, we need to find out all we can about who wrote them, when, and where.

There are two ways of going about such an inquiry, and both must be used. The first is search for what is called *external evidence*. What references do other ancient writers make to our sources? What do they tell us about date, authorship, and place of composition? Such evidence is called *external* because it is outside the book we are interested in. In contrast with this is *internal evidence*. Books contain within themselves clues as to their date and authorship; for example, books which refer to the atomic bomb will be subsequent to 1945. The allusions may be to ideas or events as well as to things. For the determination of authorship the occurrence or nonoccurrence of distinctive ideas and the distinctive style of an author are clues. These latter have only negative value unless we have some other undisputed pieces of the author's work. Thus, style and ideas may help decide whether the Gospel of John and the first Epistle of John are by the same author; but they cannot throw any light on whether their author was John, the son of Zebedee, some other John, or someone whose name is quite unknown.

MARK

In turning to a study of these questions about the Gospels, it is necessary to keep a firm grip on the result already attained: that Mark is (from internal evidence) the oldest Gospel. What are we told about Mark by the early Church writers? (There are no ancient references whatsoever to the Gospel writers outside of the Church Fathers.) The earliest writer to refer to the Gospel of Mark is a certain Papias, bishop of a city in Asia Minor, who wrote probably about A.D. 140. We do not have Papias' book, but we have a quotation from it preserved in the *Church History* of Eusebius, written about A.D. 300. In other cases we can check Eusebius' quotations; and we find him to be generally careful and accurate, so that we may be reasonably sure that we know what Papias said. But since Papias tells us that Mark was written about seventy years before his time, we need to inquire as to the source of Papias' knowledge. Papias tells us that he got his information from "the elder." At this point our chain breaks. We simply do not know surely who "the elder" was, or whether the elder based his assertion on sound knowledge or not. It does not add to our confidence that Eusebius remarks that Papias "was a man of very little intelligence, as is clear from his books." But what Papias says is this: "Mark became Peter's interpreter and wrote accurately all that he remembered, not, indeed, in order, of the things said or done by the Lord. For he had not heard the Lord, nor had he followed him, but later on, as I said, followed Peter, who used to give teaching as necessity demanded but not make, as it were, an arrangement of the Lord's oracles, so that Mark did nothing wrong in thus writing down single points as he remembered them. For to one thing he gave attention, to leave out nothing of what he had heard and to make no false statements in them."[1]

The other important ancient witness is Bishop Irenaeus of Lyons, who wrote a book against heresies about A.D. 180, in which, speaking of Peter and Paul in Rome, he says, "After their decease Mark the disciple and interpreter of Peter also handed down to us in writing what Peter preached."[2]

If we turn now to consider the internal evidence, we find that at best it only partly confirms the external evidence. We cannot compare this Gospel with anything else written by Mark, for the simple reason that we have nothing else written by him; nor is there anything in the book to connect it with him, or for that matter, any other specific person. Many scholars do assert some connection of Peter with the book, but it must be admitted that the evidence they offer is not likely to convince anyone who chooses to be skeptical. In any case, it is clear that some of the statements in the book cannot be based on Peter's direct recollection. To take the most striking example, the story of the Resurrection appearance to the women who went to visit the tomb cannot rest on Peter's own firsthand knowledge. Neither was he present at Jesus' trial. There is also reason, as we shall see, for believing that many of the little narratives of which the Gospel is composed enjoyed a wide and independent circulation before they were included in Mark's Gospel.

There is rather general agreement that a date just before or just after A.D. 70 is correct. This is about six years after the Neronian persecution in which Peter is believed to have lost his life, and to this extent agrees with Irenaeus' statement. It is to be noted, however, that the key to dating on the basis of internal evidence is the relation of Mark 13 to the destruction of Jerusa-

[1] As quoted in Eusebius, *The Ecclesiastical History,* III, xxxix, 15, K. Lake (trans.), Loeb Classical Library, Putnam's, 1926, vol. I, p. 297.

[2] Irenaeus, *Against Heresies,* E. R. Hardy (trans.), in *Early Christian Fathers,* Library of Christian Classics, Westminster Press, 1953, vol. I, p. 370.

lem. Since some scholars see in this chapter clear evidence that it reflects conditions just before the destruction, while others see in the same passages evidence that it was written just after the destruction, it seems plain that the evidence is not quite as clear-cut as we would like it to be. Somewhere in the neighborhood of A.D. 70 is probably right; but there are degrees of probability, and here the degree is not the highest.

As for Rome being the place of composition, here again the evidence is not as strong as we would like to have it. It is generally accepted—primarily, one suspects, because evidence for any other place is, if possible, even more scant.

If, then, we conclude that Mark was written in Rome, about A.D. 70, perhaps by a man named Mark who had some connection with Peter, we should do so with the recognition that our grounds for it are by no means as firm as we would like them to be; and we can hardly expect to build on them any structure that can be called on to bear much weight.

MATTHEW

When we turn to Matthew, Papias is again our chief authority. At the end of the passage already quoted, Eusebius continues: "This is related by Papias about Mark, and about Matthew this was said, 'Matthew collected the oracles in the Hebrew language, and each interpreted them as best he could.'" It is natural to suppose that he was here intending to refer to the Gospel of Matthew; but if so he is clearly wrong, for the Gospel of Matthew, as has been seen, is based directly upon Mark and thus must have been written in Greek. Moreover, it is hard to suppose that if one of Jesus' immediate followers, such as Matthew, had written a Gospel, he would simply have copied large portions of the work of a man who wasn't there. And if, by any chance, this is what he did, then his work has only the authority of his sources, not that of an eyewitness.

For the date we have only general considerations: this Gospel must be later than Mark. If Mark was written in A.D. 70, Matthew must be later than that. How much later is hard to say; A.D. 85–90 is a common estimate.

It is generally inferred that Matthew was written in Antioch. The early Church in Antioch, as both Acts and Paul's letter to the Galatians show, was a mixed Jewish and Gentile group. Such seems to be the background of this Gospel. In many respects it is the most Jewish of the Gospels, but in other respects it looks forward without reserve to the spread of the Church among the Gentiles. Such a book would fittingly find its origin in such a community. One small detail is perhaps significant. In the story of the question about whether Jesus should pay the temple tax, told in Matthew 17:24–27, it is presupposed that a coin called a *stater* was exactly equivalent to two didrachmas. It was only in Antioch and Damascus that this equation held.

LUKE

There is no early external evidence for the Gospel of Luke. By the end of the second century, it is one of the four recognized Gospels, ascribed to the physician Luke, the companion of Paul. Indications of when and where he wrote it are lacking.

Internal evidence is not of much help. The author's understanding of Paul (as shown by Acts) is at best superficial. This does not prove he was not a companion of Paul, but neither does it prove that he was. As for his being a physician, it has been asserted that this is verified by the fact that Luke's vocabulary has much in common with the vocabulary of the Greek medical writers. The contention breaks down, however, since examination of other Greek writers of the period shows the same phenomena. We would have to say that if this argument proves Luke was a physician it proves that other writers were physicians too. Many of the supposed medical words occur in the Septuagint, in Josephus, Plutarch, and the satirist Lucian. The argument is worthless.

One may ask how the name of Luke got attached to the book if he did not write it. If the author were ever unknown, it might be expected that it would be ascribed to someone more prominent than Luke. This argument has some force; but it is also true that a line of inference can be traced from references in the New Testament which might have led an inquirer to the "discovery" that Luke must have been the author. Lukan authorship is possible, perhaps probable—but not proven.

We have no knowledge as to where the book was written and no very plausible conjectures. As to date, we are in the same position we are with regard to Matthew. Our only sure clue is the fact that it was written later than Mark, therefore later than A.D. 70. Some things in Luke have been taken to imply some acquaintance with the works of Josephus. If this is correct, it would require a date somewhere about A.D. 95 or after, a date which is not unreasonable in any case.

RESULTS OF THIS APPROACH

The results of these discussions are not very substantial, and it is important to see why they are necessary. Why can we not simply assume that Papias and Irenaeus and others doubtless had good reasons for their assertions even if we cannot discover them? There are two answers to this. In the first place, historians have learned that, in general, untested assumptions are more often wrong than right, even when they are made with the best intentions in the world. Moreover, as has been said, the controversy during the second century with the Gnostics led the anti-Gnostic party to appeal to three apostolic standards: the creed, supposedly what the apostles taught; the episcopate—that is, the bishops who had succeeded the apostles; and the canon—the list of books written by the apostles. The orthodox party was sure that it was true to these standards. If there was a Gospel highly valued by the orthodox, then they were certain it must have been written by an apostle. Starting with this belief that the books *must* have had apostolic authors, any hint derived from rumor, tradition, or the books themselves that could connect them directly or indirectly with an apostle would be accepted uncritically in the heat of controversy. It was not a case of deliberate falsification but of willingness to be easily satisfied with regard to conclusions they were sure were right in any case. Of course, such procedure did not satisfy the opponents; but it must be remembered that the battle was won, not by the superior logic of the orthodox party but by its exercise of disciplinary powers. Anyone who would not agree was simply shoved out. Those who were left were easily convinced because they wanted to be. If we want to have solid foundations beneath our assertions about the life and teaching of Jesus, we must try to find some way of getting on to firm ground.

THE GOSPEL OF JOHN

We must, of course, ask our questions about the Fourth Gospel; but in considering the traditions, it is particularly necessary here to remember that all of them come to us from this side of the great divide which the Gnostic controversy provides. The possibility of wishful thinking must be allowed for.

The earliest statements about the authorship of the Fourth Gospel are found in Irenaeus: "John, the disciple of the Lord, who had also lain on his breast, himself published the gospel, while he was living at Ephesus in Asia."[3] This residence of John in Asia was put at the end of the first century and the beginning of the second.

There are, however, some problems about this statement. In the first place, there are traces of a tradition in out-of-the-way

[3] *Ibid.*

places that John, the son of Zebedee, was martyred before A.D. 50 and therefore could not have been bishop of Ephesus half a century later and written the Gospel then. We have a conflict in tradition; but it is easy to see, if it came to be officially recognized by the end of the second century that the Fourth Gospel was the work of John, how any reports contradicting this would be ignored as obviously wrong, and would survive, if at all, only in obscure places. On the other hand, if it had always been clearly known and understood that John had lived to a ripe old age in Ephesus, it is hard to see how a conflicting tradition would ever arise anywhere.

Another fact which must be considered is that Papias, though he seems to say nothing about the composition of this Gospel, indicates that there were two Johns in Ephesus. It was a common-enough name; and, without our system of family names, confusion would be easy.

Certainly the internal evidence is more easily reconcilable with authorship by someone other than the apostle, though the point can hardly be demonstrated apart from a more detailed study of the book than is possible at this point.

The traditional date, about A.D. 100, seems more probable than the traditional authorship. A scrap of papyrus from the early part of the second century containing a part of the Fourth Gospel shows that it cannot have been much later than A.D. 100. That it comes from the end of the century is implied by the nature of the references to Jesus' opponents as "the Jews." This is not the way they are referred to in the Synoptic Gospels. The Sadducees have disappeared. Again, the main points at which there is conflict between Jesus and his opponents are those which were at issue at the end of the century, not those which are found in the Synoptic Gospels and in Acts. A confirming detail is the reference in John 9:34 and 16:2 to excommunication from the synagogue. There is no evidence that this was ever the practice before A.D.

85–90, when a "Test Benediction" was drawn up by Rabbi Simeon the Less, at the request of Rabbi Gamaliel II, with the express intention of excluding heretics (among whom were Jewish Christians).

Evidence for and against Ephesus, Alexandria, or Antioch as

This fragment known as Rylands Greek Papyrus 457 is from the eighteenth chapter of John. It can be dated by means of the handwriting to about A.D. 125. It is not, of course, part of the original manuscript but it shows that the Gospel must have been completed before that date. (Courtesy of the John Rylands Library, Manchester, England)

the place of composition is divided, and no certainty can be reached.

The results of this examination of the evidence as to authorship, date, and place of composition of the Gospels are disappointing. They can be summed up by saying that the Gospels were written by people who were not eyewitnesses, a generation or two after the events they tell about, far from the scenes they depict, in an alien language and under the influences of a strange culture. Nevertheless, it is possible to find in the Gospels sound materials for a knowledge of the life and especially the teachings of Jesus, but we shall have to do so by some way other than simply taking the Gospels as we have them to be direct reports written by people who were there.

To start with, we have the general confirmation of the basic outline of the Gospel story from the Jewish and Roman sources we have considered. But this does not take us very far; and no further progress is possible until we deal with the question, already suggested, as to whether the Synoptic picture of Jesus, or that of the Fourth Gospel, is fundamental. Was Jesus' message that the kingdom of Heaven was at hand and men should prepare for God's deliverance, or was it the exhibition of his divine sonship and the summons to recognize this?

HISTORICAL VALUE OF THE FOURTH GOSPEL

When the issue is formulated in these terms, it is hard to see how the Johannine picture as a whole can be original. At various points of detail, some scholars think the Fourth Gospel has preserved a sounder tradition; and this is entirely compatible with the priority of the general Synoptic interpretation. But if the more exalted picture given by the Fourth Gospel is true, it is hard to see how three Gospels giving a "lower" interpretation ever got written, and still harder to see how they ever came to be accepted throughout the Church.

That the trend of Christian thought was toward the exaltation of Jesus is clear within the Synoptic Gospels themselves. Details which Mark reports which seem to imply some limitation on Jesus' powers, such as the statement that he could do no miracles in his home town, or stories of cures which are not completed by the simple pronouncement of a word, are eliminated in Matthew and Luke. To suppose that the Jesus presented in the Fourth Gospel is the original, of which the Synoptics are a watered-down version, is to go against the evidence of the Synoptic Gospels themselves as to the direction taken by Christian interpretation.

This general impression is strengthened when the two versions are compared to the actual religious situation in Palestine in the early part of the first century. The Synoptic Gospels, in their picture of the Jewish parties, the main points of friction between Jesus and his opponents, the questions under discussion, the use of Scripture, the emphasis on moral conduct, and the expectation of the coming of the kingdom, seem thoroughly rooted in Palestine of that time as we can reconstruct it from other sources.

This is not true of the background of the Fourth Gospel, despite the discovery that there are elements common to this Gospel and the Dead Sea Scrolls. This opens up some interesting possibilities but does not invalidate the general conclusion, because these common points are also widely spread over the Near East. They are not native to Judaism, and only go to show that influences which entered into the Johannine interpretation of Jesus were also at work elsewhere in Judaism. But the substitution of *eternal life* for *the kingdom of God;* the de-emphasis on the ethical elements in Jesus' preaching; the view that the primary function of the Scriptures is to testify of Jesus rather than reveal God's will; the use of the clearly Hellenistic idea of the Logos (*Word*); the presentation of Jesus as the divinely-sent being whose function it is to convey to men a mystical life with God, rather than as God's chosen instrument for securing to his people the blessings which would fall to those who served him perfectly—all seem secondary. The background of the Synoptic Gospels is akin to what has been called *normative Judaism*, while the background of the Fourth Gospel represents a kind of Judaism more akin to Hellenism. Which of these is more likely to be original seems to leave little room for doubt.

To say that the Fourth Gospel hardly gives us an accurate picture of the life and teaching of Jesus is not to say that it is worthless. Even after we have arrived at conclusions as to what he said and did, we still have the problem of estimating the significance of these words and deeds. The Fourth Gospel comes into its own as an interpretation of Christian experience.

HISTORICAL DATA IN THE SYNOPTIC GOSPELS

The recognition that the Synoptic Gospels are our primary sources for the words and deeds of Jesus does not, however, as has been shown, solve all our problems. We still need some way of breaking through the barrier of the lateness and anonymity of our primary sources. Helpful in this direction is the type of study known as *form criticism.*

The first step is the recognition that the short sections of which these Gospels are composed show signs of being older than their present setting. If one compares the Gospels, it soon becomes clear that the sections vary much more at their beginnings and their ends than in the central core. If these links between sections are detached, each story is complete in itself and stands on its own feet. This would not be true of the paragraphs of a fresh composition, planned as a whole and set down for the first time. It means that the so-called authors were really compilers of older material rather than authors in the usual sense.

Once the string is broken, the beads fall apart; but we are now in a position to look for clues as to the age of the individual beads. We are no longer tied to the date of the whole string as the date of the beads. They are certainly older than the stringing, but this in itself does not tell how much older. As it turns out, not all the beads are the same age. But how can that be determined?

In the first place, the units are classifiable into a limited number of forms; and in some cases, at least, form gives a clue to age. Some narratives serve as the setting for a saying of Jesus, while others are told for the interest of the story. Compare these accounts of the healing of a blind man:

And as he came out of Jericho with his disciples and a crowd
of people, there sat a blind beggar at the wayside. When he
heard that Jesus of Nazareth was passing, he cried out after
him, "Jesus, Son of David, have pity on me!" Then Jesus
stopped, and said, "Call him here." They called to the blind
man, "Come, cheer up, he is calling you." He threw aside his
mantle, sprang up, and came toward Jesus. And Jesus asked
him, "What is it you want with me?" The blind man replied,
"Master, that I may be able to see." Then said Jesus to him,
"Go your way, your faith has restored you." And at once he
was able to see, and followed him on his way."[4]

In this story the emphasis is on the man's faith and the word
of Jesus which it calls forth. In the following story the interest is
centered on the miracle and the process by which it was accomplished. It contains no saying of general import such as, "Your
faith has restored you."

As they came to Bethsaida, they brought a blind man to him
and begged him to touch him. So he took the blind man by
the hand and led him out of the village. Then he put spittle
in his eyes, laid his hands upon him, and asked, "Can you see
anything?" And he looked and said, "I can make out people,
for I see something like trees moving about." Then Jesus again
laid his hands upon his eyes; and he looked sharply in front of
him; so he was healed and was able to recognize everything
clearly.[5]

Such miracle stories as the latter are typically Greek, while the
anecdote serving to give point to a teacher's saying is well known
in Jewish sources. A story strongly molded by, if not originating
in, a Greek environment, has *prima facie* a poorer claim to au-
thenticity.

[4] M. Dibelius, *The Message of Jesus Christ,* F. C. Grant (trans.), Scribner's, 1939, p. 19.
[5] Dibelius, *op. cit.,* p. 99.

Other sayings of Jesus are preserved without a narrative setting. Many of these are found in the Sermon on the Mount. Many have the parallelism of Hebrew poetry and also have a quality which makes an unforgettable impression. Such sayings have a strong claim to genuineness.

> I say to you, love your enemies
> And pray for those who persecute you,
> So that you may be sons of your Father who is in heaven;
> For he makes his sun rise on the evil and on the good,
> And sends rain on the just and on the unjust.
>
> If anyone strikes you on the right cheek, turn to him the other also.
>
> It is easier for a camel to go through the eye of a needle than for a rich man to enter the kingdom of God.
> (Matt. 5:44–45, 5:39*b*; Mark 10:25.)

A clearly marked form is the parable. Such stories were often told by Jewish teachers. Thus:

> R. Eleazar b. Azariah said: . . . He whose wisdom is more abundant than his works, to what is he like? To a tree whose branches are abundant but whose roots are few; and the wind comes and uproots it and overturns it. . . . But he whose works are more abundant than his wisdom, to what is he like? To a tree whose branches are few but whose roots are many; so that even if all the winds in the world come and blow against it, it cannot be stirred from its place.[6]

There is evidence that, in the process of transmission, Jesus' parables were worked over and adapted to later situations; but in many cases it is not hard to see what has happened, so that the parables turn out to be one of our most important sources for a knowledge of Jesus' teaching.

[6] "Pirqe Aboth" 3:18, in H. Danby (trans.), *The Mishnah*, Oxford, 1933, p. 452.

One narrative stands out for its greater length, the connection between the elements, and its intrinsic importance. This is the so-called Passion narrative, the story of Jesus' Last Supper with his disciples, and his arrest, trial, and execution. Even the Gospel of John, for all its differences in detail, shows the same underlying pattern at this point. Whenever and however the Gospel of John and the Synoptic Gospels diverged, the same general view of Jesus' last days seems prior to both of them.

There is much of the Synoptic material, then, whose form indicates that it originated in Palestine, and thus earlier than the development of the Gentile Christianity for which our Gospels were written. A similar conclusion can be drawn from the background of many of the units themselves. They reflect Jewish customs, Jewish scenes, and Jewish interests, and consequently could not have originated or even taken form in a Gentile environment.

To have established a Palestinian origin for the tradition about Jesus does not solve all problems by any means. Nevertheless, it does afford an additional ground for confidence that we have authentic materials, since we know independently that the sayings of Jewish teachers were customarily carefully preserved in oral form.

Another gain from the discovery that our Gospels are composed from previously independent units which circulated widely among the followers of Jesus is the recognition that the old tradition is not simply the recollection of some individual or individuals set down a number of years after the event. It is the common tradition of the community which grew up shortly after his death among those who had actually seen and heard him. This provided a control whose importance is shown by a comparison of our Gospels and the later apocryphal Gospels and Acts. Where this control was lacking, the result, as has been seen, was an extravagant growth of legend whose results can only be described as ridiculous.

It is not enough, however, to show that, in general, we may expect to find sound tradition where we can find evidences of a Palestinian background; nor is a story or saying valueless in all cases where such a background is lacking.

We need, therefore, some tests which can be applied to the materials which seem to be old, by which we can recognize the presence of distortion even in traditions rooted in Palestine. What passes these tests has a strong presumption of being genuine, especially when the material thus isolated leads to a consistent picture which will account for the later development of the Christian community.

Negatively, we will be suspicious of material with the following characteristics: where sayings have as their background not the coming kingdom but concern for the life of the settled community; where sayings reflect later interpretation of the life of Jesus; where sayings are simply expressions of common wisdom in popular form; where the radical demand is replaced by common sense and prudence. Positively, genuine tradition will be generally free from non-Christian and secular influences; it will have characteristics aiding retention in the memory; and it will be in forms suitable for use in the Church's message of salvation.

Finally, it is reassuring that the picture which emerges is confirmed in its main outlines by Paul:

> The Pauline testimony, therefore, is all of a piece. He attests the character of Jesus, something of His life and death, and something of His teaching; and he assigns Him His place in history as a crucified Messiah. This testimony is of the utmost importance, since we know that Paul came into the Church (which he already knew before his conversion) within seven years (probably less) from the Crucifixion; that he was well acquainted with Peter, John, and James, the brother of Jesus; and that for all their differences of opinion, he never differed from them in his conception of the fundamental tradition.[7]

[7] C. H. Dodd, *History and the Gospel*. Nisbet, 1952, p. 68.

It is to be noted that, while these various tests give us some assurance that we know what Jesus taught and in general the kind of things Jesus did, we have no such assurance as to the order of events in his life, apart from such obvious facts as that the Crucifixion and events associated with it marked the end of his life; his baptism preceded his preaching; he taught in Galilee and died at Jerusalem. But beyond such generalities we have little information. Papias' statement that Mark did not write in order is confirmed by what we know about the history of the tradition. But we have seen that Mark's order is the basis of Matthew's and Luke's, so that if we cannot rely on Mark we are no better off with the others. If this at first seems a great loss, it is not really so, as can be seen as soon as we ask how much light the present order of events really throws on the nature of Jesus' career. To put the question in another form: how would the essentials of our picture of Jesus change if it were shown that the events of the "Galilean ministry" actually occurred in quite a different order? The harmonizers of the Gospels would have a different set of problems, but nothing important would be changed.

CHAPTER 6

The Jewish Background: General

IF WE ARE to interpret the Gospels correctly, we must have some
knowledge of the social and religious conditions out of which
they grew. These conditions provided an all-pervasive atmosphere which is essential to a comprehension of the career and
teaching of Jesus and of the activities of his early followers after
the Resurrection.

THE GEOGRAPHICAL SETTING

Palestine is a small country. From Nazareth to Jerusalem is
only a matter of seventy-five miles as the crow flies. The country
is rugged; a mountain ridge forms its backbone; extensive level
areas are few. Fields are stony, often terraced. Trees are scarce.
The climate differs in different parts of the land, being mild and
even along the coast, more extreme in the highlands, and tropi-
cal in the deep gash through which the Jordan River flows.
Summers are dry and rainless. A rainy season extends from October to April. The winds are generally westerly. Occasionally
the hot, dry, violent sirocco blows in from the east across the
desert, bringing dust and sand, endangering health, and threat-

ening growing things. The coastal plain is well watered, but after the winter rains the highlands are soon parched. Wadies which are rushing torrents during the rainy season disappear completely during the summer months. Permanent springs are few. Water must be carefully stored in cisterns.

The general lay of the land can be easily understood from examination of a cross section of Palestine, say at Jerusalem.

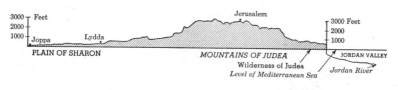

CROSS SECTION OF PALESTINE (at Jerusalem)

There are thus four main divisions, with the central highland rising from the coastal plain to over 3000 feet above sea level, and with the Jordan Valley dipping to some 1300 feet below sea level. The central highland is broken just below Nazareth by the plain of Esdraelon. The hills to the north of Esdraelon are known as Galilee. To the south of the plain, the rolling country, which gives way to low mountains with open plains between, is known as Samaria. These rise to an old and broken tableland which is Judea. To the south this runs out into desert.

The Jordan River rises in the mountains north of Galilee, and passes through the swamps of Lake Huleh at about sea level. From there it descends to Galilee, nearly 700 feet below sea level, whence it drops by a winding, tortuous course to the Dead Sea.

The plateau to the east of the Jordan hardly figures in the New Testament.

The chief political divisions at the time of Jesus' ministry were the tetrarchy of Galilee and Perea, under Herod Antipas; Judea, under a Roman procurator; the Decapolis, a league of some ten

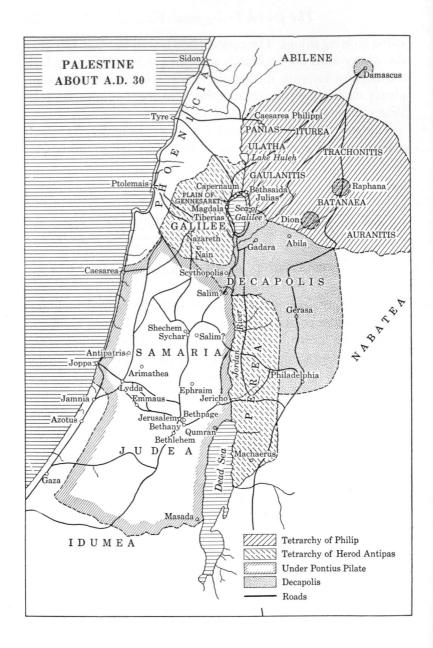

PALESTINE
ABOUT A.D. 30

Sidon

ABILENE

Damascus

Tyre

PHOENICIA

Caesarea Philippi

PANIAS — ITUREA

ULATHA
Lake Huleh

TRACHONITIS

Ptolemais

GAULANITIS

Raphana

Capernaum
PLAIN OF
GENNESARET

Bethsaida
Julias

BATANAEA

Magdala
Tiberias

*Sea of
Galilee*

Dion

GALILEE

AURANITIS

Nazareth

Abila

Gadara

Nain

Caesarea

Scythopolis

DECAPOLIS

Salim?

Gerasa

Jordan River

Shechem
Sychar

Salim?

N A B A T E A

Antipatris

S A M A R I A

P E R E A

Joppa

Arimathea

Philadelphia

Lydda

Ephraim

Jamnia

Emmaus

Jericho

Azotus

Jerusalem

Bethpage

Bethany

Qumran

Bethlehem

J U D E A

Dead Sea

Machaerus

Gaza

Masada

I D U M E A

/////	Tetrarchy of Philip
\\\\\	Tetrarchy of Herod Antipas
≈≈≈≈	Under Pontius Pilate
::::	Decapolis
——	Roads

independent cities with Greek culture; and the tetrarchy of Philip to the northeast of the Sea of Galilee.

Many cities and towns figure in the Gospel story. Important in Galilee were Nazareth, where Jesus grew up; Capernaum on the Sea of Galilee, which seems to have been his headquarters

The problem of water supply in Palestine has always been acute. This artificial pool near Bethlehem for the storage of water goes back to about the second century B.C.

during his ministry; and Bethsaida on the north shore of the lake, where he also worked. To the north, in Philip's territory, there was "Philip's Caesarea" (Caesarea Philippi), and on the Mediterranean coast the ancient cities of Tyre and Sidon.

In the territory under the Roman procurator lay Caesarea, on the Mediterranean, the seat of government. Shechem in Samaria would be avoided by pious Jews. Jericho in the Jordan valley lay at the junction of several important roads. Travelers from Galilee to Jerusalem who wished to avoid Samaria would pass through Jericho. The religious center of Judaism was Jerusalem, site of the great Temple devoted to the sacrificial worship of God and the only place where such worship could be offered. Five or six miles to the south of it lay Bethlehem, while around the corner of the Mount of Olives was the little village of Bethany, where during the last week of his life Jesus spent the nights because of the crowded conditions in the city during the Passover season.

Jerusalem was normally a city of about 30,000 population, but at the Passover season when pilgrims were present from all over the world there were perhaps ten times that number. It was a walled city, lying on two hills between the valley of Hinnom which enclosed it on the west and south, and the ravine of the Kidron running down the eastern side and joining the valley of Hinnom below the southeast corner. Within the walls the city was divided into two quite unequal sections by the Tyropoeon valley which joined the other two valleys where they ran together. The largest part of the city was on the western hill, but the temple lay at the northern end of the eastern hill. Running along the eastern side of the Kidron valley was the Mount of Olives. These were the scenes among which Jesus' life was lived.

THE HASMONEAN KINGDOM

One determining factor in the life of the Jews during the period of the Gospels was the memory of the Maccabean period. The efforts of the Seleucid king, Antiochus IV, to encourage Greek ways and stamp out Judaism, culminating in the pillaging and desecration of the temple, the prohibition of circumcision, and the destruction of copies of the Scriptures, enforced with great cruelty, led to a revolt which began in 168 B.C. Due to the involvement of Syria elsewhere, the revolt under the leadership of a father and his five sons whom history knows as "the Maccabees" (from the nickname of one of the sons) was successful.

Not only was religious independence regained and the Temple reconsecrated in 165 B.C., but by 143 B.C. political independence was won. For the first time since the days of Solomon, the Jewish kingdom was extended to its ancient boundaries and was ruled by native rulers, free from foreign control. Unfortunately, the kingdom so auspiciously begun became increasingly worldly and

An open valley among the hills of Samaria. Site of the very old city of Shechem and the scene of Jacob's well. (Ewing Galloway)

oppressive. The Hellenism which Antiochus IV did not succeed in forcing on the Jews from without, now began to make progress from within. There was increasing opposition from the emerging party of the Pharisees. Queen Alexandra (76–67 B.C.) favored the Pharisees, but on her death there was a dispute over the succession to the throne. Appeal was made by both parties to the Romans, whose power in Asia was increasing rapidly. The Roman commander Pompey finally resolved the problem by taking over the Jewish kingdom in 63 B.C. From that time until the middle of the twentieth century, Palestine was never again under Jewish control.

This Hasmonean kingdom, as it is frequently called, left an important legacy to future generations. In the first place, the brief period of independence called forth an intense nationalistic feeling—a strong national self-consciousness, and pride in what had been accomplished against such great odds. Along with this went

The northern end of the Sea of Galilee, with the Galilean hills in the background. (Courtesy of the Israel Government Tourist Office)

the hope that, as they had accomplished with God's help the seemingly impossible in throwing off the Syrian yoke, so they might throw off that of the Romans, so galling after their few years of freedom. When later, led by these hopes, they did revolt, the result was disastrous.

Another effect of their experience with the Syrians and the later phases of their own native dynasty was an intense opposition to all things Greek. There was a deepened and strengthened conviction that they were God's people and that, as such, they must keep free from all the ways of the heathen.

THE ROMAN OCCUPATION

Palestine in Jesus' day had been under Roman control for nearly one hundred years. The central position of the country, between Asia Minor, Syria, and Mesopotamia on the one hand and Egypt on the other, made control over Palestine vitally important if Rome was to maintain its position in the Middle East.

The Romans showed a genuine concern for law and order. The first duty of the head of the government was to preserve these. If he could not do so he was summarily removed. In general, it was not the Roman policy to interfere any more than necessary with local customs. As far as possible, the local law held sway and was administered by native courts. The traditional religion was recognized and protected. If the Jews did not like the Roman administration, it was not because it proposed any radical interference with established ways. The high priest was one official whom the Romans controlled because it was essential that they have someone in this position with whom they could work.

Control of Palestine rested on military power. The Roman administration was in many ways what in modern terms would be called an occupation government. As such, it was under the direct control of the emperor, as commander in chief of the army. He, of course, did not rule it in person, but delegated power either to native puppet rulers or to Roman high commissioners known as *procurators*.

Herod the Great was a puppet king. He was a skillful ruler who, despite his unpopularity with his Jewish subjects, managed to hold his throne from 37 B.C. to 4 B.C. He was loyal to Rome, eager to promote Hellenistic culture, and also anxious to keep on good terms with the Jews. He engaged in numerous building projects, rebuilding the city of Samaria which he named Sebaste (derived from the Greek equivalent of Augustus) for the emperor. He built Caesarea on the coast, as a seat of government, together with a number of other towns and fortresses. One of his most important projects was his rebuilding of the Temple at

The Jordan River, near the southern end, in July.

Jerusalem. Begun in 20 b.c., the magnificent central structure was finished promptly, but the surrounding buildings were not finally completed until a.d. 64, just a few years before it was all destroyed.

At Herod's death, his territory was divided among his three sons. To Herod Antipas he left Galilee and Perea. To Philip went the territory north and east of the Sea of Galilee. Samaria and Judea were to go to Archelaus, with the title of king. Rome recognized the division of territory but refused Archelaus the title king, calling him *ethnarch* ("head of a nation") instead.

Archelaus proved unable to keep his territory in order. Complaints against his oppression mounted and led to serious disturbances. In A.D. 6 he was removed and replaced by a procura-

Tiberius, Roman Emperor during the period of Jesus' activity. Pontius Pilate, Governor of Palestine at this time, was his representative.
(Brown Brothers)

tor. In A.D. 26 Pontius Pilate was appointed to this position, which he held for ten years. From the beginning he had trouble with his subjects, but in A.D. 36 the attempt to disperse a Samaritan mob led to a bloody massacre. Pilate was removed and sent to Rome for trial. His final fate is not known.

Herod Antipas ruled Galilee from 4 B.C. to A.D. 39. He was an able ruler, and Galilee was prosperous during his reign. His marital affairs were a source of difficulty. After having married the daughter of King Aretas of the neighboring territory of Nabatea, he fell in love with his niece Herodias and divorced the Nabatean princess. Herodias proved to be a loyal and devoted wife to him, but his divorce involved him in a war with Aretas which resulted in defeat for Herod. At the time of Jesus' ministry, this was in the past and Galilee was at peace.

As a result of intrigue by Herod Agrippa, brother of Herodias, Antipas was deposed in A.D. 39. Agrippa was able, dissolute, and unscrupulous. The emperor Caligula appointed him to succeed Philip as king and then gave him the territory of Antipas. In A.D. 41 Claudius gave him Judea and Samaria, so that he ruled over most of his grandfather's territory. He persecuted the followers of Jesus and executed James, the son of Zebedee. He died suddenly in A.D. 44.

Thereafter, there were a series of Roman procurators until the revolt in A.D. 66 which led, in A.D. 70, to the destruction of Jerusalem and the Temple.

ECONOMIC CONDITIONS

The economic life of Palestine in the time of Jesus was dependent chiefly on the products of the land.

Agriculture was basic. Methods of preparing the soil and harvesting were quite primitive. Plowing was hardly more than scratching the soil. Reaping was done with a sickle. Threshing consisted in spreading the grain on a flat rock or floor and driving over it a sort of sledge pulled by an ox or donkey. Winnowing was accomplished by tossing the grain in the air, and then sieving the remainder.

Much of Palestine is rocky hillside; and to use this, terracing was necessary. Water was scarce and irrigation was resorted to. Galilee was more fruitful than Judea.

The chief agricultural products were grains, such as wheat

and barley; vegetables—cabbage and lettuce, carrots, onions, garlic, cucumbers, melons, squash, lentils, beans and peas; fruits —grapes, olives, figs, pomegranates. From the grapes, wine was made; and they were also dried as raisins. Olives were grown for the oil which was pressed from them.

Grazing was also an important occupation. Sheep and goats

This terraced Judean hillside indicates the difficulties under which agriculture was carried on. The trees are olive trees.

grazed in mixed flocks. Clothing was made from wool and tents from goat hair. Meat from both sheep and goats was used for food, as was goat's milk and the cheese made from it. Their skins were the sources of leather and were also used as "bottles" for the storage of liquids.

Poultry was raised. Commercial fishing in the Sea of Galilee was an important source of food.

Palestine is not rich in minerals; but salt, asphalt, tar, and phosphorus were obtained from the Dead Sea.

Threshing grain in the ancient manner. (Courtesy of J. Floyd
Moore)

Most of the inhabitants of Palestine in Jesus' day could be
described as peasants. They held small pieces of land which they
worked themselves. A few bad years could reduce them to a state
where they had to sell their property. Their holdings were too
small to be divided, and their children had to become hired la-
borers—if there was anyone to hire them. If there was not, the
choice was between beggary and brigandage. Some landowners
did well, increased their holdings, bought and sold the surplus of
the peasants, and had money to lend. There were few large land-
holders. The general trend, however, was toward the concentra-
tion of wealth, with the rich getting richer and the poor, poorer.
Slavery was also found.

The artisans who practiced various handicrafts formed an important class. "We find, almost contemporary with Jesus, mention of no less than forty kinds of craftsmen in the Jewish literature: Tailors, shoemakers, builders, masons, carpenters, millers,

bakers, tanners, spice-merchants, apothecaries, cattlemen, butchers, slaughterers, dairymen, cheesemakers, physicians and blood-letters, barbers, hair-dressers, laundrymen, jewellers, smiths, weavers, dyers, embroiderers, workers in gold brocade; carpet makers, matting makers, well diggers, fishermen, bee-keepers, potters and platemakers (who were also pottery dealers), pitcher makers, coopers, pitch refiners and glazemakers, makers of glass and glassware, armorers, copyists, painters and engravers."[1]

Trade and commerce were flourishing in first-century Palestine. Some were peddlers, others kept shop. In addition to this internal trade, there was a fairly lively foreign trade, especially in grain, oil, wine, fruit, and salted fish.

The Jordan Valley near Jericho. Tradition says Jesus was tempted on the mountain in the background. The grazing flock contains both sheep and goats, as is usual in Palestine. (Ewing Galloway)

[1] J. Klausner, *Jesus of Nazareth,* Macmillan, 1925, p. 177, to which this section is chiefly indebted.

Taxes were oppressive. The Romans collected a water tax, a city tax, a tax on meat and salt, and a house tax. Taxes were levied on imports and exports. The privilege of collecting such duties was sold by Rome to the highest bidder. This system was a breeder of extortion and led to the low opinion of tax collectors

Ruins of a colonnaded street in ancient Gerasa, east of the Jordan. Gerasa was one of the ten Greek cities of the Decapolis. (Ewing Galloway)

("publicans") reflected in the Gospels. Goods in transit were taxed at every frontier. The total tax burden was very great, averaging, it is said, 40 percent of a man's income.

Although the land was fairly productive, it was overpopulated. This, with the heavy taxation and the increasing number of people without land or other steady source of income, produced a situation which made the population receptive to fomentors of revolt as well as to preachers of the coming of God's reign.

SADDUCEES

Out of the turmoil and experiences of the eighty years of independence under the Maccabees, there emerged a number of groups, often, though not quite accurately, called sects or parties. The first of these was the Sadducees. They seem to have been the wealthy landed aristocracy. As such, it is not surprising that they were intensely conservative. Politically they were allied with the rulers, whether Hasmonean or Roman, for their interests were best served by the preservation of the *status quo*. This association with the rulers exposed them to the full force of the Greek culture which was so attractive, and they tried to come to terms with it. Religiously they were also conservative, resisting any attempt to interpret the Law so as to make it better adapted to the conditions and needs of the times. They recognized only the Pentateuch as authoritative, and this they interpreted more literally and less leniently than the Pharisees. They explicitly rejected such doctrines as that of a future resurrection of the dead, a last judgment, any form of eternal life, and the existence of angels and spirits, on the ground that these were not warranted in Scripture.

PHARISEES

In contrast to the Sadducees, the Pharisees were the progressive group. They held that God's Law covered all phases of human life, and that by an elaborate system of interpretation one could discover God's will in all sorts of cases which were not explicitly covered. Their study of the Law was essentially an effort to adapt it to new conditions. They recognized the authority of a traditional, oral interpretation. Thus, in the New Testament they appear as recognizing a gradation in the force of oaths, as straining drinking water to prevent swallowing an unclean insect, as practising ritual washings of cups and dishes, as fasting, and as observing the Sabbath very strictly. They recognized first the Prophets and later the Writings as Scripture. They made place for new festivals not prescribed in the Law, such as Dedication (Hanukkah) and Purim. They speculated about the Messiah, and insisted that a resurrection of the dead was taught in Scripture. They were, in general, inclined to ignore the government so long as it did not outrage their religious feelings or interfere with their religious practices. They saw in the Roman rule God's punishment for the transgression of his Laws on the part of his people, and looked for relief rather in efforts to secure obedience than in revolt. Not all could live up to the Pharisaic ideal, but the Pharisees were widely looked up to and admired, even by those who could not meet their standards. After the destruction of the nation following the revolts in A.D. 66–73 and A.D. 132–135, it was the Pharisaic point of view which survived and is represented in Talmud and Midrash.

Despite the fact that the Pharisees were looked up to by the masses, from the point of view of the Pharisees themselves no person who did not study and observe the Law in all the detail prescribed by their interpretation could be truly pious. Such a person was known as an 'am ha-arets (literally "man of the land"). Since his nonobservance of the Law as interpreted by the Pharisees made it likely that he was unclean, and since uncleanness was contagious, the pious Pharisee held himself aloof from the 'am ha-arets.

ZEALOTS

Differing both from the Pharisees and Sadducees were the Zealots. The Zealots were superpatriots, men of direct action. They felt that as God had come to the aid of their forefathers when they had raised the standard of revolt, so he would again, if only his people would take the initiative against the Romans.

When, after years of agitation, they had their way, the outcome was the destruction of the city and Temple in A.D. 70 and the destruction of the city again in A.D. 133, with complete exclusion of the Jews from the Roman city built on the same site to replace it.

ESSENES

Ancient writers, both Jewish and pagan, tell us of the existence of still another group known as the Essenes, although these are

The barren shores of the Dead Sea, with the hills of Judea in the background. (Ewing Galloway)

not mentioned in the New Testament. These people, we are told, occupied a settlement near the Dead Sea, while others were also to be found in various Palestinian villages. They lived an ascetic life and, on joining, turned over all their property to the community. Admission was only after a lengthy period of probation. After a year the novice was admitted to the ritual baths of purification; and only after a further period of two years was he permitted to share in the sacred common meal. These washings and meals were their chief religious exercises, with prayer and the reading and study of Scripture. They did not participate in

Air view of the settlement at Qumran. The long rectangular area at the bottom of the complex is the assembly room and banqueting hall. Jutting down from the left-hand end of this is a pantry where a full set of dishes was found. Several of the other large rectangular areas, as well as the circle, were cisterns for water storage. (Courtesy of the Palestine Archaeological Museum)

the Temple sacrifices, not because they held to more spiritual principles of worship but because they held that the Temple worship was polluted. Their interpretation of the Sabbath law was much more rigid than that of the Pharisees.

The discovery, early in the present century, of a document

34846

The first column of the "Rule of the Community" which regulated
the lift of the sect at Qumran. (Courtesy of John C. Trever)

referring to the covenant of a group which had migrated to "Damascus," and, more recently, the discovery of a whole series of ancient scrolls and fragments in caves near the Dead Sea, has put the whole matter in a clearer light. Also found was an extensive building at Qumran which was the headquarters of a community which most scholars recognize as these same Essenes. More recently, excavations at Ain Feshkha have brought to light a related building there.

The community seems to have been founded during the days of the Hasmoneans under the leadership of one known as the Teacher of Righteousness, who saw no hope of living a life pleasing to God under the conditions prevailing, and retreated with some kindred spirits to the Judean wilderness. He believed that through him God had revealed the full depth of meaning in the prophets, and that these spoke of the events of the last times in which men were living. The Essenes' faith was based on a renewal of God's ancient covenant, by which a remnant is to be preserved and prepared for the coming end of the present order. God's sole sovereignty is stressed. All men are predestined by him to have a part in the lot of the righteous or the lot of the wicked. These two are subject to two spirits: the spirit of light and good, and the spirit of darkness and evil. In the present age the spirit of evil is in control, although there are limits to its power over the righteous. But the sect looked forward to the imminent coming of the final days. At that time the affairs of the community would be led by an anointed priest and an anointed lay ruler, the "messiahs" of Aaron and of Levi, respectively. The word *messiah* here simply means one duly consecrated for the office; it does not have the connotations which the word acquired when applied by Christians to Jesus. The end will be preceded by forty years of war, during which the various heathen nations will be destroyed. Thereafter, God will dwell forever with the righteous. That there will be a final judgment is clear. This, of course, implies that death is not the end; but whether the sect believed in the survival of souls (immortality) or the reunion of souls and bodies (resurrection) is not clear.

The life of the community consisted of a combination of manual work and worship, including the continuous study and interpretation of Scripture. The work consisted in provision for the needs of the members, with a pottery, dyers' shop, laundry, stables, and especially a large scriptorium for the copying of manuscripts. The settlement at Ain Feshkha was the community farm. All of the community life was regulated by an interpretation of the Law much stricter than that of the Pharisees.

The leaders of the community were apparently priests, as experts in what was clean or unclean. There was a council of twelve or fifteen men. An official called the *mebaqqer* (which might be translated *episcopos,* "inspector, overseer") probably was the head of the council. There was also an assembly of the whole community.

As will appear later, there are a number of points where there is or may be a relationship between aspects of the life and thought of this community and features in early Christianity. It is also probable that in the understandable enthusiasm generated by these remarkable discoveries there is a tendency in some quarters to exaggerate their significance.

CHAPTER 7

Judaism

THE MOVEMENT which produced the books of the New Testament came into being within the framework of Palestinian Judaism. Jesus of Nazareth and his earliest followers were born and grew up in Jewish homes and in a Jewish society. To understand the beginnings of Christianity we must understand Judaism.

Judaism is the religion which developed in the last six centuries before the beginning of the Christian era, on the basis of the beliefs and practices of the Hebrews, influenced by the great prophets, the Exile, and the subsequent efforts of the Jews to maintain themselves under the domination of Persia, Greece, and the Seleucids. A brief period of independence followed; then Rome gained and held control, finally to destroy the Temple and the Jewish state. In these years Judaism had so developed that it was capable of a continued life detached from any national center.

The core of this religion was the belief that God had revealed to men his will for them. This revelation was called *Torah*. *Torah* is teaching, law, and specifically the Law of Moses (Pentateuch). The substance of religion is conformity to this revealed will of God.

The primary source of a knowledge of God's will was thus Scripture (what Christians call the *Old Testament*); but Scripture, like any other law, needs supplementation and interpretation. It was clear, for example, that Torah prohibited work on the Sabbath day. But a little reflection shows that innumerable cases will arise which cannot be decided until there is a definition of *work*. Nor is it enough to establish an abstract definition of *work*. In the end, it is particular cases which must be decided. These establish precedents for similar cases, and by analogy and otherwise can be extended to situations not contemplated when the law was laid down. A modern example would be the United States Constitution. This embodies the fundamental principles of our government, but it would be of no practical value without a system of courts to provide an interpretation of it. It is also necessary that the duly-issued interpretation should enjoy all the authority of the document from which it was derived. So the *torah 'al peh* ("oral torah") had ascribed to it the same authority as the words of Scripture on which it was based. In calling this interpretation *oral torah,* both a unity and a difference were asserted. It was *torah,* God's will; but it was not the revelation as written in Scripture. For three centuries or thereabouts, it was forbidden to write down the interpretation, or at least to quote it from a written statement. "Written things must not be recalled from memory, verbally transmitted words must not be recited from writing."[1]

Finally, however—about the end of the second century—a codification of the traditional interpretation in Hebrew, known as the Mishnah, was produced. In the course of the next three centuries, this was discussed and commented on in Aramaic; and the Mishnah, with this commentary or Gemara, make up the *Talmud.* In the first century these written collections were not

---

[1] Gittin, 60b, quoted in M. Jastrow, *Dictionary of the Targumin, Talmud, etc.,* Pardes, 1950, s.v. *peh.*

in existence, but the full authority of the traditional interpretation was generally acknowledged. Only the Sadducees held that the Torah needed no interpretation. Other sects differed at specific points, the Essenes having an interpretation which was frequently stricter than that of the Pharisees.

The content of God's revelation of his will was twofold. In the first place, God had made known what he wanted men to believe. The content of this required belief was very simple: men must believe that God was one, the creator and sovereign of the universe. Any doctrine that threatened the idea of God's unrivaled unity was ruled out.[2]

Beyond this basic point, orthodoxy in first-century Judaism was not constituted by what a man believed but by what he did. To Christians, who for a number of reasons have put the stress on what is believed, this is difficult to grasp. But one cannot understand Judaism if he supposes that he will find its essence in an answer to the question, "What did (or do) Jews believe?" The Jew did not think chiefly of what he was required to believe, but of how God wanted him to act. If, for purposes of convenience, we distinguish between moral conduct and ritual acts, it must not be thought that this corresponded to any essential difference. Both ritual and morals were equally God's command and were equally obligatory.

Judaism carried out this principle with great consistency. The result is sometimes called *legalism,* and hard things are said about it. But many Christians are quite as legalistic as Jews are supposed to be, even though the requirements of God are held to be different in the two cases. It is also an error to suppose that Judaism presented God as only a judge who went strictly by the law, so that to transgress the law at one point was to be forever guilty of all of it. As will appear, this was not the general Jewish understanding of man's relation to God.

[2] The Pharisees later made belief in the resurrection of man's body a requirement.

GOD'S COVENANT

One central tenet of Judaism had to do with God's choice of Israel. The Jews were his people in a unique sense. With them he had made a covenant, and to them he had given his Law. He had promised their forefathers the land of Palestine, and had assured them that the day would come when he would vanquish their enemies and would cause his people to dwell in peace and righteousness. Since this choice seemed to subject God to the charge of partiality, it came to be held that God had offered the Torah to all peoples but that only Israel had accepted it and undertaken to keep it. But, in any case, this sense of belonging to God's chosen people, with the obligations it involved and the privileges which it conferred, was a central fact in the Jewish outlook.

GOD

While it is true that correctness of belief was not stressed, this did not mean that such concepts as *God* were without content. God was the holy God revealed in Scripture. He had shown himself just and merciful. He had created the world, revealed himself through chosen spokesmen such as Moses and the prophets, and even now rules the world he has made. If, as some supposed, the present world was controlled directly by an evil power, that was by God's sufferance, for his own good reasons, within limitations which he set; and the time would come when he would take things again into his own hands.

Despite speculation in some quarters, under foreign influences which tended to exalt God to the point that he was remote from the world, dealing with it only by angels and other spirits, God was generally conceived as he is depicted in Scripture—guiding the destinies of men and nations himself, combatting evil, always accessible in prayer to those who turned to him in supplication and repentance. "The exaltation of God was not his exile. He who dwells in the high and holy place, dwells no less with him that is of a contrite and holy spirit. His almighty power and his humility go together; he is lofty enough to think nothing beneath him, great enough to think nothing too small to be his concern."[3]

ANGELS AND DEMONS

But though God could deal with men directly, and was always accessible to the pious in prayer, this did not mean that he made no use of agents, either in his dealings with men or with the world. The ministers he used were called *angels*. They formed a celestial court which offered God praise and worship, went on his errands, and formed a heavenly council which he regularly consulted—though all decisions were his own. The doings of the angels were the subject of many stories, but these were never of any great religious significance. "Doubtless the belief in the attendance of a guardian angel helped the pious to realize God's constant providential care, and the recording angel, keeping a memorandum of all a man's words and deeds to be reported to God, may sometimes have steadied a vacillating conscience; but for the rest, angels, whether in sermons or folklore, hardly belonged to religion at all; they were not objects of veneration, much less adoration."[4]

Another class of supernatural beings was constituted by the *demons*. As to the origin of these invisible but malicious creatures, there was a difference of opinion. As to their existence there was complete unanimity. Men were believed to be surrounded by myriads of them. They lurked especially in ruins, latrines, and wherever there was water, always preferring the darkness to the light. They tempted men to evil and caused disease and madness in man and beast. It was believed they could be warded off

---

[3] G. F. Moore, *Judaism: In the First Centuries of the Christian Era,* Harvard University Press, 1927, vol. I, p. 442.
[4] *Ibid.,* vol. I, pp. 410 ff.

by amulets, and expelled by properly qualified persons. God would protect those who obeyed his commandments against their machinations.

THE NATURE OF MAN

All men were believed to be of one stock, created by God in his image and in his likeness. Man was soul and body, both being essential to a whole man. The idea that the body is something which must eventually be left behind if man is to realize his true possibilities was entirely foreign to Judaism except where it yielded to Greek influences.

Because of the "evil impulse" planted in man, all men sin; but not all men are sinners. The righteous man repents and is forgiven. The sinner hardens himself against God and ends as an open rebel against him.

Sin in Judaism was primarily a religious rather than a moral concept. It was a violation of God's holiness. Paul was not un-Jewish when he wrote: "All [men] have sinned and fall short of the glory of God." (Rom. 3:23.) More specifically, sin was any failure to conform to God's will, whether deliberate or unintentional. If God did not want something done, he did not want it done. God had declared (Num. 19:16) that anyone who came in contact with a grave would be "unclean" seven days. While in a state of uncleanness, he was debarred from approaching God in any way. If he did so, he sinned. Graves were supposed to be marked with lime so that they could be recognized; but suppose the marking had not been made properly, and inadvertently you had walked over a grave or sat on it. If, during the next seven days, you went to the Temple to make an offering in payment of a vow, you would commit a sin. Of course, God knew that such things would happen; and he had provided a remedy for it, in the prescribed regular sacrifice of goats on the three great Feasts and at the New Moon. Both sin and application of the remedy might be quite unconscious, but this to us strange conception is a necessary consequence of the basic principle that sin is doing what God doesn't want done. He still didn't want it, even if you were unaware of doing it or could not help doing as you did. (Childbirth, for example, causes uncleanness, though not because God disapproves of having children— quite the contrary.)

Not all sins, however, are in this class. Too often men transgress the Law of God knowing only too well that they are doing so. In such cases, it was believed that repentance was both the sufficient and the necessary condition for restoration. Without repentance, the prescribed expiations were worthless. With repentance, the ritual was not absolutely essential. After the destruction of the Temple had made all performance of the ritual impossible, repentance was all that God required.

Repentance in this sense meant more than regret that you had done what you did. One of the chief words for repentance came from a verb which meant "to turn around." Repentance was thus a reorientation of the will rather than a feeling of sorrow. It meant to stop going in the direction you were headed and turn around and head in the opposite direction. To repent with the intention of sinning again was completely worthless.

Such repentance, sincere and thoroughgoing, availed for any sin whatsoever. The Jerusalem Talmud tells of the repentance of King Manasseh, the worst of the kings of Judah. He had encouraged idolatry and human sacrifice, practiced sorcery, and even erected an idol in the Temple. On his deathbed he was in great distress and remembered that it was said that God was a merciful God and would have mercy on whoever returned to him. So he called upon God. "The ministering angels stopped up the windows of the firmament to keep Manasseh's prayer from coming up to God, and said to God, Is there repentance for a man who set up an idol in thy temple? God answered, If I do not receive him in repentance, I shall bolt the door to all penitents.

What did God do? He made a kind of loophole beneath the glorious throne and heard his supplication."[5]

MAN'S DUTY

For our purposes, it is convenient to divide the discussion of man's duty into two parts—observances and moral conduct. But this is not a distinction which had any religious significance for Judaism. All were alike God's will, and doing God's will was the meaning of religion.

For the individual, the prime observances were circumcision and the Sabbath. He was also expected to observe a complicated system of rules intended to preserve or restore cleanness. This concept had no moral or hygienic content whatever. God had declared that certain things, such as contact with death, exercise of reproductive functions, some kinds of food, and leprosy produced a state of uncleanness which unfitted the person for any approach to God until appropriate measures for removing the uncleanness were taken. Anything or anyone in a state of uncleanness conveyed it to others unless proper precautions were observed. Within this system were the dietary laws which prohibited the eating of various kinds of food—pork, any kind of flesh not slaughtered by draining off the blood, garden herbs on which the tithes had not been paid—these are only a few of the nonkosher foods.

In addition to the Sabbath, there were the great annual festivals: the Passover, celebrating the deliverance from Egypt; the Feast of Tabernacles (or Booths, temporary shelters which were occupied during the seven days of the festival) at the time of the vintage and the oil-pressing; and the one-day Feast of Weeks. In addition to these festivals prescribed in Scripture, there was Hanukkah (Dedication) (John 10:22), instituted by the Maccabees to celebrate the reestablishment of worship in the Temple.

[5] *Ibid.*, vol. I, p. 524.

Purim, commemorating the deliverance of the Jews from the plot of Haman, was another non-Scriptural celebration.

The Day of Atonement (Yom Kippur) was the great fast day. While the Temple stood, there was a special ritual for this day which was supposed to remove any uncleanness from the Temple and "all the iniquities of the people of Israel, and all their transgressions, all their sins." (Lev. 16:21.) In the synagogue the emphasis was on confession of sin and prayer for forgiveness. One of these prayers is as follows: "Thou knowest the secrets of eternity and the most hidden mysteries of all living. Thou searchest in the innermost recesses, and triest the reins and the heart. Naught is concealed from thee, or hidden from thine eyes. May it then be thy will, O Lord our God and God of our fathers, to forgive us for all our sins, to pardon us for all our iniquities, and to grant us remission for all our transgressions."[6] The period of penitence began ten days before, at the New Year's festival, Rosh Hashana.

MORAL DUTY

Man's moral duty was both social and individual. He owed obedience to his rulers, whether they ruled an independent state or were foreign conquerors. Only if the government demanded violation of God's law was it to be defied. In one's dealings with his fellows the principle was "You shall love your neighbor as yourself." (Lev. 19:18.) Hillel's answer to the prospective convert who wanted to have the whole law summarized while he stood on one foot was: "Do not do to your fellow what you hate to have done to you."

Such general statements do not actually serve as a guide to conduct by themselves. Summaries, in general, are no substitute for that which they are supposed to summarize. What they mean

[6] Quoted in *ibid.*, vol. II, p. 60, as found in the modern prayer book.

has to be determined in detail from other sources. If we examine the specific rules which governed conduct in particular cases, we find that the standards were high. They covered family life, commercial transactions, general relations between persons (even including matters such as gossip and slander), the practice of charity, and the pursuit of justice, truth, and peace. It is, of course, harder to discover how well these standards were kept. No one would expect to find that they were always maintained; but there is good reason to believe that, in this case, the level of performance was generally better than average.

Various motives were appealed to, to secure obedience. The obvious consequences of violation of the accepted standards were pointed out, the rewards for those who were obedient to the divine commands were stressed, reverence for God and his will were appealed to. Characteristic was the appeal for the "hallowing of God's name." Good conduct called forth respect for the God who had ordained it; wrongdoing reflected on him. For this reason, the Jew was to be particularly careful in his relations with Gentiles, lest God be brought into disrepute.

PERSONAL RELIGION

Beside the prescribed duties in the realm of observance and morals, every religion allows for more personal, voluntary expressions. These we may describe as the practice of piety.

The real basis for Jewish piety in the first century was the recognition of God as the heavenly Father. "The Fatherhood of God" was no discovery of Jesus. It is, of course, found even in the Old Testament. "Thou, O Lord art our Father." (Isaiah 63:16.) "I thought you would call me, My Father." (Jer. 3:19.) "He shall cry to me, 'Thou art my Father, my God, and the Rock of my salvation.'" (Ps. 89:26.) Rabbi Judah ben Ila'i says of God's care for men, "It is like a man who was walking on the way and letting his son go on before him; came robbers in front to take the boy captive, he put him in behind him; came robbers in front and wolves behind, he took him up in his arms; he did begin to be troubled by the heat of the sun, his father stretched his own garment over him; was he hungry he gave him food; thirsty, he gave him to drink. Just so God did, as it is written."[7] There follows a list of Scripture passages where these various deeds of God are described.

Typical expressions of piety are prayer, fasting, almsgiving, and study. In prayer, one approaches God, the Father in Heaven; in fasting, one humiliates himself before him; in deeds of loving-kindness, one becomes the imitator of the heavenly Father. To study the Torah is to study God's revelation of himself and of his will. "The Law of God perpetually in man's mind guides him on his way, guards him in his sleep and converses with him when he wakes—guides him in this world, guards him in the hour of death, will be with him when he wakes in the days of the Messiah, and converses with him in the world to come."[8]

In the home, religion found many expressions. The rules for cleanness and uncleanness and the special days would serve to make the overshadowing presence of God real to the members of the family. So would the blessings with which each meal began and ended, the private prayers, and the parental instruction of the children.

The general spirit of Judaism was joyous. Misfortune was to be accepted as God's necessary chastisement of his children who needed to be trained in the way they should go. The Law was not felt to be oppressive, but the will of the Father in heaven, in the obeying of which they were to find joy. The Sabbath was God's gift to his children. Fasting and mourning on the Sabbath were forbidden. It was to be a day of sheer gladness. Judaism had no place for an asceticism based on the idea that matter was evil and natural pleasures were therefore bad. One Rabbi even said:

[7] *Mekilta, Beshallah* 4. Quoted in *ibid.*, vol. II, pp. 203–204.
[8] Moore, *op. cit.*, vol. II, p. 247.

"A man will have to give an account on the judgment day of every good thing which he might have enjoyed and did not."[9]

WORSHIP AND INSTRUCTION

Judaism had two institutions for the worship of God—Temple and synagogue. The two were entirely different in origin, and with this went a difference in the way in which God was wor-

Galilee: ruins of the ancient synagogue of Beth Shearim in the foreground. (Courtesy of the Israel Government Tourist Office)

shiped. They were never rivals, but when the Temple was destroyed Judaism was not essentially affected. There was one thing common to the two types of worship—in neither was any image of the deity permitted.

The Temple at Jerusalem was the center of the sacrificial worship commanded in the Old Testament. There was no true

[9] *Ibid.*, vol. II, p. 265.

temple anywhere else; nor could there be, because it was believed that God had chosen this one spot for this purpose.
Sacrifice elsewhere would be worse than none at all.

The worship at the Temple was not in any way equivalent to
"going to church" on Sunday. It was never a religious duty to
attend the Temple on the Sabbath (properly, from sundown
Friday till sundown Saturday). There was no preaching and no
pews. Sacrifice took place every day, with special sacrifices on
special days—after the New Moon and on the great festival days
and on the Sabbath. Provision was made that representatives of
the nation should be present, but an audience was no more
essential than for the Catholic Mass (which is also thought of as
a sacrifice). It was not performed for the purpose of instructing,
comforting, or inspiring the people. Its purpose was to establish
and maintain right relations between man and God in the way
the Old Testament plainly stated God had commanded it to be
done.

Those who performed these sacrifices were the priests. No
one decided to become a priest (*cohen*), for priesthood was
hereditary. A member of a priestly family could only take a bride
from another priestly family. There was no possible way for one
who was not born a priest to become one. Moreover, the priests
had no other duties than to perform the stated sacrifices when
their turn came. They did not preach, officiate at weddings, bury
the dead, visit the sick, give moral counsel, or organize the
church schools. Since there were many more priests than were
necessary at any one time, most of them lived away from Jerusalem and came up to officiate from time to time as their turn
came, about twice a year. Each term of service lasted about a
week. At the great feasts all priests were on duty. When sacrifice
was performed on behalf of individuals, the priest received a share
of the offering. In general, the priests, whether actively officiating
or not, were entitled to tithes. Tithes on all agricultural produce

were paid to the Levites, who in turn gave a tithe of their tithe to the priests.

The origin of the synagogue is obscure. We may guess that it originated in spontaneous gatherings during the Exile in Babylon. Nor can we follow the process by which it became an official public institution in which, by the first century, the real center of Jewish religious life lay. In contrast to the Temple, it was the scene of a rational worship without sacrifice or offering. In the synagogue, instruction in religion was the most prominent feature. It was an expression of the fundamental character of Judaism—the conception that the content of religion is the revealed will of God. The synagogue was the place where the content of his will was learned.

The priests had no official role whatever in the worship of the synagogue except to give the benediction and to blow the trumpets on a fast day. Each synagogue was presided over by a *head of the synagogue* (the "ruler of the synagogue" in Mk. 5:22), the *rosh-ha-keneset*. Sometimes there was a committee, "heads of the synagogue." These officials presided over the exercises, maintained order, invited strangers to speak, and so on. There was also a salaried official, the *minister* or *attendant* (Luke 4:20), the *hazzan-ha-keneset*. In his charge were the building and its furniture, especially the sacred scrolls of the Scriptures. He announced from the roof, by trumpet blast, the beginning and end of the Sabbath. He gave the priest the signal to pronounce the benediction and, on fast days, to blow the trumpets. Ordinarily the Scripture was read by a reader chosen from the congregation, but the *hazzan* might have to do duty here if there were not enough readers. It appears, then, that the ancient synagogue was essentially a lay organization.

The synagogue service was based on prayer, reading of lessons from Scripture, and, if a competent person was present, a sermon. The prayer was introduced by the Shema, the central confession of Judaism: "Hear, O Israel, the Lord our God, the Lord is One, and thou shalt love the Lord thy God with all thy heart, and with all thy soul, and with all thy might."[10]

In the prayer, "the three prefatory benedictions bless the God of the Fathers, Abraham, Isaac and Jacob; the Mighty God, who

It has sometimes been supposed that Jesus attended this ancient synagogue at Capernaum, but it dates from the second century of our era. (Courtesy of the Israel Government Tourist Office)

nourishes the living and revives the dead; the Holy God. Petitions follow for knowledge, repentance, forgiveness, deliverance from affliction, healing, for a bountiful year, the gathering of the dispersed of Israel, the restoration of good government, the destruction of heretics and apostates, for the elders of the people and upright converts, for the rebuilding of the Temple and the

[10] Deut. 6:4–5. Translation of the Jewish Publication Society.

reign of the Davidic dynasty, for the hearing of prayer, the restoration of sacrificial worship; closing with thanksgiving for God's goodness and loving kindness, and a final prayer for the peace and welfare of all God's people."[11]

The Scriptures were read in Hebrew, followed by a translation into the common tongue, which in the first century was Aramaic, a Semitic language related to Hebrew somewhat as Spanish is related to Italian. A lesson from the Law (Torah) was read, followed by a lesson (*Haftarah*) from the Prophets.

"Preaching in the synagogue was not the prerogative of any class, nor was any individual regularly appointed to conduct this part of the service, but it was only natural that those whose life study had been the Scriptures and the religion of their people should be found more profitable for instruction than unschooled men, and that such as had the gifts of interesting and edifying discourse (Haggadah) were more popular than those who excelled only in juristic refinements."[12]

Because synagogues were found everywhere, and because they ministered directly to human needs, Judaism was able to survive the destruction of the Temple and the sacrificial system. It was believed that God in his own providence had permitted the destruction of the Temple, thus making physically impossible the carrying out of his instructions. But in the synagogue he had come to be known in another way, and this made possible the survival of Judaism.

THE JEWISH HOPES FOR THE FUTURE

Few topics in the history of religion are so misunderstood as this one. Nothing is so confusing as to have the same term used in different senses by different groups; and that is precisely what

[11] Moore, *op. cit.*, vol. I, pp. 293–294. This refers specifically to the later form of the prayer, but the substance of it is very old.
[12] *Ibid.*, vol. I, p. 305.

has happened here. Such terms as *salvation, redemption, Messiah, Son of man, kingdom of Heaven,* and even *resurrection* have quite different meanings for modern Christians from what they had for Palestinian Jews in the first century. To add to the confusion, these words have been the center of debate between Christians and Jews, as well as between various groups of Christians; and their use tends to call forth all the deep-seated emotions of these long and bitter conflicts.

Another difficulty which plagues the attempt to bring clarity into this field is the fact that actually there never was a simple, clear-cut formulation of thought on the matter. There were varieties of opinion on various points, and any systematic discussion of the topic is bound to result in some oversimplification.

The key to the subject is to be found in the Jewish understanding of God's promises to their forefathers. He had promised Abraham descendants in number like the sands of the sea, whom he would establish in Palestine and bless there. The history of the Jewish people had been a series of recurring disasters, ending with the Roman domination under which Jesus and his contemporaries lived. These calamities were explained plausibly enough as due to God's necessary punishment of his people for their obvious unfaithfulness; but most of the prophets looked forward to a time when a righteous nation would dwell as God's people, and the ancient promises would be completely fulfilled. The heathen nations that oppressed Israel would be overthrown; or, in the terminology of the prophets, Israel would be delivered, redeemed, saved. These concepts referred not to the attainment by the individual of a blessed life either here or in some realm beyond the skies, nor even to his being cleansed from sin, but to God's fulfillment of his promises to establish the nation in the land which he had promised their fathers.

In this general form, these hopes were doubtless common to all Jews, though for the Sadducees we have no explicit testimony one way or the other. But as to just how this hope was to be realized, and the degree of vividness with which it was held, there was wide divergence.

One fundamental difference is expressed in the two phrases, the *kingdom of Heaven* and the *age to come*. The first of these looked forward to the fulfillment of God's promises in the unfolding of history. God would act to deliver his people from their oppressors in the same way he delivered their ancestors from Egypt. He would make his power felt as he had done many times. He would doubtless act through a chosen leader, as he had with Moses or David. But this establishment of the kingdom of Heaven involved no new kind of activity on God's part.

To speak of the coming deliverance as the kingdom of Heaven is to invite from the modern Christian an almost inevitable misunderstanding. When a first-century Jew spoke of the kingdom of Heaven he was speaking of a condition in which God reigned on earth. He called it the kingdom "of Heaven" because it was the kingdom of God who dwelt in heaven. It was felt that the very word *God* was too sacred for everyday use, and various substitutes were in common use—*the Holy One, the Power,*[13] and *Heaven* among others. In the Gospels it is Matthew who regularly refers to the *kingdom of Heaven*. Mark and Luke have *kingdom of God* in their reports of the same saying or parable. The kingdom of Heaven, therefore, is not a kingdom which is *in* heaven, but the reign of God *on earth*.

Because it was God's reign, it is a mistake to suppose that the fact that it was to be on earth meant that it was materialistic. No doubt, when God fulfilled his promises of blessing to his chosen people, there would be no grinding toil, nor any lack of any of God's good gifts which he made to gladden the heart of man. No doubt, too, there were those to whom the chief appeal of the kingdom was the possibility it offered of such satisfactions. More-

[13] Compare Mark 14:62: "You will see the Son of man sitting at the right hand of Power"—i.e., God. There is an article before *Power* in the Greek, although this is generally untranslated in English versions.

over, it is much easier to depict the material blessings of the promised future than to depict the spiritual condition it would represent. But primarily, the emphasis was on God's rule in men's lives. The establishment of the kingdom of God (or of Heaven) meant, first of all, that God's will would be done "on earth as it is in heaven."

"Its principal features are the recovery of independence and power, an era of peace and prosperity, of fidelity to God and to his law, of justice and fair dealing, and of personal rectitude and piety. The external condition of this is liberation from the rule of foreign oppressors; the internal condition is the religious and moral reformation or generation of the Jewish people itself."[14] There is nothing materialistic in the idea that God is to rule in men's hearts and lives, even though the scene of their activity be earth.

In the course of time, even the nationalistic emphasis of this hope came to be paralleled by another "of larger scope and more religious character." The time would come when all men everywhere would acknowledge God and be obedient to him. "Then he will raise up a kingdom to all eternity over men, he who once gave a holy law to the godly, to whom he promised to open all the earth."[15]

"In this sense the consummation of the kingdom of Heaven may be best expressed for our understanding as the universality of the true religion, not alone professed by all men but realized in their lives in all their relations to God and to their fellowmen."[16] It was expected that the inauguration of this golden age would be preceded by the coming of Elijah. The expectation is based on Malachi 3:1–3; 4:5, but this does not specify just what Elijah was to do, and opinions varied. Some thought he would settle questions of clean and unclean, others thought he would

[14] Moore, *op. cit.,* vol. II, p. 324.
[15] Sibylline Oracles, iii, 767. Quoted in *ibid.,* vol. II, p. 372. The "godly" are, of course, Israel.
[16] Moore, *op. cit.,* vol. II, p. 372.

determine which families were of pure Jewish stock—"for which," as Moore says, "undoubtedly inspiration was necessary." The thought that he was to bring Israel to repentance is not found in the earliest references, but it had become current by the beginning of the first century. Another feature expected as part of the Messianic period was a great Messianic banquet. This belief is found in the Gospels,[17] but without trace of fantastic forms it later took. Other features of this hope were the miraculous fertility of Israel's land, the return of the people from exile and dispersion, and the liberation of Israel from the dominion of foreign nations.

THE MESSIAH

Those who looked forward to the coming of the kingdom of Heaven frequently—though by no means always—thought that God would choose someone to act as his agent in the prospective deliverance or to preside over the kingdom thereafter, and would anoint him for that purpose, since anointing was the accepted mode of signifying the divine appointment among the Jews. The high priest was called the *anointed priest* in Leviticus, and the anointing of Saul and David to the kingship is described. King Cyrus of Persia, who is depicted as God's chosen instrument for the deliverance of Israel from the Babylonian yoke, is referred to as "My Anointed." In Daniel 9:25–26, there is a reference to an anointed prince or an anointed one. There is no definite article to indicate that this prince is to be identified with some definite figure otherwise known, and the context suggests that this anointed one was to be a priest.

This all seems clear enough until it is realized that the Hebrew word *anointed*, according to one way of transcribing it, is *Messiah*. Because Jesus' followers identified him with the expected anointed deliverer—and then, with the development of Chris-

[17] Matt. 8:11, Luke 14:15–24, Mark 14:25.

tian theology, recognized him as the Son of God—new connotations came to be attached to the word which were not part of its original meaning, even though they be rightly applied to Jesus. Originally it had no suggestion of metaphysical sonship, or any implication of divinity, but simply called attention to the divine appointment. That the divine appointee would be other than a human being seems not to have occurred to anyone.

In one respect, perhaps, this latter statement may be too sweeping. Recent studies have led many Old Testament scholars to the conclusion that the Hebrews thought of their kings as being divine figures. This meant, however, that they were representatives of God, channels of divine power and blessing, raised above all common men—even that the king on his enthronement was adopted as God's son—but in any case the king's "divinity" was not that of a pre-existent being of like substance with God, who became incarnate at some point of time. This latter is entirely a Christian notion.

As has been said, there was no unity in the expectation of such a figure. The Old Testament contains no reference to the Messiah[18] under that title, though in numerous passages it is clearly stated that the restored kingdom would be presided over by a king of Davidic ancestry, or even by David himself. In such passages, this Davidic king appears as the ruler of the established monarchy, not as the agent by which it would be established.

In other cases, the kingdom is pictured without any reference to who would be king over it. Some of the rabbis seem to have thought the king would be Hezekiah.[19] Others call him Menahem. Some descriptions of the future kingdom expect it to be presided over by a high priest. Thus the "revelation" known as

[18] This is easily checked by a concordance. If a concordance to the AV is used, two references (Dan. 9:25, 26) will be found; but these depend on the illegitimate insertion of a definite article in English where there is none in Hebrew. The new concordance to the RSV correctly gives no references to the Messiah in the whole Old Testament.

[19] Berakot 28b. Quoted in Moore, *op. cit.*, vol. II, p. 348.

The Testaments of the Twelve Patriarchs (Test. Lev. 18) speaks of the Lord raising up a priest to rule as king, and interprets Isaiah 11:2 of him. The sect which produced the Dead Sea Scrolls looked forward to two anointed ones, one a priest and the other not, with the priest playing the more prominent role. Thus, at the time of Jesus, the Messianic expectations of Israel were still fluid.

THE AGE TO COME

It was this fluidity which made possible the development, especially under the impact of the terrible disaster of the fall of Jerusalem in A.D. 70, of a quite different view of the way in which God's deliverance must come about. The goal of the deliverance is now spoken of as the *Age to Come*. Israel's experience of the might of the heathen empires, now represented for the Jews by Rome, led to the conviction that the only hope lay in the direct intervention of God, not simply to overthrow the Roman armies, but to root out the evil power itself. This was thought of in such radical terms that it was believed that all men would be assembled for a great and final judgment, at which the good and the evil would be permanently separated and the wicked destroyed or sent off to eternal punishment. Then the world itself would be wiped out, and a new one created in which the righteous would dwell with God. In this form of hope, nothing was said about any anointed ruler, but he who was to preside over the judgment was known as the *Son of man*. He was thought of as a supernatural figure, but even so there was no suggestion of divine sonship or sharing in God's nature. Eventually[20] the Son of man was identified with the Messiah.

In some cases the two forms of hope were combined. It was believed that the Messiah would reign over God's people for a

---

[20] Just when is uncertain. The first indubitable evidence of an identification is found in the Christian Gospels, but this is not proof that it originated there.

limited period, at the end of which the judgment would take place and the present world would be destroyed and replaced by a new one. This is the scheme presupposed by the Christian book, the Revelation of John, where the period of the Messiah's rule is set as one thousand years.[21] A similar scheme is represented by the Jewish apocalypse, II Esdras, where, however, the period of Messianic rule is said to be four hundred years. In this detail, as in most others, there was no uniformity of expectation.

One feature of the hope of the Age to Come which also appears in the Gospels and Revelation has to do with events which were expected to precede it. These are called in later references the "birth-pangs of the Messiah," or the "Messianic woes." The birth-pangs of the Messiah do not refer to sufferings connected with the Messiah's birth, but to the sufferings of Israel which were expected to precede the revelation of the Messiah. Terrible diseases, monstrous births, the cessation of childbirth, natural disasters, famine, war, division of families, the suppression of the wise and the exaltation of folly, were some of the dire calamities to be expected in this time.

THE RESURRECTION OF THE DEAD

Closely connected with these hopes of the fulfillment of God's promises to his chosen nation was the hope of individual return from the grave. This had not always been the expectation of the Hebrew people. Like all primitive people, the Hebrews thought of the living being as consisting of a body inhabited quite literally by a spirit. When a person died, the spirit left the body and it was believed that normally it went off to a dim cave beneath the earth called *Sheol*. Here all spirits came, to endure a miserable existence forever after. The Greeks had a similar

---

[21] In Latin, *millenium,* a period of a thousand years. The "coming of the millenium" means the beginning of this limited period, not a transition to a final utopia.

belief; and the Odyssey tells how Odysseus, needing some help from a deceased friend, found his way to this underground cave. When he appeared, his friends, thinking him dead, greeted him with wailing, telling him that the most miserable mortal was better off than they were. Their misery was not due to the fact that they were being punished for their misdeeds, but simply that life without a body was inconceivably drab.[22]

It was during the Maccabean revolt that this dreary view began to be replaced by another. Surely the valiant warriors who gave their lives in this struggle should share in the good time to come. There was no limit on the power of God, so it was natural to expect him to restore the fallen heroes to life when his kingdom on earth was established. As for the traitors and apostates, it came to be felt that they deserved particular punishment; and this expectation was soon extended to the wicked generally. It turned out that the Maccabean struggle did not usher in the hoped-for golden age; but the belief persisted among the Pharisees that when God's kingdom finally came, the spirits of the righteous dead would be raised up and reunited with their former bodies, to live forever on earth, while the evil would be destroyed or receive the punishment they so richly deserved.

Not all Jews in Jesus' day accepted this relatively recent innovation in thought. The Sadducees, as has been said, especially rejected all such notions and declared—rightly—that they had no foundation in the Law. When the Sadducees came to Jesus (Mark 12:18–27) and told the story of the woman who was married in succession to seven brothers, and asked, at the end, "Now in the day of resurrection, whose wife is she going to be?" they were not seeking information but trying to dispose of the whole notion by reducing it to an absurdity. And Jesus' reported argument that the dead do rise was of the same nature as a rab-

[22] It is a mistake, therefore, to translate either *Sheol* or *Hades* (the Greek equivalent) by *hell* as is done in the Authorized Version of the Bible. Hell is a place of punishment for the wicked. Sheol and Hades were believed to receive the spirits or shades of all, without moral distinction.

binical argument. Jesus argued that since God said to Moses,[23] "I am . . . the God of Abraham, the God of Isaac, and the God of Jacob," they must still have life[24] ahead of them, else the present tense would be inappropriate. Rabbi Gamaliel II is reported to have rested his case on Deuteronomy 11:9: "The land which the Lord swore to your fathers to give to them." Since they were dead, the only way God's promise could be fulfilled would be for him to raise them up.

[23] Exodus 3:6.

[24] It must be constantly kept in mind that in Judaism "life" was inconceivable apart from a body. Even Christians, who have come to believe in a spiritual existence in heaven, conceive it as lived in a spiritual body. Spiritual bodies seem to have all the characteristics of physical bodies except that they are not called physical.

CHAPTER 8

The Career of Jesus

O UR SURVEY of the sources has led to the conclusion that the tradition as to the teaching of Jesus is more reliable than the tradition as to the order of the events of his life. It will not therefore be possible to give a connected picture of the course of his career. Nevertheless, there are certain general topics which need discussion.

CHRONOLOGY

The effort to establish the basic chronology of Jesus' life is beset with all sorts of difficulties and leads to no absolutely certain results.

We can fix the date of his Crucifixion at about A.D. 30; and if we allow a margin of a year either way, we can be practically certain we are right. There are two uncertainties here. First, whether the meal Jesus ate with his disciples the night before he was arrested was a Passover, as the Synoptic Gospels state (Mark 14:12 ff. and parallels), or whether the supper took place the night before the regular Passover, as John presupposes (John 18:28; 19:14). Both agree that the Crucifixion took place on Friday, and astronomical calculation ought to be able to tell us when Passover fell on Friday or Saturday, as the case may be. Usually it has been supposed that the meal was the regular Passover, but there is still the difficulty that the Jewish religious calendar was based on actual observation of the new moon. We can calculate when the new moon should have first been visible, but clouds or other accidents might have delayed the actual observation for a day or so. So the best we can say is that A.D. 30 seems rather more probable for the year of the Crucifixion than any other.

Neither do we know exactly the length of Jesus' active ministry. The Synoptic Gospels mention only one Passover; John mentions three. A year would be more than enough to allow for everything to happen that is reported.

The date of Jesus' birth is even more difficult. The one thing we can be reasonably sure of is that he was not born A.D. 1. Our familiar reckoning was not adopted till over five hundred years later and was the result of calculations which did not take into consideration all the data. Luke puts the birth at the time of a census by Quirinius which we know took place in A.D. 6. He also states that John the Baptist came forward in the fifteenth year of the Emperor Tiberius, which would be A.D. 28–29. Jesus' ministry began shortly after, when, says Luke, he was "about" thirty years of age. The word *about* does not suggest that Luke had exact information, but this is the basis for the usual chronology. Just to complicate the picture, Matthew's account explicitly puts Jesus' birth before the death of Herod the Great, which took place in 4 B.C. Efforts to identify the star the Wise Men followed with some astronomical object are failures, in spite of the fact that planetarium directors favor a triple conjunction of Venus, Jupiter, and Saturn which took place in 6 B.C. How the close approach of three planets for a period of a few days could give rise to the story of a single star which acted as a guide is hard to see. The main value of this "explanation" is that it makes a good show in the planetarium.

PLACE OF BIRTH

Matthew and Luke agree that, in fulfillment of the current Jewish Messianic expectation, Jesus was born in Bethlehem. Nowhere else in the New Testament is birth in Bethlehem mentioned or implied, either in Mark or John or Paul or any other book. Mark, indeed, speaks of Jesus in Galilee returning to his *patris*,[1] a word which means "native place." This presumably was Nazareth, as the common designation "Jesus of Nazareth" seems to imply. The Fourth Gospel reports that ". . . some said, 'Is the Christ to come from Galilee? Has not the scripture said that the Christ descended from David, and comes from Bethlehem?'" (John 7:41–42.) If John had believed that Jesus was born in Bethlehem, it is hard to suppose that he would not have stated the fact at this point (or elsewhere) to make it clear that here, as usual, Jesus' opponents were wrong. Actually, the tradition that Jesus was born in Bethlehem seems to have been an inference. Believing without question that Jesus was the Messiah, and understanding Micah 5:2 as a prophecy that the Messiah was to be born in Bethlehem, Christians apparently concluded that he must have been born in Bethlehem, without any explicit evidence. What evidence there is, other than the bare statements of the later writers, suggests that he was born in Nazareth.

THE LANGUAGE OF JESUS

There is every reason to believe that Jesus' native language was Aramaic, the language of Palestinian Jews of the period. This is a language related to Hebrew in somewhat the same way as Italian is related to Spanish. A few Aramaic words ascribed to Jesus have come down to us in the form of a transliteration into Greek letters: "Talitha, cumi" (Mark 5:41), "Ephphatha"

---

[1] The word also has the meaning "homeland," but this meaning is hardly appropriate for a town, and it is not so used in the New Testament, at least.

Nazareth nestles in the hills of Galilee. (Courtesy of the Israel Government Tourist Office)

(Mark 7:34), "Abba" (Mark 14:36), "Eli, Eli, lama sabach-thani?" (Matthew 27:46).

He may possibly have known some Hebrew, the sacred language in which discussions of the Law were carried on among the experts. He could also have known some Greek, as many did; but he surely did not use it in addressing the Galilean multitudes.

This means that his sayings, which have come down to us in Greek, must at some time have been translated from the one language to the other, with doubtless some loss and distortion in the process.

JESUS AND JOHN THE BAPTIST

The Gospels make it clear that there was a close relationship between the work of Jesus and that of John the Baptist.

Somewhere about A.D. 28 a certain John appeared in the Jordan Valley, proclaiming the necessity for confession of sin and repentance, in view of God's coming judgment. As a symbol (if nothing more) of their repentance, they were directed to be washed (baptized) in the Jordan River. This preaching found a wide response until John was arrested on orders of Herod Antipas, who ruled the territory in which John was active. According to the Gospels, the reason for the arrest was John's criticism of Herod's marriage to his brother's divorced wife, a marriage prohibited by Jewish law. Josephus says nothing of this but indicates that Herod feared that John's popularity might be made the basis for a revolt. Whatever the reason, John was eventually executed.

Among those who came to be baptized was Jesus. To later Christians this was a twofold embarrassment. In the first place, its apparent implication that Jesus felt the need of repentance conflicted with the theological belief that Jesus was sinless; and secondly, it made it possible for later followers of John the Baptist to ridicule Christian claims that Jesus was the Messiah, since, they claimed, his baptism by John clearly marked Jesus as a subordinate to their own master.

These two motives have affected the Gospel tradition in various ways. Matthew tries to avoid the implication that Jesus was conscious of any need for repentance by a dialogue in which John hesitates to baptize Jesus, and Jesus reassures him, "Let it be so now; for thus it is fitting for us to fulfill all righteousness." (Mt. 3:15.) The Fourth Gospel omits any direct report of the baptism and insists that John recognized and confessed his subordination to Jesus. "He must increase, but I must decrease." (Jn. 3:30.)

All the Gospels seem to suppose that John was given a sign from heaven at the time of Jesus' baptism that Jesus was the Messiah. It is therefore puzzling that both Matthew and Luke have the statement, derived from Q, that while John was in prison he sent disciples to Jesus to inquire whether he was the Messiah. It is generally supposed that this is because his initial assurance had given way to doubt, because Jesus had not fitted into the traditional pattern of the Messiah. But there is nothing said about this in the sources, and it puts John in the position of doubting, not Jesus, but a sign from heaven. The probability is that John had never previously recognized Jesus as the Messiah. What his reaction to Jesus' response was we do not know. Jesus' answer is not a flat-footed *Yes* or *No*. He says, "Go and tell John what you hear and see: the blind receive their sight and the lame walk, lepers are cleansed and the deaf hear, and the dead are raised up, and the poor have the good news preached to them. And blessed is he who takes no offense at me." (Mt. 11:4–6.)

It is clear that, whatever the relationship between Jesus and John, Jesus was not simply continuing in the latter's footsteps. Speaking of John, Jesus said:

> As they went away, Jesus began to speak to the crowds concerning John: "What did you go out into the wilderness to

behold? A reed shaken by the wind? Why then did you go out? To see a man clothed in soft raiment? Behold, those who wear soft raiment are in kings' houses. Why then did you go out? To see a prophet? Yes, I tell you, and more than a prophet. This is he of whom it is written,

> Behold I send my messenger before thy face,
> who shall prepare thy way before thee.

Truly, I say to you, among those born of women there has risen no one greater than John the Baptist; yet he who is least in the kingdom of heaven is greater than he." (Mt. 11:7–11.)

THE SCENE OF JESUS' ACTIVITY

The Synoptic Gospels present Jesus as active in Galilee for a period of unspecified duration, followed by a brief period of activity in Jerusalem, which was brought to a quick close with his death. The Fourth Gospel depicts him as moving back and forth between Galilee and Jerusalem and vicinity, with his major effort exerted in the south. To a number of scholars it seems probable that on this point John is to be preferred, at least in general. The Synoptic Gospels, if this is right, represent an oversimplified version of the truth. It should be observed, however, that the ground plan of John's Gospel seems determined by the development of a theological theme; and it may be this, rather than accurate knowledge, which determines the locale of a given scene. Furthermore, the material presented in these Judean episodes is just what forces us to question the validity of the Johannine presentation of the nature of Jesus' understanding of his mission. It seems odd to reject the content of these Jerusalem episodes, while asserting the accuracy of the setting in which they did not occur as reported. It would seem more probable, though by no means certain, that the Synoptic picture is to be preferred. Jesus may well have been in Jerusalem before that last week, in attendance at celebrations of Passover and other festivals; but we

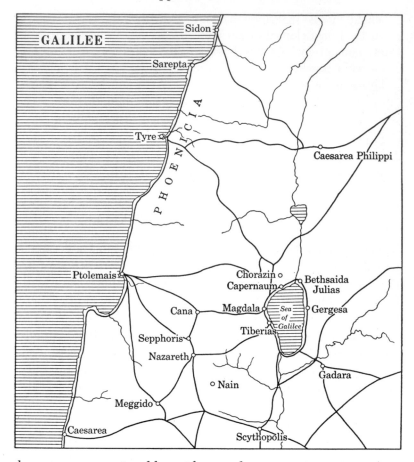

have no unquestionable evidence of any previous attempt to carry out there what he conceived to be his mission.

THE NATURE OF JESUS' MISSION

After John the Baptizer had been arrested, Jesus appeared in Galilee, summoning men to repent because the time had come for God's fulfillment of his promises. God's kingdom was at the door and men had better prepare for it.

It is difficult, if not impossible, to fit such a figure into the context of modern life. He had none of the present-day mass media for getting his message across—no newspapers or magazines, no radio or TV appearances. Strange as it may seem to some, there is no evidence that he ever reflected on the most effective way to "put over" the Gospel. Those who suppose they

The Sea, or as it might better be called, the Lake of Galilee. (Ewing Galloway)

find such evidence are simply reading into accounts, which certainly do not explicitly mention any such thing, an interpretation derived from their own attitudes and ways of doing things. This is never a safe thing to do; and it is especially dangerous when dealing with Jesus.

Neither do his activities fit into any of the familiar occupations of today. He was not the pastor of a church, nor an itinerant evangelist moving from one campaign to another. He was in some sense a teacher; but he held no degrees, gave no lectures,

138 A Historical Approach to the New Testament

and was never in a classroom. He was charged with a message from God to man about the coming kingdom and the implications of this for life.

He spoke sometimes in the synagogue, but more often he talked to people where he found them—by the seashore, in the fields, in a house, along the street. What he said was often in response to a question, or by way of comment on something that was said to him. He did not give formal lectures or develop a systematic presentation of a theological doctrine or an ethical theory. Such a body of teaching as we call the Sermon on the Mount could hardly have all been delivered at one time. The points are generally not developed or illustrated, and as presented would have left no clear impression. The mind cannot take in so many ideas at once. A comparison with the way Luke presents much of the same material suggests that the Sermon on the Mount, as we have it, was compiled by Matthew, not preached by Jesus.

In form, Jesus' teaching is concrete, unadorned, pungent. It is free from fancy language and moves clearly and directly to the main point. Study of such a parable as that of the Prodigal Son from this point of view is illuminating. Adjectives are few, those that are used are essential to the story—a *far* country, *wanton* living, the *best* robe, the *fatted* calf. Out of about 316 words in the first part of the parable only about 3 percent are adjectives—the part of speech most often used for padding and effect. Poor writers will use several times this many.

Another characteristic of Jesus' way of expressing himself is a quality which can be described as radical, intense, or extreme. "If your eye leads you astray, pull it out and throw it away." "How can you say to your brother, 'Let me take that speck of dirt out of your eye,' when all the while there is a whole log in your own eye?" "You blind guides, carefully straining out a gnat while you are swallowing a camel." Many of them have a definite touch of humor about them, like the picture of the man who was making a substantial gift to charity and hired a trumpet player to go ahead of him as he went to make his gift, so as to be sure that no one would miss his generous gesture. But Jesus was not smiling indulgently at human folly. He was in deadly earnest in his exposure of any sham or pretense behind which men tried to conceal from themselves their real motives.

One feature of Jesus' speech that attracted attention was its authority. However, so far as the word *authority* suggests something delegated or derived, it is misleading. The idea is rather that of power. Partly this was a reaction to his power to heal—to drive out evil spirits. But it was also a recognition that he seemed to be speaking at firsthand, with fresh and compelling insight. He was not repeating something from a book.

In some respects he was like an ancient rabbi (who, after all, was a teacher) and he was frequently addressed so, though there is no reason to suppose that he was ever recognized as a rabbi by the scholars. It was doubtless often a courtesy title like its modern equivalent, *Doctor*. But our sources show him acting in many ways like the rabbis who were his contemporaries. He taught in the synagogue, discussed the interpretation of the Law, using familiar rabbinic modes of argument, and gathered around him a band of students (the original meaning of *disciples*) whom he instructed.

Some of his contemporaries called Jesus a prophet; and this is probably the best term, though it is to put him in an ancient, not a modern, classification, and is subject to a host of misunderstandings of its own. When he spoke of the future, it was not for the purpose of providing advance information as to what was to come in some far-distant day when those who heard him were dead and gone. He was concerned with the future only as it would be the result of the present. As a prophet he was God's spokesman, summoning men to live as God demanded. If he spoke about the future, it was a future that was at hand, conditioning the present and bringing to clear light the ultimate realities which are so easily lost sight of in the struggle to keep alive and get ahead. In this sense *prophet* comes nearer to describing him than any such designation as priest, pastor, evangelist, teacher, or modern rabbi.

THE DISCIPLES

Christian tradition indicates that among the disciples who followed Jesus there were twelve in particular whom we also know as apostles. These apostles were accorded a special role in the early Church, and their names are given. It is to be noted that the lists as given by Matthew, Mark, and Luke do not agree in all respects. The usual harmonizations simply rest on the *a priori* theory that of course the lists really must be the same. The strange thing is that there are so few indications as to what these apostles

Several of Jesus' disciples were fishermen. Methods and equipment used have changed little over the centuries. (Courtesy of the Israel Office of Information)

actually did in the early Church, though later legends are abundant enough. Paul tells us (Gal. 2:9) that James (the Lord's brother, not one of the twelve), Cephas (generally identified with Peter[2]), and John were known as "pillars," but we have no information as to what function that implied.

But just as *rabbi* is not a comprehensive-enough title to do justice to the prophetic elements in Jesus' mission, so *disciple* in the rabbinic sense was not comprehensive enough for these companions of Jesus. They did not simply learn from him how to expound God's revelation of his will. On at least one occasion, Jesus sent out his disciples to proclaim throughout the Jewish parts of Palestine the message of the imminent coming of God's kingdom. This was their original function—not that of prospective officials in a world-wide organization to be promoted after Jesus' death.

HEALINGS

The proclamation of the coming kingdom which was central in Jesus' work was accompanied by healings of persons sick or mentally distressed. The disciples shared in this power. There is no reason to doubt that, in general, such cures took place. Faith healing has had a long and confused history, and belief in it has been exploited by many self-seekers and fakes; but that there is some genuine core seems clear. In recent times psychosomatic medicine has begun to place the whole subject against a scientific background. It is to be noted that Jewish tradition includes this aspect of Jesus' work but explains it as the result of a league with the forces of evil. For Jesus this power was not just a blessing which he was able to confer on suffering humanity, but the direct evidence that the kingdom of God was at hand. This is the meaning of the clash between Jesus and the scribes who came

[2] *Cephas* is a transliteration into Greek of an Aramaic word for "rock"; *petros* is a Greek word meaning "stone."

down from Jerusalem (Mark 3:22–27). According to the Gospels they accused him then of "driving out demons by Beelzebub, the prince of demons." The cases were cases which we would diagnose as mental illness. In the understanding of that day, they were the result of an evil spirit or demon getting control of a man. Relief was interpreted as driving out this spirit. Jesus does not question the interpretation. He does vigorously deny that he is able to drive out evil spirits because he has made a deal with their chief. This, he says, is silly. If it were so, the chief of the evil spirits would be working against himself. Actually, the only way anyone can enter a strong man's house and plunder it is by first tying up the strong man. It was widely believed that God had allowed Satan to take control of this world. But now that evil spirits were being driven out, it was clear evidence that God had assumed his rightful power, overthrown the powers of evil, and was thus on the verge of asserting his true sovereignty among men. "If it is by the finger of God that I cast demons out, then the Reign of God has reached you already." (Luke 11:20, Moffatt.)

Jesus saw as an essential element in his mission the effort to confront men with this fact and to awaken them to the necessity of getting ready for it. So he appeals to these "signs of the times." You can look at the sky and tell what the weather is going to be, he says, but why can't you see what is really going on under your noses? This inability of his contemporaries to appreciate the significance of their true situation is the theme of the earliest form of one of his most difficult parables, that of the Unjust Steward, who, caught in dishonesty and forced to settle up his affairs, proceeded to a further piece of dishonesty so that after his retirement he could live on blackmail. Jesus commended him, saying, "for the sons of this world are wiser in their own generation than the sons of light." (Luke 16:1–8.) Obviously Jesus was not recommending dishonesty. What he was saying was: here was a crook who was at least smart enough to see what was coming and to try to get ready for it. When are the "good" people going to wake up to what is going on around them? The fact that the man was a complete scoundrel only makes plainer the folly of the people who are supposed to be religious, but whose very concern with religion makes them oblivious to the deeper demands of God.

JESUS AND THE CHURCH

There is indeed no evidence that Jesus ever envisaged the establishment of what we know as the Church. The word only occurs in the Synoptic Gospels in Matthew, and there only in two passages which seem to reflect later conditions. One of these is in material which has no parallel in the other Gospels. In the other passage—Peter's recognition of Jesus as Messiah (an incident found in all three Synoptic Gospels)—only Matthew has anything about a church. Luke uses the word freely in Acts, after the Resurrection, but never attributes it to Jesus or represents him as anticipating its formation. All the probabilities point to Luke's being correct in this usage. Moreover, whatever may have been Jesus' teaching about when the kingdom of God was to come, the early Christians expected to see it within their own lifetime. This would hardly have been the case had Jesus instructed them to proceed to the organization and expansion of a body destined to endure through the ages.

The most that seems possible is that, when it became plain that Israel as a whole was not going to respond to Jesus' message, Jesus may have looked on those who did respond as forming the nucleus of a new Israel that would inherit the promises God made to Abraham and his descendants. But that he did anything to organize groups of these, or to promote meetings of them, there is not the slightest evidence. Only his immediate disciples formed anything like a permanent fellowship, and at first this was on a very informal basis.

Caesarea Philippi: the south gate. The bridge was built under Herod the Great. One of Jesus' few excursions outside Jewish territory was made to this region. (Ewing Galloway)

JESUS AND THE GENTILES

In view of the fact that Christianity spread widely among non-Jews, and in fact soon became entirely a Gentile movement, it is surprising to find no anticipation of this in Jesus' preaching.

Jesus seems to have had no deep prejudice against Gentiles. He commended one Roman officer for having greater faith than he had seen in Israel. A Samaritan (ordinarily considered to be even lower than a Gentile) is the hero of one of his best-known parables.

Luke states that on one occasion Jesus himself intended to make a journey through Samaria, but the Samaritans would not receive him. On another occasion he made a journey to the vicinity of Tyre and Sidon, and while there healed a woman's daughter, but only after the enigmatic statement, "Let the children first be fed, for it is not right to take the children's bread and throw it to the dogs." (Mark 7:27.)

On the other hand, he seems clearly to have thought of his own mission strictly in terms of Israel. In sending out his disciples to proclaim the coming kingdom, he instructed them, "Go nowhere among the Gentiles, and enter no town of the Samaritans, but go rather to the lost sheep of the house of Israel." (Mt. 10:5–6.) The later controversy between Paul and Jerusalem over the Gentile mission seems to confirm the view that Jesus never in any way spoke of a prospective appeal to the Gentiles. If it was implicit in his teaching, he did not bring it out.

RESPONSE AND OPPOSITION

Jesus' announcement of the coming kingdom met with a varied response. At one point it is said that the common people heard him gladly. Elsewhere the Gospels indicate that great

The road from Jerusalem to Jericho winds through the wilderness of Judea. In ancient times brigands often attacked travelers passing along it. See Luke 10:30. (Ewing Galloway)

multitudes followed him. Both of these statements are editorial comment rather than part of the old tradition. But there is also evidence in the criticisms of the more orthodox that Jesus found a considerable following among tax collectors, prostitutes, and others who were considered beyond the pale of respectable society. Much of their interest may have been temporary. It is a puzzling fact that the future of Christianity lay not in Galilee, where Jesus seems to have met with some success, but in Jerusalem where the violence of the opposition led to his death.

This opposition took various forms. At certain points he differed sharply from each of the chief parties in the Judaism of his day.

One important party was the Zealots, who believed in a violent uprising against the foreign power which ruled God's people. Although Luke indicates that one of Jesus' disciples was a Simon the Zealot, his allegiance to Jesus must have involved a change of view. Jesus' instructions to turn the other cheek, to carry the soldier's pack a second mile, to love one's enemies, would hardly fit in with the Zealot program. Perhaps at one time some Zealots might have thought that Jesus' proclamation of the coming kingdom was something they could work with. If so, they were permanently alienated when Jesus replied to the question whether Jews should pay the Roman poll tax by calling for the coin by which it was to be paid. Since the coin contained the emperor's image, he suggested that the question should be settled by giving the emperor what belonged to him. No Zealot would have accepted this as a satisfactory answer.

Another important group—which, strangely, does not appear directly in the New Testament—is the Essenes. The revival in some quarters of the old speculation that Jesus had some connection with the Essenes is hardly one of the valuable contributions of the Dead Sea Scrolls to New Testament study. The community revealed in the Qumran documents withdrew from the world; Jesus did not. They would doubtless have held that their righteousness exceeded that of the Scribes and Pharisees; but with their meticulous care to preserve ritual purity, this was hardly in the direction that Jesus called for.

With the Pharisees he differed at many points in the interpretation of the law, though this in itself was not necessarily serious. More serious was the fact that Jesus was known to associate with the wrong sort of people. If "a man is known by the company he keeps" and "evil companions corrupt good morals," respectable people had every reason to steer clear of Jesus. Tax collectors, who did the dirty work of the foreign government and were dishonest and extortioners in their own right, loose women, and people who in general were careless about God's Law were among his followers. Being charged with this, Jesus replied—doubtless not without a touch of irony—"Those who are well don't need any doctor, just those who are sick." Some of his best-known parables are directed to this criticism, among them the Lost Sheep and the Lost Coin, the Two Debtors, the Pharisee and the Publican, and the Two Sons (the Prodigal Son).[3] Most serious was the charge that his cures were the result of sorcery; this was strictly prohibited by the Law and carried the death penalty.

Jesus differed sharply with the Sadducees on the question of whether there was to be a general resurrection of the dead, but here he would have the backing of the Pharisees. The chief ground of Sadducean opposition grew out of the fact that this group of wealthy, landed aristocrats saw that their best interests would be served by collaboration with the Roman government in the maintenance of the *status quo*. So far as Jewish opposition was a factor in Jesus' death, it would seem to have been the Sadducees, rather than any other party, who were responsible.

THE LAST JOURNEY TO JERUSALEM

For reasons which are hardly clear, Jesus, in the spring A.D. 30 (probably), went up to Jerusalem. Whether he simply intended

---

[3] Luke 15:1–10; 7:39–47; 18:9–14; 15:11–32.

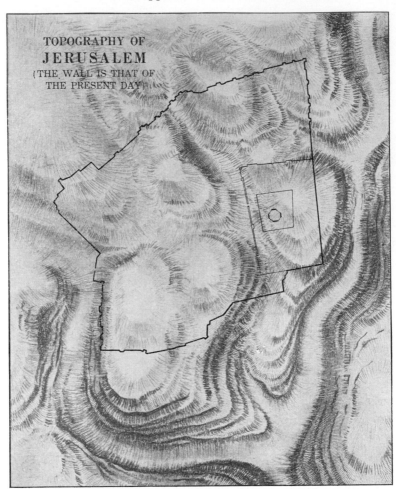

TOPOGRAPHY OF
JERUSALEM
(THE WALL IS THAT OF
THE PRESENT DAY)

to attend the Passover, or to transfer his activities to the center of Jewish religious life, we do not know. If Mark 10:32–34 is historical, he went anticipating his death; but in the light of subsequent events, it is hard to be sure that this kind of detail does not represent the reading back of later reflection as to what must

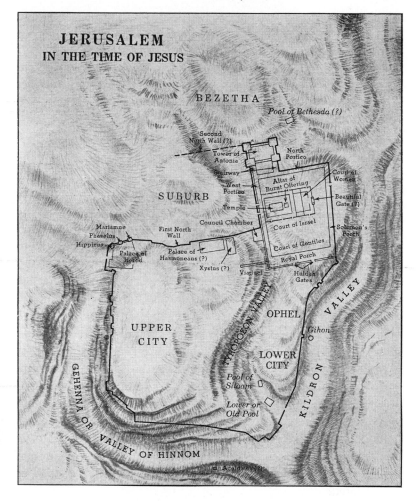

JERUSALEM
IN THE TIME OF JESUS

BEZETHA

Pool of Bethesda (?)

Second
North Wall (?)

Tower of
Antonia

North
Portico

Stairway

West
Portico

Altar of
Burnt Offering

Court of
Women

SUBURB

Temple

Beautiful
Gate (?)

Council Chamber

Court of Israel

Solomon's
Porch

Mariamne
Phasælus

First North
Wall

Court of Gentiles

Hippicus

Palace of
Herod

Palace of
Hasmoneans (?)

Royal Porch

Xystus (?)

Viaduct

Huldah
Gates

TYROPOEON VALLEY

OPHEL

KIDRON VALLEY

UPPER
CITY

Gihon

LOWER
CITY

GEHENNA OR

*Pool of
Siloam*

KIDRON

*Lower or
Old Pool*

VALLEY OF HINNOM

have been in Jesus' mind. Unfortunately, this is not a safe way to write history.

It is equally difficult to allow for the influence of such considerations in examining the story of Jesus' approach to Jerusalem. As told by all three of the Synoptic writers, this represents a public claim on Jesus' part to be the Messiah. He deliberately undertakes to fulfill the prophecy in Zechariah 9:9 (quoted in Matthew, but probably presupposed by Mark and Luke). It seems significant, however, that Matthew's Gospel, which in 21:1–9 makes the fulfillment of Messianic prophecy most explicit, is the Gospel which reports in 21:11 that the crowd said, "This is the prophet Jesus from Nazareth of Galilee." In the first century no one would have described the Messiah as a prophet. This description of him as a prophet does not conflict with the acclamation, "Hosanna! Blessed be he who comes in the name of the Lord. Blessed be the kingdom of our father David that is coming!" (Mark 11:9–10.) Jesus had indeed proclaimed the coming of God's kingdom; and the rejoicing of the mob may well have been directed to him as the bringer of the good news, not to him as the prospective ruler. Finally, it is to be noted that, if the incident had been an overt Messianic declaration, deliberately planned and calling forth enthusiastic response, the Roman authorities could hardly have been unaware of it or let it pass without prompt and decisive action to suppress it. To say that they failed to do so because they did not want to stir up trouble at a crucial time ignores the fact that, if this was a Messianic demonstration they already had trouble, and would not have dared to wait hoping that nothing worse would happen before they had a chance to quietly pick up the leader. The suggestion that Jesus intended this as a proclamation that his Messiahship was to be nonpolitical does not help, either; for this is not a distinction which the Romans—or the crowd—would have understood or appreciated.

THE CLEANSING OF THE TEMPLE

All three Synoptic Gospels place this incident at the beginning of Jesus' last visit to Jerusalem—though Mark puts it on the day following his arrival, while Matthew and Luke seem to place it on the day of his arrival. John tells a similar story, placed at the very beginning of Jesus' ministry. The accounts are so similar that it is impossible to think that they are independent stories of two different incidents—apart from the intrinsic improbability of such an action being repeated. Faced with the necessity of a choice, most scholars are agreed that the Synoptic date is correct. In general, the structure of the Fourth Gospel seems to be determined by a theological scheme rather than a firm chronology.

Mark 11:18 indicates that it was this action which set in motion the determination of the religious leaders to get rid of him; and this may well have been the case. Neither Jesus' differences with the Pharisees over the interpretation of the Law nor his supposed claim to be the Messiah would seem to offer sufficient ground for Jews wanting to execute him. But an attack on vested interests (money-changers and sellers of sacrificial animals were surely concessionaires, not squatters) would certainly have aroused the wrath of those in charge of the Temple and marked Jesus as a potential troublemaker who had better be put out of the way before he started something which might get out of hand.

In this action there was no Messianic claim, explicit or implicit. Neither was it an attack on sacrificial worship, express or implied. Rather, it was a protest against commercialization and extortion.

THE LAST SUPPER

All the Gospels tell the story of a last meal of Jesus with his disciples. As soon as one tries to go beyond this general fact to the details of what was said and what it meant, he finds himself involved in a morass in which it is very difficult to reach solid ground. The problem is not made easier by the fact that this meal is believed to have been the origin of a sacrament which has been highly valued by most Christians, and by some has been taken as embodying the essential content of the Christian religion. In such an emotionally charged atmosphere, a clear view of the truth is hard to come by.

In the first place, our sources are far from presenting a clear and consistent picture of what was said and done. Our earliest written account is Paul's, found in I Corinthians 11:23–26. Jesus offers his disciples broken bread as his body broken for them, and after supper a cup of wine as the new covenant in his blood, and directs them to repeat these acts in remembrance of him. Mark, the oldest of the written Gospels, tells of Jesus giving bread and cup. Of the bread, he says it is his body, without further explanation. Of the cup he says, "This is my blood of the covenant, which is poured out for many." (Mark 14:24.) He goes on to say that he will not drink wine again until the day when he drinks it new in the kingdom of God. Nothing is said about repeating the rite in remembrance of him. Matthew's account is derived from Mark's. He adds, as words of Jesus, that his blood, poured out for many, is for the forgiveness of sins.

Luke's account seems clearly to be based on some source other than Mark. Moreover, there are serious questions as to the original form of Luke's text. The most striking variation is the mention of the sharing of a cup *before* the distribution of bread. A formidable array of manuscripts tell of the sharing of a second cup after the bread; but many authorities on the text believe that this is a scribal addition to bring Luke into line with the other Synoptic Gospels, especially since, as Luke tells it, the first sharing of the cup is not connected with any reference to a covenant nor to Jesus' blood. In the manuscripts which have only the one cup, preceding the bread, Jesus simply says of the bread, "This is my body" (Luke 22:19a), without further interpretation. The manuscripts which refer to a second cup precede the reference by a continuation which explains that his body "is given for them" and enjoins them to "do this in remembrance of me" (Luke

Looking from Jerusalem across the Kidron Valley to the Mount of Olives. Two rival sites for the Garden of Gethsemane are marked by churches. The tower on the right at the top of the hill is at the traditional scene of the Ascension. (Ewing Galloway)

22:19*b* RSV margin). In spite of the weight of manuscript evidence, the shorter form of the text is more probably correct.

The Gospel of John also tells of a last supper of Jesus with his disciples, but without any mention of broken bread or cup, or any reference to their significance, or any injunction to repeat the action in remembrance of him. On the other hand, John goes much farther than the Synoptics in stressing the significance of taking Jesus' body and blood, but puts this in connection with the Feeding of the Five Thousand (John 6).

The earliest traditions as to the celebration of the Lord's Supper by Jesus' followers do not help much. The early chapters of Acts describe a common meal, but do not indicate that this had any of the features of Jesus' Last Supper with his disciples. Paul's story in I Corinthians 11, although it gives the earliest written account of Jesus' last meal with his disciples, implies a real meal, not a ritual conducted by a duly consecrated official. Pliny's report to Trajan of his examination of suspected Christians says that they gathered to take food, but "it was ordinary and harmless food," and he says that on his order they abandoned the practice. The Didache, an early Church "manual of discipline," composed after the Gospels but earlier than the latest book of the New Testament, gives directions for celebrating the "Eucharist." It does not quote the words of Jesus, but gives prayers for blessing the cup and the bread, which are mentioned in that order. The prayers emphasize the life, knowledge, faith, and immortality which God has made known through Jesus, and the need for unity in the Church which is representative of the coming kingdom. No reference is made to any sacrificial aspect of Jesus' death.

An additional complication is that the Synoptic Gospels clearly present this last meal as a celebration of the Jewish Passover. John is equally explicit in stating that it took place on the previous day. (Cf. Mark 14:12, 14; Luke 22:1, 7; John 13:1; 18:28; 19:14.) Many scholars have been inclined to accept the Johannine dating at this point, largely because the trial and execution of Jesus on the day of the Passover (which began with the meal in the evening) seems unlikely on the basis of Jewish practice as described in the Mishnah. However, an important recent discussion[4] argues that the meal was a Passover, and that the Markan account, except for a few later additions, represents the most primitive form of the tradition, going back to a Palestinian environment. Those who disagree would either take the position that the whole story is late in origin, reflecting Hellenistic sacramental conceptions, or else appeal to the ritual meal celebrated by the sect (probably Essenes) at Qumran as providing an analogy of another sacred meal celebrated by a religious group in anticipation of the imminent end of the present world and the establishment of God's kingdom.

It would doubtless be comforting to be able to show that, despite all the seeming confusion in our sources, there is a simple solution of all these difficulties; but it would seem to be a comfort that we shall have to do without. Doubtless some conclusions are more probable than others, but anyone who looks at several discussions of the subject will discover that the probabilities are estimated quite differently by different students. The one certain conclusion would seem to be that there is no certainty as to what was said and done on this occasion.

GROUNDS FOR EXECUTION

There is reason to think that the early Church, for obvious reasons, tended to throw the entire blame for the execution of Jesus on the Jews and represent the Roman administration as being reluctantly pushed into it. This can hardly be the case, for Pilate was not likely to have yielded so easily to Jewish pressure. In any case, crucifixion was a Roman punishment; and to say that a man was crucified is as clear evidence that the execution was the result of conviction by "due process" as would be the

[4] J. Jeremias, *The Eucharistic Words of Jesus*, A. Ehrhardt (trans.), Blackwell, Oxford, 1955.

statement that a man died in the gas chamber or the electric chair of one of our states.

The matter is further confused by the statement that the Jewish authorities considered him guilty of blasphemy. According to the Mishnah, there was no blasphemy unless the name of God was pronounced. To refer to God as "the Power" would not constitute blasphemy under this definition, even though what was said was presumptuous or derogatory. Properly speaking, then, the claim to be the Messiah, to destroy the Temple, or even to be seated at God's right hand was not blasphemy. It is true that the Mishnah's definition is later, and it is also true that courts have been known to go beyond the law. The decisive fact against his conviction on the charge of blasphemy is the fact that he was handed over to the Romans for crucifixion, instead of being stoned. From our point of view, it might seem to make little difference. In the end the prisoner was executed. That was not the Jewish point of view. Blasphemers ought to be executed because it was God's command. But the method of execution was as much a part of the command as the prohibition of the offense. God accepted no substitutes.

It looks, therefore, as if the report of a charge of blasphemy was a later development. Perhaps his followers were suspected of healing by pronouncing God's sacred name (which would be blasphemy), and this was read back into the earlier situation. The execution certainly was the result of a Roman sentence, on the charge that he was at least a potential revolutionary. Passover seasons were tense; the governor's first responsibility was the preservation of law and order. The simplest way to prevent trouble would be to do away with a suspected leader before the trouble started. Probably Jesus was brought to the attention of Pilate by leading Jews, chiefly Sadducees, alarmed over Jesus' attack on vested interests in the Temple, which could easily have been regarded as the probable forerunner of further and more serious trouble. At any rate, Jesus died on a Roman cross under the ironic placard, "The King of the Jews."

CHAPTER 9

The Message of Jesus

Jesus is to be understood primarily as the herald of God's coming reign—that is, of God's exercise of complete sovereignty over all human life. But he did not simply assert God's imminent assumption of his sovereignty. He tried to show men what God's rule meant and what must be done if they were to be prepared for what was coming. It was a message addressed directly to those who heard him, not over their heads to people who would read about it hundreds or thousands of years later.

As long as one is ignorant of the thought and ways of first-century Palestine, it is easy to read the Gospels as if they were general pronouncements of abstract universal truths; but the more one learns about the life of the period, the more firmly Jesus' teachings are seen to be anchored in their times.[1]

---

[1] If this seems at first disturbing, it needs to be recognized that, after all, Christianity has always claimed to be founded on the fact that, in Christ, God actually came into the world, taking on human form. If this is meant seriously, it cannot be taken to say that Christ had a body of flesh and blood which was inhabited by a self-consciously divine spirit. This is an ancient heresy which was long ago rightly condemned. Christ had not just a human body but a human nature. He spoke the language of his environment, but this meant that he had to use words in a whole framework of concepts and assumptions if he were going to say anything intelligible at all. Words arise in a living body of thought and can no more exist in isolation than cells can live apart from the body. So to find Jesus expressing himself not only in the words but in the thought forms of the time is only what we should expect.

This Jewish background comes out, in the first place, in the local color of the sayings and parables: the Palestinian method of scattering the grain before plowing; the mud-brick houses that a thief could dig into; the use of roof tops; absentee landlords; the magnificence of the gold on the Temple; mixed flocks of sheep and goats; the Roman soldiers, with their galling right to commandeer the services of the civilians to carry their equipment; the sudden, violent storms characteristic of an inland lake surrounded by mountains; the fishermen busy at the endless task of keeping nets mended—these are only a few from the examples that occur on every page of the Synoptic Gospels.

Other evidence of the relation of the teaching of Jesus to the Jewish background is found in the form of his sayings. Even phrases reflect this all-pervading atmosphere. Typical expressions which turn out to have been in common use are *inherit the kingdom, flesh and blood, to taste death. Unrighteous mammon* seems to have been the same sort of cliché that Tyndale's translation of it as "filthy lucre" has become in English. There are also bits of Aramaic, as has been said, and translated expressions meaning God, such as *the Power* and *Heaven.* The mustard seed is a frequent symbol of the very small, and the tree or the mountain of that which is great. Babylonian Jews refer to the impossibility of getting an elephant through a needle's eye. Here we have a combination of Jewish and non-Palestinian background. Babylonian Jews were familiar with elephants; Palestinian Jews were not, but were familiar with camels.

THE REIGN OF GOD

But the relation of Jesus' message to his environment goes much deeper than such matters. His central proclamation of the coming reign (kingdom) of God reflects it clearly.

In the first place, Jesus never really explains what is meant by the *kingdom.* Obviously, he took it for granted that everyone knew. He could not have done that unless he was using the term in a generally understood sense. The notion that Jesus offered a completely new interpretation of this concept is mistaken and rests on a twofold error. First, the Jewish hope of the coming kingdom, or better reign of God, is misrepresented as a crude materialism; and then notions which developed later in Christianity, partly under the influence of Greek thought, are read back into Jesus' teaching. There is indeed a wide difference between these two, but neither represents the real position of first-century Judaism or of Jesus.

There is one text which is often cited to indicate that Jesus taught a "spiritual" kingdom in place of a "material" kingdom. This saying is given only by Luke. As translated in the 1611 version it reads: "And when he was demanded of the Pharisees, when the kindom of God should come, he answered them and said, The kingdom of God cometh not with observation. Neither shall they say, Lo here! or lo there! for, behold, the kingdom of God is within you." (Luke 17:20–21.) The crucial phrase is the one translated "within you." Although this is not an impossible rendering of the Greek words in isolation, it is hardly an appropriate answer to the question asked. What they were asking was, "How can we tell when God is going to assert his power and cause his will to be done on earth as it is done in heaven? What are the events which will lead up to this?" Jesus answers, "There is no 'program' which can be recognized as having begun to unfold, from whose beginnings you can forecast the date of the end. The kingdom of God is within your grasp."[2] The questioners should submit themselves to God's will then and there, instead of trying to prognosticate the future. If they had replied, "Why, we Pharisees have already taken the yoke of the kingdom upon

[2] The translation "within your grasp" is based on studies in the papyri of the use of this preposition with persons, and is confirmed by the comments of early Church fathers, who knew Greek as a living language. See H. J. Cadbury, "The Kingdom of God and Ourselves," *Christian Century*, 67 (1950), 172.

us, we already have done what we as individuals can do," Jesus might have answered, "That is just the question. You tithe garden herbs with great care, but in the process you have lost sight of the real meaning of God's will."

Neither does Jesus' teaching about the "kingdom of Heaven" refer to a realm beyond the sky which men may enter at death. As has been said, *Heaven* is a reverent substitute for the word *God,* and *kingdom of Heaven* expresses no other idea than *the reign of God.* That this is so, is plain again because Jesus never criticized the idea that was current. He never said, "You think God's kingdom is to be realized on earth but you are wrong. It is to be realized in heaven, after death."[3]

What Jesus did say, as Moffatt translates it, is: "Thy Reign begin, Thy will be done on earth as in heaven" (Matt. 6:10), where the second clause is, in accord with Hebrew verse forms, parallel in meaning to the first. The kingdom was to come on earth, and for those not then living it would be entered by resurrection—that is, by the reuniting of bodies with their spirits—to live forever on a new earth.

Jesus' proclamation of the imminent coming of God's kingdom meant, then, that the time had come when God was about to assume the power which was really his, and make his righteous will effective throughout the world. The distinctive thing about Jesus' teaching of the kingdom of God was not an original conception of its nature as "spiritual," or as otherworldly, but rather the announcement that *it was at hand.* Its coming was not some far-off event. The time was now. "After John was arrested, Jesus came into Galilee, preaching the gospel of God, and saying, 'The time is fulfilled, and the kingdom of God is at hand; repent,

---

[3] It is often asserted that Jesus did try to say this but that the disciples did not understand him. This is incredible and also disastrous to all attempts on our part to understand him. The disciples might have found this difficult to believe; but if they could not understand at least what was denied, they must have been supernaturally stupid. And what becomes of Jesus as "the master Teacher" if he could not put a basic idea over to his chosen followers? Furthermore, if his disciples did not understand him, we never will, for everything we know of him comes to us filtered through their minds.

and believe in the gospel.' " (Mark 1:14–15.) On one occasion Jesus said, "Truly, I say to you, there are some standing here who will not taste death before they see the kingdom of God come with power." (Mark 9:1.) Again he says: "Truly, I say to you, this generation will not pass away before all these things take place." (Mark 13:30.)

Once one becomes aware of it, this sense of the imminence of God's decisive action dominates much of what Jesus has to say. Jesus does say that only God knows the exact hour; but this is not to be interpreted as if *at hand* then meant sometime in the next several thousand years. If Jesus meant what he is reported as saying, he expected God to act in that generation. Just when God would act—whether within five minutes, two months, or three years—Jesus did not profess to know; but he said plainly it would be before all his hearers were dead.[4]

JUDGMENT

Between the present and the coming of the kingdom lay God's judgment, which every man must face. "When the Son of man

---

[4] The difficulty here is not that his words are not plain enough, but that their plain meaning conflicts with theological presuppositions. Since the kingdom did not come in that generation, Jesus must have been mistaken on this point; and this cannot be reconciled with the omniscience that, as a divine being, he is supposed to have exercised. This is not the place for theological discussion, but it should be obvious that incarnation must involve being subject to some limitations. What those were should be determined not by *a priori* speculation as to what ought to have happened, but by what actually did. But even on *a priori* grounds, it should be remembered that the orthodox creedal statements insist on the full reality of Jesus' human nature. An omniscient "human nature" would not be human.

Although things did not, as a matter of fact, happen as Jesus seemed to expect them to, this does not make his words without meaning on this point. Everyone has read stories of the patient who had been leading a meaningless and frivolous life and who was told by the doctor that he had only a limited time to live. In the light of the pending fate, he takes a look at himself and undertakes to make the remaining time count for something. Usually the story has a happy ending, and the hero escapes his doom and lives on, according to his new insight. In this case, though the doctor's diagnosis is false, it enables the man to discover a deeper truth. So it can be with Jesus' expectation of the imminent end of the present world order.

comes in his glory, and all the angels with him, then he will sit on his glorious throne. Before him will be gathered all the nations, and he will separate them one from another as a shepherd separates the sheep from the goats." (Matt. 25:31–32.)

"Truly, I say to you, in the new world, when the Son of man shall sit on his glorious throne, you who have followed me will also sit on twelve thrones, judging the twelve tribes of Israel" (Matt. 19:28).

"Then he began to upbraid the cities where most of his mighty works had been done, because they did not repent. 'Woe to you, Chorazin! woe to you, Bethsaida! for if the mighty works done in you had been done in Tyre and Sidon, they would have repented long ago in sackcloth and ashes. But I tell you, it shall be more tolerable on the day of judgment for Tyre and Sidon than for you.'" (Matt. 11:20–22.)

"I tell you, on the day of judgment men will render account for every careless word they utter." (Matt. 12:36.)

REPENTANCE

One part of Jesus' message was thus the proclamation that God's assumption of his rightful sovereignty over man was imminent. The other complementary part was a summons to men to repent in view of this fact.

Here again, Jesus' assumptions were those of contemporary Judaism. Any failure to conform to God's will, whether deliberate or not, was sin. God had provided remedies for sin. Jesus never criticizes the Temple sacrifices; but for him, as for the Pharisees, the necessary and sufficient condition for restoration of the sinner to God's favor is repentance. But efficacious repentance meant a radical reorientation of one's whole life in accordance with God's will, not just a return to conventional standards of righteousness, with pious sorrow over past lapses. Even the righteousness of the scribes and Pharisees, who were generally acknowledged as particularly zealous and sincere, was not enough. There were no limits to the efficacy of repentance. But at one point Jesus clearly goes beyond the position of the rabbis of the period. This is in the assertion that the Son of man came to seek and to save that which was lost. It is also the implication of the parables of the Lost Sheep and the Lost Coin. Whereas Judaism was convinced that God was ready to meet the sinner halfway and accept his repentance, the sinner was generally expected to make the first move. Jesus asserts that God himself is always trying to make the first move, trying to lead the sinner to repentance; and he sees his own work as being an expression of this effort on God's part.

Herein was the ground for calling the proclamation of the coming reign of God "good news"; and the Gospels indicate that this part of Jesus' message found a wide response. "The great throng heard him gladly." "The crowd welcomed him, for they were all waiting for him." (Mark 12:37*b*, Luke 8:40.) Especially responsive were those whose occupation or way of life excluded them from the company of pious Jews: "Now the tax collectors and sinners were all drawing near to hear him."(Luke 15:1.) The sinner who knew that he was unworthy to stand in God's presence was assured that God would receive him rather than the person who supposed that by conventional religious practices he had earned God's favor: "What do you think? A man had two sons; and he went to the first and said, 'Son, go and work in the vineyard today.' And he answered, 'I will not'; but afterward he repented and went. And he went to the second and said the same; and he answered, 'I go, sir,' but did not go. Which of the two did the will of his father?" They said, 'The first.' Jesus said to them, "Truly, I say to you, the tax collectors and the harlots go into the kingdom of God before you." (Matt. 21:28–31.)

JESUS AND THE SCRIPTURES

For Jesus, the standard by which men would be judged was the Scriptures; and for offenses against its requirements they must repent. In this, Jesus was at one with other Jews. As to what constituted Scripture he seems to have recognized the same books that others included in the canon. He refers to the two divisions of the Scriptures recognized in his day: the Law and the Prophets. In addition to these, he quotes the Psalms and is quoted as alluding to Daniel. These—together with other books which constituted the third division of what we call the Old Testament, the Writings—were not officially recognized as Scripture until A.D. 97; but the council at Jamnia, where this was done, for the most part simply put its stamp of approval on what had already been recognized. Jesus and the Pharisees were not at odds on what constituted Scripture.

He quoted Scripture in defense of his own teaching, used it in criticising the teaching of others, referred to it by way of illustration, and appealed to it as authority. He used familiar quotations to summarize the essence of the Law. He is reported to have said, "Think not that I am come to abolish the law and the prophets (i.e., the Scriptures); I have not come to abolish them but to fulfill them." (Matt. 5:17.)

Nevertheless, there were vital points at which Jesus differed from other Jewish teachers about the Law. In general, he opposed the Pharisaic interpretation of the Law. He did not deny, as did the Sadducees, that the Law must be interpreted; and at some points his own interpretation agreed with that of the Pharisees. But, in general, he saw the Pharisaic approach as having lost sight of the underlying meaning and purpose of the Law.

The Pharisees held consistently to the position that God had given specific directions as to what he would have men do. Most Pharisees would probably have agreed, at least in principle, with Jesus' assertion that the Sabbath was made for man and not man for the Sabbath; but they would still have held that God had laid down the general rules for man's conduct on the Sabbath, and no other considerations could be allowed to override this primary fact. The rabbis recognized the difference between moral and ritual requirements, between intrinsically important and intrinsically unimportant actions. They were perfectly aware that, intrinsically, mercy was a greater thing than tithing garden herbs. But, not illogically, they held that, when God had spoken, such distinctions were quite irrelevant for practice. Nor could they separate the Law from the interpretation. Law always has to be applied to concrete situations not detailed in the statutes. Thus it requires interpretation; but once the interpretation has been authoritatively declared, the interpretation must be held to be of the same degree of authority as the statute, or the authority of the Law is meaningless.

In a general way, Jesus would doubtless have agreed with this. There is no indication that he ever tried to define his position on the Law with any precision. He accepted it as the revelation of God's will; he agreed that the consequences of the statements in it should be drawn so as to make it applicable to the various concrete situations of life from moment to moment. But in doing this, he was impatient with the legal point of view in deducing these applications, especially when its consequences threatened what we would call human values. The Scriptures spoke to him of the character of God, and he tested the results of logic against this character. "Go and learn what this means, 'I desire mercy, and not sacrifice.'" (Matt. 9:13.) "Woe to you Pharisees, for you pay tithes on mint and rue and every herb and ignore God's righteousness and love." (Luke 11:42[C].[5]) It would not be true to say that his opponents read the character of God differently. They simply did not recognize the character of God as a principle by which to test their deductions from the legal principles which they found stated in the Torah. Of course, the scribes did not pursue logic to the bitter end either; but for them the limits were set by practical necessity, as in the case of the ox falling into the ditch on the Sabbath, or in the case of tending

[5] Translations by the author are indicated by [C] following the reference.

farm animals on the Sabbath. For this reason, much of the Pharisaic interpretation of the Law was actually intended to make it workable in situations quite different from those in which it had arisen. But for Jesus, where ritual requirements seemed to override moral demands or to lead to human suffering, he held that somehow God's will had been misunderstood. Unfortunately, it is easier—and seemingly safer—to construe the Law as written than to interpret it in the light of God's character and purpose; and it ought not to be too hard to understand and sympathize with those who chose the more cautious way.

SOME SPECIFIC CASES

In general, then, Jesus' discussions with the legal experts were discussions of the proper interpretation of the Law, not simply the defiance by Jesus of what everyone agreed was the Law. This was so in the discussions over the observance of the Sabbath, which was one of the chief points of issue between them. The Law explicitly prohibited "work," but *work* had to be defined. In spite of the feeling of anyone who has done chores around a farm, feeding and watering the animals on the Sabbath was not, of necessity, considered work within the meaning of the Law. On the other hand, reaping and threshing were surely work. On one occasion Jesus' disciples, being hungry, picked some grain, rubbed it out in their hands, and ate it. Certainly they had gathered grain and removed the husks. To the legal experts this was obviously reaping and threshing. But when they complained to Jesus, he did not assert that reaping and threshing were not prohibited, or that one could do anything on the Sabbath that was to his advantage. Jesus' position was that where men were hungry, any such interpretation of the Law must somehow be wrong. This could not be what God's Law really meant. In arguing the point he did not appeal to some favorable decision, nor to a Scripture passage which dealt with reaping and threshing. He brought forward one of his cardinal principles for interpreting Scripture—that is, God's real will. It could not be God's will, he held, that the satisfaction of primary human needs should be subordinated to technicalities; and he quoted, as precedent for this principle, the story of how David and his men, when hungry, had even eaten the sacred "bread of the Presence." All interpretation of the Law must be in accord with basic common sense. Sheer logic is not enough, for sheer logic would certainly have ruled out pulling an ox out of a pit on the Sabbath[6] which even the scribes allowed. The issue between Jesus and the scribes was not whether the Law was valid, not whether it was to be interpreted, but how it was to be interpreted. Most other legal experts would not have agreed with Jesus' interpretation here; but the general problem of the interpretation of the Sabbath law was in the minds of Jesus' contemporaries, and there is plenty of evidence that on numerous points there were varying views even among the Pharisees.

The problem was complicated by a scribal principle which Jesus certainly would not have accepted. This was the injunction to "build a fence about the Torah." This meant that in interpreting the Law it should be done in such a way as to guard the Law as written from accidental transgression. If the Law said, "Do not boil a kid in its mother's milk," one would be kept far from the possibility of violating this injunction by prohibiting the use of meat products and dairy products at the same meal and never cooking the two kinds of food in the same pans or serving them on the same dishes. Many of the Sabbath regulations had a similar origin.

This was doubtless true of the prohibition of healing on the Sabbath except in cases where life itself was in danger. This is another point at which Jesus clashed with the Pharisees over the interpretation of the Sabbath law. They held that healing should wait till the Sabbath was over; Jesus held that this was not necessary. Doubtless his position on this point was influenced

[6] The Essenes were logical here and prohibited this as work.

by the fact that he saw these healings as a manifestation of the divine victory over evil, and nothing should hold that back. The issue is clearly summarized in the incident in Luke 13:14–16: "The ruler of the synagogue, indignant because Jesus had healed on the sabbath, said to the people, 'There are six days on which work ought to be done; come on those days and be healed, and not on the sabbath day.' Then the Lord answered him, 'You hypocrites! Does not each of you on the sabbath untie his ox or his ass from the manager, and lead it away to water it? And ought not this woman, a daughter of Abraham whom Satan bound for eighteen years, be loosed from this bond on the sabbath day?' "

But that Jesus was critical of the Pharisees' efforts to "build a fence" around the Law does not imply that he criticized even the Temple ritual as such. We are told, indeed, that on one occasion he directed a healed leper to conform to the Mosaic code in regard to purification, and on another occasion he used the conduct of the priests in the Temple as an example, without implying any criticism. He was scandalized not by the sacrifices but by the money-changers and sellers of animals. His very concern for the preservation of the sanctity of the place implies his approval of its main purpose, which was simply and solely sacrifice.

DIVORCE

Another point of legal discussion which also is firmly rooted in the problems and outlook of first-century Judaism is the matter of divorce. The statement in the Law indicates that a husband who found "some unseemly thing"[7] in his wife might give her a paper stating that he had no further claim of any kind on her and send her away. The problem is as to the meaning of *unseemly thing*. Some rabbis took this as equivalent to unchastity,

---

[7] Deut. 24:1–4 (G. F. Moore). The ordinary English versions, by translating "uncleanness" (A.V.) or "indecency" (R.S.V.) obscure the ambiguity of the original.

while others held that it meant anything about her that displeased the husband. One went so far as to say—perhaps with deliberate exaggeration—that a man could divorce his wife if she burned his dinner. When Jesus was asked for his opinion on the matter of divorce, he shifted the question onto entirely different ground, and he replied that the Law at this point was simply a concession to human weakness, not God's real will; but that God's will as revealed at creation was that marriage should be indissoluble on any ground. This line of argument, from the Jewish point of view, was a dangerous one. To appeal from an explicit statement to the real but unexpressed purpose of God is to undermine completely the whole idea of an authoritative revelation of God's will. When Paul drew this conclusion explicitly and stated, "Now we are discharged from the Law" (Rom. 7:6), there may well have been many who said, "I told you so."

GOD'S CHARACTER

Though the meaning of God's will depended on God's character, the character of God to which Jesus appealed did not in itself include any novelty. What Jesus taught about God was basically what was taught by the rabbis who were his contemporaries. This has already been presented in discussing Judaism. Where he differed was in the conclusions he drew from it.

There is nothing strange, then, even in the idea of God as Father in heaven. After all, this idea is found in the Old Testament, and there is abundant evidence that the rabbis were familiar with it and used it.[8] As the word is used in Jewish sources, it is always with a personal pronoun before it—*our, my, their, his, your* Father—just as Jesus regularly used it. It is true that

[8] Indeed, in the Synoptic Gospels the use of the expression is practically confined to Matthew, the Gospel in which various Jewish traits are most prominent. Perhaps it is Matthew rather than Jesus for whom it was a favorite expression.

the rabbis also thought of God as king and judge; but although sayings of Jesus in which these words are used have not come down to us, he did speak of God's judgment and God's kingdom. A judgment implies a judge and a kingdom implies a king.

The recognition that such expressions as *my Father* were in common use should guard us from the inference that the use of such terminology is necessarily the product of a deep and intimate sense of relationship between the speaker and God. No one draws any such inferences from rabbinic use of expressions like this. There may have been such a sense on Jesus' part, but if so it cannot be established on the basis of this usage.

It does not follow, however, that Jesus' use of the term is purely conventional. He uses it in two ways. Since man is the child of the heavenly Father, he draws inferences from this as to man's conduct and attitudes. Because God is our heavenly Father, we may trust him to provide for our needs.

> Look at the birds of the air; they neither sow nor reap nor gather into barns, and yet your heavenly Father feeds them. Are you not of more value than they? And which of you by being anxious can add one cubit to his span of life? And why be anxious about clothing? Consider the lilies of the field, how they grow; they neither toil nor spin; yet I tell you, even Solomon in all his glory was not arrayed like one of these. But if God so clothes the grass of the field, which today is alive and tomorrow is thrown into the oven, will he not much more clothe you, O men of little faith? Therefore do not be anxious, saying 'What shall we eat?' or 'What shall we drink?' or 'What shall we wear?' For the Gentiles seek all these things; and your heavenly Father knows that you need them all. (Matt. 6:26–32.)

Likewise, a man's conduct is to be determined by his sonship.

> Love your enemies and pray for those who persecute you, so that you may be sons of your Father who is in heaven; for he

makes his sun rise on the evil and on the good, and sends rain
on the just and on the unjust. (Matt. 5:44–45.)

On the other hand, for Jesus, the behavior of human fathers
shows what God may be expected to do.

What man of you, if his son asks him for a loaf, will give him
a stone? Or if he asks for a fish, will give him a serpent? If you
then, who are evil, know how to give good gifts to your children,
how much more will your Father who is in heaven give good
things to those who ask him? (Matt. 7:9–11.)

This is said particularly of God's readiness to answer prayer.
Similarly, when Jesus wants to make clear God's offer of forgiveness, he argues from the forgiveness of the human father
who had a prodigal son.

THE ABSOLUTENESS OF GOD'S CLAIMS

The true character of Jesus' teaching hardly comes out in
taking various sayings, or even various problems, in isolation.
For Jesus, there is first and foremost an absoluteness in God's
claim that colors all his teaching, and is, in part at least, responsible for the extreme form of his statements.

No one can serve two masters; for either he will hate the
one and love the other, or he will be devoted to the one and
despise the other. (Matt. 6:24.)

If anyone comes to me and does not hate his own father and
mother and wife and children and brothers and sisters, yes, and
even his own life, he cannot be my disciple. (Luke 14:26.)

The kingdom of God is like a treasure hidden in a field, or like
a pearl of great price, which must be attained at the sacrifice of
everything else. It takes precedence over the most pressing hu-

man obligations: "Follow me, and leave the dead to bury their own dead" (Matt. 8:22). Even a sound body is relatively of less importance.

> If your right eye causes you to sin, pluck it out and throw it away; it is better that you lose one of your members than that your whole body be thrown into hell. And if your right hand causes you to sin, cut it off and throw it away. It is better to lose one of your members than that your whole body go into hell. (Matt. 5:29–30.)

What is absolute is God's claim to man's allegiance. Jesus would not have understood modern proposals to separate religion and ethics, least of all *his* religion and *his* ethics. Jesus never questions or argues about the existence of God. For him this is as undeniable a fact as that the sun shines and the rain falls. These, in fact, for him are God's doing. That man is subject to the claim of God's will is not a matter for discussion. What is necessary is that man acknowledge his subjection to God and learn what it involves in every act and relationship of life.

From this follows the demand for a denial of self in all forms: "Whoever would save his life will lose it, and whoever loses his life for my sake and the gospel's will save it." (Mark 8:35.) There is no room for self-interest. "Give to every one who begs from you; and of him who takes away your goods, do not ask them again." (Luke 6:30.) There is no room for self-defense, not even for the deeply ingrained instinct to insist that we should not be victimized unjustly:

> Do not stand up to one who is evil. But if anyone slaps you on the right cheek turn the other one to him too. If anybody tries to sue you and take your coat, let him have your shirt also; and if any (Roman soldier) impresses you (to carry his pack) a mile, carry it two miles for him. (Matt. 5:39–41[C].)

Whoever is angry with his brother will have to answer to the court. (Matt. 5:22[C]. The original text said nothing about "without a cause.")

Love your enemies and pray for those who persecute you, so that you may get to be the children of your heavenly Father, for he shines his sun on the evil as well as on the good and he makes it rain on the righteous and also on the unrighteous. (Matt. 5:44–45[C].)

If God can so treat those who offend and defy *him*, who are we to be so touchy?

Similarly the emphasis is on our duties rather than our rights:

Will any one of you, who has a servant plowing or keeping sheep, say to him when he has come in from the field, "Come at once and sit down at table"? Will he not rather say to him, "Prepare supper for me, and gird yourself and serve me, till I eat and drink; and afterward you shall eat and drink"? Does he thank the servant because he did what was commanded? So you also, when you have done all that is commanded you, say, "We are unworthy servants; we have only done what was our duty." (Luke 17:7–10.)

God's absolute claim on man's self is reflected in the demand for humility. This is the reverse of the "natural" human attitude of self-assertion. Jesus rebukes the disciples who ask for preferred places when the kingdom comes.

You know that those who are supposed to rule over the Gentiles lord it over them, and their great men exercise authority over them. But it shall not be so among you; but whoever would be great among you must be your servant, and whoever would be first among you must be slave of all. (Mark 10:42–44.)

He discouraged the desire to be addressed by such titles as *Doctor,* and says, "He who is greatest among you shall be your

servant; whoever exalts himself will be humbled, and whoever
humbles himself will be exalted." (Matt. 23:11–12.)

Good deeds were not to be done in public, in such a way as to
call attention to the doer. Prayers or gifts to charity with an eye
to their publicity value would be worthless for anything else.
The Pharisee whose prayer was a reminder to God of all the
good works he had performed was rejected, while the outcast
tax collector who could only say, "God, be merciful to me, a
sinner," was vindicated. (Luke 18:10–14.)

Those who would soon find blessing in the coming kingdom
were the poor, the hungry, the mourners, the hated. (Luke
6:20–22.) It is he who humbles himself as a little child who is
great. (Luke 9:48.) Jesus himself even repudiated the salutation
Good since only God deserved it. (Mark 10:18.)

Another way in which the absoluteness of God's claim appears is in the appeal to trust God's goodness, which has already been discussed in connection with God's character. With
this is connected what Jesus has to say about wealth:

> Do not lay up for yourselves treasures on earth, where moth
> and rust consume and where thieves break in and steal, but
> lay up for yourselves treasures in heaven, where neither moth
> nor rust consumes and where thieves do not break in and steal;
> for where your treasure is, there will your heart be also. (Matt.
> 6:19–21.)

A man cannot serve God and riches.[9] A rich man has about as
much chance of getting into the kingdom of God as a camel has
of getting through the eye of a needle, except by God's undeserved favor. (Mark 10:25.)[10] It is to be noted that the tradition of Jesus' words preserves nothing to the effect that pursuit of

[9] *Mammon* is simply an Aramaic word for wealth. It is not the name of a
deity.

[10] The "Needle's-eye gate" is a figment of the imagination, which the disciples clearly had never heard of, since their reply is: "Then who can be saved?"
—not "Well, that *is* pretty hard."

wealth is legitimate if one practices what is often called "steward-ship," and he says nothing about the opportunities afforded by wealth for disinterested service. Riches are a peril, and on one occasion Jesus suggested that the best thing to do was to give them away (Mark 10:17–22).

Once when he was asked to help a man secure an inheritance rightfully his, Jesus replied. "Man, who made me a judge or divider over you?" And he went on, "Take heed, and beware of all covetousness; for a man's life does not consist in the abundance of his possessions." (Luke 12:14–15.) Jesus seems to have believed that covetousness is the root of all desire for wealth, and he would hardly have had much patience with the rationalizations by which men profess high regard for his teach-ings and at the same time evade their plain meaning.

Even basic family loyalties are subordinated to God's claims:

> I have come to set a man against his father, and a daughter against her mother, and a daughter-in-law against her mother-in-law; and a man's foes will be those of his own household. He who loves father or mother more than me is not worthy of me; and he who loves son or daughter more than me is not worthy of me. (Matt. 10:35–37.)

There is here, however, no disparagement of family ties as such. Jesus, as has been seen, held that marriage was intended to be permanent. And although he put the claims of God upper-most, he vigorously denounced practices by which children neglected their parents in the name of religion.

> He said to them, "You have a fine way of rejecting the com-mandment of God, in order to keep your tradition! For Moses said, 'Honor your father and your mother'; and, 'He who speaks evil of father or mother, let him surely die'; but you say, 'If a man tells his father or his mother, 'What you would have gained from me is Corban' (that is, given to God)—then you

no longer permit him to do anything for his father or mother, thus making void the word of God through your tradition which you hand on!" (Mark 7:9–13.)

A corollary of the absoluteness of God's claims is Jesus' call for simplicity and sincerity of speech:

> You have heard that it was said to the men of old, "You shall not swear falsely, but shall perform to the Lord what you have sworn." But I say to you, do not swear at all . . . Let what you say be simply "Yes" or "No"; anything more than this comes from evil. (Matt. 5:33–37.)

Here, Jesus is not concerned with what we would call profane language, but with the practice of calling on God to witness our statements and punish us if they are false. The implication is that otherwise we are as likely as not to be lying. Jesus calls for a single standard with regard to truth, so that a simple statement should be enough. Elsewhere he indicates his impatience with finespun distinctions wherein the use of certain words constitutes a binding oath, while others sounding just as impressive are without force:

> Woe to you, blind guides, who say "If anyone swears by the temple, it is nothing; but if anyone swears by the gold of the temple, he is bound by his oath." You blind fools! For which is greater, the gold or the temple that has made the gold sacred? (Matt. 23:16–17.)

Jesus was well aware that such strenuous demands would not always be met. For his part, God was ever ready to forgive the repentant sinner; but this entailed a corresponding readiness on the part of the sinner to forgive when he was the victim of the offense:

> Then Peter came up and said to him, "Lord, how often shall my brother sin against me, and I forgive him? As many as

seven times?" Jesus said to him, "I do not say to you seven times, but seventy times seven."

"Therefore the kingdom of heaven may be compared to a king who wished to settle accounts with his servants. When he began the reckoning, one was brought to him who owed him ten thousand talents; and as he could not pay, his lord ordered him to be sold, with his wife and children and all that he had, and payment to be made. So the servant fell on his knees, imploring him, 'Lord, have patience with me, and I will pay you everything.' And out of pity for him the lord of that servant released him and forgave him the debt. But that same servant, as he went out, came upon one of his fellow servants who owed him a hundred denarii; and seizing him by the throat he said, 'Pay what you owe.' So his fellow servant fell down and besought him, 'Have patience with me, and I will pay you.' He refused and went and put him in prison till he should pay the debt. When his fellow servants saw what had taken place, they were greatly distressed, and they went and reported to their lord all that had taken place. Then his lord summoned him and said to him, 'You wicked servant! I forgave you all that debt because you besought me; and should not you have had mercy on your fellow servant, as I had mercy on you?' And in anger his lord delivered him to the jailers, till he should pay all his debt. So also my heavenly Father will do to every one of you, if you do not forgive your brother from your heart." (Matt. 18:21–35.)

It is because of the absoluteness of God's demands that, for Jesus, motive and inner attitude are of equal importance with outward deed. This is the origin of his criticism of a purely formal conformity to the Law. Law prescribes certain things to be done or not done, and the implication is that where there are no specified requirements one is free to do as one pleases. In Jesus' thought, man is never free to do as he pleases. God is not to be satisfied with external performance—he demands the whole man. It is not enough just not to murder or commit adultery—

God calls for a heart free from anger and lust, as well as a heart free from duplicity, the spirit of retaliation, hatred, and covetousness.

PERSONAL PIETY

Prayer, fasting, and almsgiving (giving to charity) were the typical expressions in Judaism of what may be called personal religion, or personal piety. The practice of religion, of course, always includes the fulfillment of moral obligations; but it also finds expression in some specifically religious exercises.

In the practice of prayer, there is no reason to suppose that there was any sharp difference between Jesus and the rabbis. Later reflection has attributed to the prayers of Jesus greater fervor and sincerity; but this is deduced from theological premises, not inferred from evidence. True, Jesus criticizes the prayers of many for vain repetition, ostentation, and hypocrisy; but the leading rabbis would surely have seconded his protests on these points.

In general, we do not know the content of Jesus' prayers; but the one that is quoted in full (Matt. 6:9–13; cf. Luke 11:2–4) is remarkable rather for its accord with Jewish piety than for any difference in content or feeling. To address God as the Father in heaven and pray that his name might be hallowed are both typically Jewish forms of expression. Petition for the coming of God's kingdom had a place in Jewish prayers; and that kingdom was thought of by Jews as, first and foremost, the condition in which God's will would be done on earth as it was done in heaven. "The Lord will become king over all the earth; on that day the Lord will be one and his name one." (Zech. 14:9.) To pray to God for the necessities of life, for forgiveness, for deliverance from temptation and from evil, even to say the concluding doxology which the oldest manuscripts show is certainly not a part of the original prayer, is to do nothing which would seem in the least strange to Jewish ears. Every phrase has close parallels in Jewish prayers or in the Talmud. If the Lord's Prayer had been preserved in Jewish sources instead of in the Gospels, no Jew would ever regard its content with any slightest suspicion.

With regard to fasting, the Gospels seem to imply (cf. Mark 2:18–20) that Jesus did not fast; but we have no record that he criticized the practice. His remarks about it are again a criticism of ostentation and insincerity, and he asserts that those who fast for the standing this will give them with others may expect to get just what they are really looking for and nothing more. With regard to giving to charity, Jesus proclaims the same principle.

EMPHASIS ON THE INDIVIDUAL

Jesus' teaching is directed toward individuals. This does not mean that it has no social implications, but that his approach was to persons, not to social institutions. He produced no blueprint for the ideal society and formulated no program leading in such a direction. He did not pronounce against slavery, propose to overthrow the Roman Empire, or attack private property. It is not to be assumed, however, that he thereby set the stamp of his approval on the *status quo* either of his day or of ours. In fact, as has been said, he looked forward to an imminent and violent alteration of the *status quo*. God was suddenly going to assume the sovereign power which was rightly his. When he ruled in men's hearts, there would be no slavery, no Roman Empire, and no accumulation of property as a source of security, power, and self-gratification. His concern was that when the Son of man came he should find faith on earth. If men were set, above all, on attaining God's kingdom and his righteousness, all other things, as far as needful, would be added. Jesus' concern was with this primary condition.

Similarly, Jesus sees God as concerned with individuals. Not a sparrow falls without God knowing it, and men are of more value than many sparrows. There is more joy in heaven over one repentant sinner than over ninety-nine conventionally religious people who don't see the need to repent. The all-important thing is that each man should find his right relationship to God.

Neither does Jesus appeal to social motives. He does not directly appeal to our sympathy with the need of the neighbor, nor call attention to his rights. He does not point out the bad effect of our evil deeds on the victims. He stresses the bad effects of our deeds on us. He does not enjoin us to love our enemies because that is the best way to convert them into friends, but simply because *we* are God's children and should act as he does. Jesus seems oblivious to the bad effects that it will have on the oppressor to let him get away with his oppression. His only question is as to what hatred and self-assertion do to the person who hates, or who defends himself and his "rights."

Nevertheless, it would be a great mistake to suppose that Jesus was concerned only with a purely individualistic, pietistic religion, which minded its own business and was indifferent to politics and social problems. One of the tests of whether a man had really acknowledged God's sovereignty was whether he had fed the hungry, given drink to the thirsty, welcomed the stranger, clothed the naked, visited the sick and prisoners. If these things are good, the alleviation of the conditions which produce them is surely good also, especially if we think that the world is likely to go on for some time. Such conditions are produced, in part at least, by the operation of social forces, and must be remedied by social action.

It is not hard to see how Jesus' attitude is relevant to these matters. He would not be satisfied to deal with such problems in terms of political controversy and legal right. The presupposition of politics and legal right is a clash of conflicting interests and its adjudication by these devices. Jesus would insist that the problem is not to find some way in which your covetousness and mine may each find maximum satisfaction. The problem is to get rid of covetousness on everyone's part.

There are also implications as to the method of dealing with such things. Jesus insisted that good ends could not be achieved by evil means. A bad tree necessarily produces bad fruit. He relied on rebuke, persuasion, individual conviction, and love, rather than on coercion by law, violence, external moral codes, or propaganda. Slavery has been done away with in the United States by coercion, and we have the race problem. The destruction of German militarism by military force led straight to fascism, communism, and the second World War, with a third looming as a continuing threat. We fight for freedom and find when the fight is over that we are bound in chains of our own making. "The form of evil changes, but the evil nature crops out in another form."[11]

THE SANCTIONS OF JESUS' TEACHING

A sanction in the legal sense is that which induces obedience to a law or custom. A sanction may be formal or essential. The difference is roughly between the immediate and the ultimate reason for obedience. Thus, the formal sanction for obeying the traffic laws is the prescribed penalty for disobeying them, but the essential sanction is the basic reason for having traffic laws at all: the preservation of life, health, and property.

Jesus appeals to a variety of motives. Formally these may be related to the kingdom of God. The kingdom is at hand; and those who want a place in it, with enjoyment of its rewards and escape from its penalties, must conform to God's demands.

The essential sanctions lie deeper. At bottom is simply the fact that men, in the ways that are open to them, should be like God. "Love your enemies . . . that ye may be the children of your Father in heaven." This is the real reason we should do what

[11] H. J. Cadbury, "The Social Translation of the Gospel," in *Harvard Theological Review* (1922), 10. I am much indebted to this article in this section.

is right. But this in turn presupposes that we will want to be children of our Father in heaven and that we can know what he is like. At this point, Jesus appeals to a native ability to see what the good is and feel its appeal: "Why do you not judge for yourselves what is right?" (Luke 12:57.)

Jesus does not indicate that his own insight into the character and will of God was anything which was supernaturally communicated to him. His own sayings suggest that his insight rested on the ability (rare enough, indeed!) to see the implications of the obvious. He saw the birds provided for, the flowers in their beauty, and inferred that God would also provide for men's need of food and clothing. Since a man would help his neighbor in need even when it was inconvenient, since even an unjust judge would listen to the pleas of the persistent widow, so God could be expected to answer the prayers of his children. When Jesus offered these analogies with the expectation that his hearers would be convinced by them, it is entirely likely that this was because he himself had already found them enlightening. His constant use, then, of analogy and parable is an effort to get his listeners to see for themselves, with inescapable clarity, what the truth is. Once so seen, it will need no further argument or demonstration. In the end, the sanction for Jesus' ethical teaching is simply that we see that it must be so and feel the inner compulsion to obey it.

When the truth is so seen and so felt, obedience will be a spontaneous expression of one's nature, not a contrived conformity to an external code:

> No good tree bears bad fruit, nor again does a bad tree bear good fruit; for each tree is known by its own fruit. For figs are not gathered from thorns, nor are grapes picked from a bramble bush. The good man out of the good treasure of his heart produces good, and the evil man out of his evil treasure produces evil; for out of the abundance of the heart his mouth speaks. (Luke 6:43–45.)

THE ORIGINALITY OF JESUS' TEACHING

As has been said, one who knows nothing of first-century Palestinian Judaism finds it easy to suppose that what seems new to us was new to everyone who heard it. But the more we know about Judaism in Jesus' day, the more parallels we can find to Jesus' sayings, until it sometimes begins to seem that Jesus was nothing but a repeater of other men's thought. Even Jesus' demand that we should be loving, that we may be the children of our Father in heaven, has its parallel: "We are to be like him: as he is merciful and gracious, so be you also merciful and gracious."[12]

The conclusion that there was nothing essentially original in Jesus' teaching would be erroneous, however. It is said that Julius Wellhausen, the great German scholar, replied to the statement that there was nothing in the teaching of Jesus which was not in the Talmud by saying, "True, but how much more there is in the Talmud." Originality may be exhibited in selection. No one would say that the sculptor is not original because there is nothing in his statue that was not in the block of marble which he had to start with. By taking away much of the material, he makes something truly new of what is left.

We would do wrong, moreover, to uphold the greatness of Jesus by trying to show that everyone else was small. To be better than what is pretty bad is much less of an achievement than to be better than what is already very good. Many of the rabbis had keen minds, sincere devotion to God's will, and penetrating insight into what God's will was. Yet their very effort to know God's will involved them in a complicated system that easily got between them and God. Jesus cut through much of this religious

[12] Abba Saul, one of the disciples of Akiba. Mekilta on Ex. 15:2, and elsewhere, quoted in Strack-Billerbeck, *Kommentar*, vol. I, p. 372. This is only one of a number of similar sayings. Abba Saul is, of course, a century later than Jesus. The point is not whether Jesus said it first, but that the soil from which such a saying sprang, doubtless independently in the two cases, was already prepared for them both.

apparatus, though the subsequent history of Christianity suggests that his approach also has its dangers.

The judgment of Claude Montefiore, a modern liberal Jewish scholar, is enlightening:

> There are combinations in the picture of Jesus which, as a picture at any rate, seem to be unique; and which I am inclined to think are not merely picture but portrait. I mean such combinations as his humility and his sense of authority, his sternness and his gentleness; his great pity and his great purity; his tinge of asceticism and his lack of asceticism; his constant living with God and his compassionate forthcomingness to many sinners; his hatred of sin and his active friendliness and sympathy for the outcast and the lost.[13]

Jesus' originality, then, is not so much a matter of complete novelty of statement as of insight in selecting what was essential from the matrix in which it was embedded and in presenting this from a single and radical point of view.

JESUS' UNDERSTANDING OF HIMSELF

Perhaps in all the study of history there is no more difficult problem than that of trying to determine just what Jesus of Nazareth thought about himself. We do know with more assurance what his early followers thought about him. They believed that he was the Messiah, the descendant of David, and also the Son of man who was soon to return on the clouds of heaven, to judge the living and the dead; and they equated the two, although as far as we know this equation was new. Holding these opinions, they inevitably believed that Jesus, when he was alive, had been aware of his nature and destiny. If he spoke of the Messiah, they were sure he had been speaking of himself. If he looked forward

[13] C. G. Montefiore, "The Originality of Jesus," *Hibbert Journal*, 28 (Oct., 1929), 101.

to the coming of the Son of man, he must have been referring to his own return. Their memories and reports of his sayings would inevitably be colored by their understanding. The difficult problem is to determine whether, or to what extent, the tradition about Jesus' words is affected by such influences. Once the question is raised it will not down, and it cannot be settled by simply appealing to the reports of what Jesus said. You do not establish the accuracy of a report by repeating it.

Now, a few things seem fairly clear. Jesus held that God's reign was at hand. Satan had already fallen, and evil spirits were under control. Between the present and God's full control lay the judgment over which the Son of man was to preside. All this Jesus announced, with a clear assurance that God had laid on him the burden of so doing.

Beyond these few facts which are in fairly clear light, lies thick darkness. It is to be observed that these announcements could be made, and made with the sense that it was at divine command, without necessarily implying that the one who made the announcement thought of himself either as the Messiah or the Son of man. We can simply raise the main questions and point out some factors relevant to an answer. But the evidence is not sufficient to arrive at a certain conclusion.

Did Jesus think of himself as the Messiah? If he did, it is clear that he never made public announcement of the fact. There are a number of signs which point to this. One seems decisive by itself. That is the impossibility of finding witnesses at his trial who would testify consistently to any such statement on his part.

There is still the possibility that, even though Jesus did not make public proclamation of his Messiahship, he did accept this designation from his disciples, instructing them in its true meaning which, it is said, was for him quite different from its usual meaning. But this raises the question as to why he should claim the title and repudiate its meaning? The answer that Judaism had missed the true meaning will hardly do. Words do not have some intrinsic meaning, of which everyone may be unaware so that everyone may use them wrongly. Words mean what people use them to mean. If Jesus did not think his role was the role which was generally ascribed to the Messiah, then he may have been something better, but he was not the Messiah. The truth is, *Messiah* is hardly an appropriate term to describe Jesus' activities; and it would really be much simpler to suppose he never used it.

One puzzling incident is thus reported: "As Jesus taught in the Temple, he said, 'How can the scribes say that the Christ is the son of David?' David himself, inspired by the Holy Spirit, declared,

'The Lord said to my Lord,
Sit at my right hand,
Till I put thy enemies under thy feet.' " (Mark 12:35–36.)

Here the obvious meaning is that Jesus challenged the Pharisaic contention that the Messiah was to be a descendant of David. But this is just what his followers soon believed that he was. It is hard to suppose that the words are not authentic, but even the repudiation of Davidic ancestry for the Messiah does not go far in showing what Jesus proposed to put in its place. It certainly does not show that he claimed to be the Messiah in some other sense, or that he had in mind the later Christian concept.

If it be asked why the conclusion was ever reached that Jesus was and had been the Messiah, if he had never said so, the answer might be that it was an inference from the Resurrection. Whatever the nature of the experience which led to the conclusion that Jesus had risen from the grave, his followers were convinced that it was a fact. Once they were, Jesus would have been marked out as a unique being; and they would have had to ascribe some unique role to him. The conclusion would be easy that he was the Messiah or Son of man to whom he had referred, or both. This, of course, is conjecture; but it makes it clear that it by no means follows that the only way to explain the conviction of his followers about him is to suppose that he himself had told them what they came to believe.[14]

Another set of puzzles is presented by Jesus' references to the Son of man. It is to be observed that this term is confined almost exclusively to the Gospels, and in the Gospels it is never in the mouth of anyone but Jesus. In some sayings, it seems to be the use of a familiar Hebrew, and especially an Aramaic, idiom by which *Son of man* meant simply "human being." This is a very plausible interpretation of the saying in Mark 2:27–28, which then would have meant originally, "The sabbath is made for man, not man for the sabbath; so man is superior even to the sabbath."

In another group of passages, Jesus speaks objectively of the Son of man, as if he himself were other than the Son of man: "Whoever is ashamed of me and of my words in this adulterous and sinful generation, of him will the Son of man also be ashamed, when he comes in the glory of his Father with the holy angels." (Mark 8:38.) When the high priest asked, "Are you the Messiah, the Son of the Blessed?" Jesus is reported to have replied: "I am; and you will see the Son of man sitting at the right hand of the Power, and coming with the clouds of heaven." (Mark 14:61, 62.) If the saying is authentic, and Jesus thought he was the Son of man, why this very awkward shift from the first to the third person in one short sentence? The assertion frequently made that in Aramaic it was customary to refer to one's self in the third person by this phrase is dubious, and in any case hardly covers such a shift in expression in the same sentence.

In another group of passages, Jesus is quoted as speaking of the Son of man as having to undergo suffering and death. Here, particularly, the difficulty is to determine what influence subse-

[14] If this is correct, then such a report as that found in Mark 8:27–30 ("Peter's confession") must belong to the post-Resurrection period.

quent events may have had on the tradition of Jesus' words. Jesus suffered and died. Christian theology understood this as the fulfilment of the prophecy of the Suffering Servant found in Isaiah 53. How was this conclusion reached? Did Jesus, foreseeing his fate, instruct his disciples that this fate was to be expected and explain it in these terms? Or did his followers, convinced by their experience of the Resurrection that he was the Messiah or Son of man or both, but puzzled to find a place for the death of such a figure, discover in the Isaiah passage a satisfying interpretation of an otherwise insuperable obstacle to their faith? It is not a question of what the Gospels represent Jesus as saying. That in many respects is fairly clear. The problem arises when some questioner who is not excessively skeptical, but does not want to be led astray by wishful thinking, asks for some confirmation that Jesus really said what he is reported to have said. To say that we must not question what the Gospels say is to put the whole question beyond the reach of historical study, for that rests on evidence which is objective in the sense that it is there for everybody. But once it is recognized that the question as to what Jesus said about himself and the Son of man must be answered on the basis of evidence, it must be admitted that the evidence is indecisive. We cannot be sure whether Jesus identified the Son of man with the Suffering Servant, and himself with both, or not.

CONCLUSION

The picture of Jesus' teaching which, with all its uncertainties, emerges from the historical study of our sources is very different from the picture often presented in Christian preaching; but it is a challenging picture nevertheless. Despite Jesus' presentation of his message in terms of concepts familiar in first-century Judaism—inevitable, if it was to be meaningful to those who heard it—it still speaks strongly of God's sovereign will and man's duty to accept that will and follow it wherever it may lead and at whatever cost. His message challenges us to give our allegiance and trust to a God who gives good gifts to his children and who, despite the absoluteness of his demands, freely forgives the repentant sinner and even seeks him out while he is still in his sin. It shows us one whose loyalty to such insight cost him his life, and who, though reviled, reviled not again. Finally, it leaves us with the ultimate question: Was this life and this teaching the expression, under the conditions of human life, of what God really is? Was Jesus' very humanity divine?

CHAPTER 10

The Followers of Jesus in Palestine After the Resurrection

 XACTLY what happened to the disciples of Jesus immediately after his execution is not altogether clear. There is no doubt that they scattered. They had come from Galilee with Jesus. Perhaps some or all of them returned there. Soon, however, they were back in Jerusalem, at the center of a rapidly growing movement which marked the beginning of the Christian Church.

SOURCES

Almost our only source of information about this period is the Book of Acts.[1] It is beyond reasonable doubt that this book was written by the same author as the Gospel of Luke. Indeed, the two books were really Parts I and II of a single work, planned as a whole, with a common theme. Acts will then have been written slightly later than the Gospel, presumably between A.D. 90 and A.D. 100. It is the early part of the book which tells of the followers of Jesus in Jerusalem and which concerns us now. There

---

[1] Very important, though limited in scope and bristling with problems of interpretation, are Paul's statements in I Cor. 11 and 15.

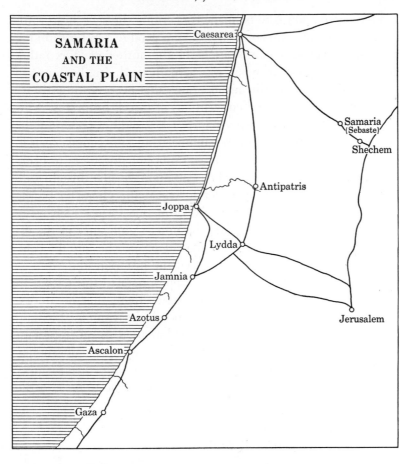

SAMARIA
AND THE
COASTAL PLAIN

Caesarea

Samaria
(Sebaste)

Shechem

Antipatris

Joppa

Lydda

Jamnia

Azotus

Jerusalem

Ascalon

Gaza

is nothing to indicate that the author's knowledge of these events as recounted here was derived from direct participation in them. We simply do not know where he got his information, and attempts to discover the author's sources from internal evidence are ingenious but hardly sufficiently convincing to bear much weight. Under these circumstances, we must rely on general probability and plausible inference from the situation and later developments.

One observation is to be made concerning the speeches in this as well as in other parts of Acts. There is good reason for thinking that these represent compositions of the author of Acts rather than direct reports of what was actually said. In the outward form of his narrative, the author shows that he is writing history according to the accepted conventions of Greek historians. Now the Greek historians, in reporting speeches, did not pretend to be reporting verbatim or even summarizing an actual speech. Rather, speeches were used for a number of purposes: to bring out the significance of the whole situation, to give insight into the meaning of specific acts, or to reveal the character of the speaker.[2] Since the speeches in Acts function in just such ways, helping the reader to appreciate the inner significance of the occasion, it seems altogether likely that these speeches are the compositions of the author. It is true that the historian undertook to provide speeches which would be appropriate to the setting in which they were placed. To the extent, then, that he understood the conditions rightly, the speech he composed would throw light on the general situation; but there is an important difference between a firsthand report and even the most competent account at secondhand, especially if the latter had an ulterior purpose. Unfortunately, this is what we seem to have in the speeches in Acts.

BASIC CONVICTIONS

One point, at least, seems clear. Whatever the nature of the disciples' experiences of the Resurrection, and whatever the circumstances under which they took place, there is no possibility of doubting that when the followers of Jesus assembled in Jerusalem they were completely convinced that he had escaped the bonds of death and had appeared to them. On this point it is to be

[2] M. Dibelius: *Studies in the Acts of the Apostles,* Scribner's, 1956, pp. 139 ff.

remembered that the Gospels do not give the earliest written account. That is found in Paul's letter to the Corinthians. What he tells them, he says, is what he himself had received, that Christ "appeared to Cephas, then to the twelve. Then he appeared to more than five hundred brethren at one time, most of whom are still alive, though some have fallen asleep. Then he appeared to James, then to all the apostles. Last of all, as to one untimely born, he appeared also to me." (I Cor. 15:5–8.)

If one were to undertake to discuss in detail the character of these appearances, it would doubtless be important to note that Paul gives no indication that he thinks of the appearance to him as in any way different from the others, although none of his references to it suggests a physical rather than a spiritual manifestation. The account in Acts of Paul's experiences quite excludes the former. But this is not a problem on which the historian can embark with any profit. He must simply note that, in whatever way the belief may have arisen, these men were utterly sure that Jesus had escaped the grave and been exalted to the right hand of God. Moreover, they believed that the expected deliverance was now surely at hand and that it would be brought about with the return of Jesus, under whom God's promised establishment of his kingdom on earth would take place. Their expectation was not directed to some indefinite distant future, but rather to something which was to occur within their own lifetimes. Here again, Paul is an early witness. In what is probably his earliest letter, he describes how "we who are alive" will fare at the coming of Christ (I Thess. 4:17), where the use of *we* indicates that Paul counted himself among those who would share this experience.

To the proclamation of this message of the Resurrection and exaltation of Jesus and his imminent return as the Messiah, the little band of followers devoted themselves with zeal and considerable success. Acts tells how the beginning of this activity followed an outpouring of the Holy Spirit on the disciples at the time of the Jewish Feast of Weeks, on the fiftieth day (Greek: *pentecoste*) after the offering of the barley sheaf on the second day of the Passover. According to Acts, this was marked by an outbreak of "speaking in tongues" which is represented as the ability to speak, or at least be understood, in foreign languages. But elsewhere in Acts, and especially in Paul (I Cor. 14), *speaking in tongues* means simply an ecstatic babbling, specifically said to be unintelligible to ordinary people (I Cor. 14:2). Since this would explain the charge (Acts 2:13, 15) that the speakers were drunk, it would seem as if there were some confusion in the Acts account.[3] It may be that both here and in the incident in the synagogue at Nazareth at the beginning of Jesus' ministry (Luke 4), told in his first volume, Luke is deliberately building scenes which serve to state symbolically his main themes: in the first volume, the rejection of Jesus by the Jews because he reminded his hearers of God's concern for Gentiles; in the second volume, the actual spread of this good news to peoples of every language, and the final rejection of the original heirs of God's promises.

But whether or not it began with a temporary manifestation of the power to proclaim the Gospel in foreign tongues, or in some ecstatic outburst, the followers of Jesus soon began a vigorous and successful proclamation of the good news that the beginning of God's reign, proclaimed by Jesus, was now indeed at hand, and would take place under the leadership of Jesus himself. In so doing, however, they did not regard themselves simply as the messengers of something wholly in the future. They themselves represented the beginning of the new order, in concrete embodiment. These were the last days, in which God was pouring out his spirit in accordance with his promise in the prophet Joel (Acts 2:17–21, Joel 2:28–32), and the gathering of Jesus' followers was the first fruits of the coming harvest.

Often misunderstood is the relation of this little band to Juda-

[3] It is to be noted that Peter did not try to show that this explanation was ridiculous. He simply offered a different interpretation.

The Dome of the Rock is on the site of Herod's Temple. The rock over which it is built was a sacred spot before Solomon built the first Jewish temple there. (Ewing Galloway)

ism. They were not conscious of themselves as belonging to a new rival religion. On the contrary, they thought of themselves as being in every respect Jews. No doubt they believed that they understood more fully than other Jews the meaning of their religion, but in their own minds they had not ceased to be Jews. Likewise, other Jews did not regard them as having ceased to be Jews. The point can hardly be overemphasized that the fact that they recognized Jesus as the Messiah did not at that time automatically exclude them from the Jewish community, either in their own eyes or in the eyes of those who disagreed with them. Undoubtedly most Jews thought the followers of Jesus were wrong, even deluded; but there was nothing essentially unorthodox in their position at this time. Other Jews, before and since, have recognized other Messiahs without excommunication; and it is very significant that James, "the Lord's brother," who soon became the head of the group of Jesus' followers in Jerusalem, was recognized by the Jewish community as a man of exceptional piety by Jewish standards, and his death at the hands of some Jewish fanatics just before the outbreak of the disastrous revolt against Rome was generally mourned by the leading Jews. So Josephus tells us, and there is no reason to suspect him of any pro-Christian bias. The breach between the two groups had a different origin, as will appear later.

Meanwhile, the growing group of those who acknowledged Jesus as the Messiah, soon to come in glory, met regularly for prayer, frequented the Temple, and shared a common meal in remembrance of Jesus' last meal with his disciples before his arrest and execution, and in anticipation of the Messianic banquet at his return.

THE SHARING OF GOODS

One feature of this fellowship is described in Acts: "And all who believed were together and had all things in common; and

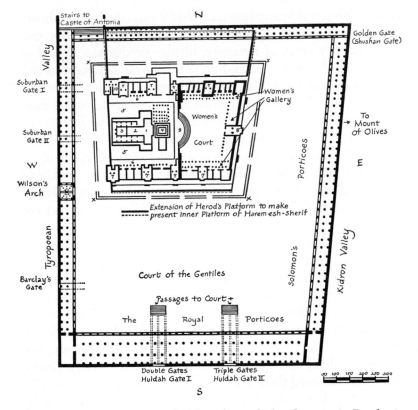

Conjectural Plan of Herod's Temple and the Courts. 1. Porch; 2. Holy Place; 3. Holy of Holies; 4. Altar of Burnt Offering; 5. Court of the Priests; 6. Court of Israel, or Men's Court; 7. Sanctuary Gates; 8. Nicanor Gate or Gate Beautiful (?); 9. Nicanor Gate (?); 10. Guard house. (From Harper's Bible Dictionary*)*

they sold their possessions and goods and distributed them to all, as any had need" (2:44–45). "There was not a needy person among them, for as many as were possessors of lands or houses sold them, and brought the proceeds of what was sold and laid it at the apostles' feet; and distribution was made to each as any had need" (4:34–35). This has sometimes been described as "communism"; but it is in any case clear that it was based on no theory of how the economic life of man should be organized, for economic activity must, of necessity, involve production as well as distribution. Moreover, according to the words ascribed to Peter in the story about Ananias, who sold property and professed to turn over the whole proceeds while actually keeping back a part, Ananias was under no obligation to give all that he had to the community: "Ananias, why has Satan filled your heart to lie to the Holy Spirit and to keep back part of the proceeds of the land? *While it remained unsold, did it not remain your own? And after it was sold, was it not at your disposal?"* (Acts 5:3–4. Italics added.) His fault lay in professing to give all when he had not done so.

The motives behind this sharing of goods on the part of the followers of Jesus seem to have been various: in the first place, a depreciation of the importance of wealth, based on the attitude of Jesus; second, a sensitiveness to human need, also derived from him; and third, the conviction that the end was at hand, when property would be worthless. To this was joined the conviction that it was of first importance to proclaim the good news. We may infer, then, that the group provided for the needy among them, and liberated those who had the necessary gifts for service of the Gospel. The funds for these activities were provided by wealthy members, who sold property as needed and contributed it to a common fund. This represented, of course, a steady depletion of capital; and it may not be unconnected with this that later Paul is moved to take up a collection among the Gentile churches for the "poor" in Jerusalem.

THE HELLENISTS

Such idealistic schemes rarely work perfectly, and this seems to have been no exception. The sixth chapter of Acts tells us that there was complaint on the part of some of the group, who were known as Hellenists, that needy widows among them were not receiving proper attention in the daily distribution of food. "The Twelve" proposed, therefore, the appointment of a committee of seven to take care of the matter, and this was done.

The account raises a number of problems, two of which must be considered here. In the first place, it gives us a glimpse of the government of the group. The account before us shows the group under the leadership of the Twelve, who had been set apart by Jesus, with a certain Matthias taking the place of the traitor Judas. Later James, Jesus' brother, appears as the head. Paul says that when, after his conversion, he visited Jerusalem, he consulted with James, Peter, and John, who were regarded as "pillars."

There is also what appears to be an "assembly" of the whole body of the faithful mentioned here in Acts 6:2, 5, as well as in a number of other places in Acts—e.g., 4:32, 15:12, 15:30— whose approval was sought, not only when, as in the present case, innovations were under consideration, but doubtless in other matters also.[4]

The other question which this passage raises is, "Who were the Hellenists?" It has usually been supposed that these were simply Greek-speaking Jews, or converts from such. But the word does not mean that by derivation; and once the question is raised, there is singularly little which can be offered in support of this interpretation. What the word really seems to mean is "one who lives in a Greek way." It refers not to language but to cultural background. If that is so here, these Hellenists would have been early converts direct from heathenism. As such, they would not be concerned with the minutiae of the Jewish Law. One of them, Stephen, was soon martyred because he was ac-

---

[4] The facts are obscured by the RSV, which offers five different equivalents for the same Greek word that appears in each of these passages: *body* (6:2), *multitude* (6:5), *company* (4:32), *assembly* (15:12), *congregation* (15:30).

cused of predicting the destruction of the Temple and favoring changes in the customs which Moses delivered to the Jews.[5]

RELATION TO JUDAISM

If from the first there were followers who were not observant Jews, it becomes easier to understand some things about the relations between this group and orthodox Judaism. It cannot be too strongly stressed that acknowledgment of Jesus as Messiah was not in itself ground for persecution at this time, nor was failure to accept the Pharisaic interpretation of the Law. Neither Sadducees nor Essenes did this, and they were not being subjected to persecution. Nor were Hellenistic Jews regarded as being in any way without the pale. To explain the violence of the persecution we need some threat to the very heart of Judaism, while at the same time the leaders of the persecuted movement were unaffected. Such a threat, offered by non-Jews in the early Jerusalem Christian group, would seem to meet the requirements. It would also explain why Paul should be concerned to extend the persecution to Damascus and perhaps elsewhere.

This is not to say that there were not real points of conflict between the Jews among Jesus' followers and those whom they regarded as their fellow Jews. The reiterated charge that the Jews had wrongly put Jesus to death, and that they ought to repent of this deed, was not likely to produce good feeling. The claim that Jesus had been exalted to the right hand of God, while techni-

---

[5] Acts, of course, represents these charges as untrue. But the question is hardly the simple one: Did Stephen commit or encourage what both parties would agree was a violation of the Law? The question was: Who understands the true purport of the Law aright? If the Hellenists were converted pagans, they would have recognized "the Law" as God's revelation; but this does not mean that they would thereby recognize the same set of obligations as did the Pharisees. That elsewhere in Judaism there were groups who neglected and even justified the neglect of such central observances as circumcision and the food laws, is shown by Philo's castigation of the *"anomoi"* (the "lawless"). But what is reprehensible among "birthright" members of a group is intolerable when practiced and promoted by later comers.

cally not a breach of monotheism, was not unnaturally considered dangerous. Manifestations of the Spirit, and the healings, carried on by the disciples, were suspected of being the result of traffic with evil powers. Most frustrating was the Christian interpretation of Scripture, just because there was no way in which either party could prove its interpretation right or the other wrong. Finally, the very success of the Christian propaganda must have been most annoying. But in spite of conflict revolving about such matters, there was no final breach between followers of Jesus and Jews on Palestinian soil. What happened was the withdrawal of the Christian group when the war with Rome broke out in A.D. 66, with the result that Jerusalem lost its central position in the new movement. There is a period of obscurity; and when the haze begins to clear, Christianity is a Gentile religion, with several chief centers entirely outside Jewish territory.

One factor which prepared the way for this shift in the center of gravity was the persecution already mentioned. Leaders of the persecuted group were forced to flee from Jerusalem, and began a vigorous mission elsewhere in Judea, including the coastal plain, and also in Samaria. The striking thing is that those who remained behind in Jerusalem recognized this Samaritan mission and sent Peter and John to supervise it. When the movement first spread beyond Palestine we do not know, but we do know that there were soon thriving groups at least in Damascus and Antioch. The development of Gentile Christianity, however, is another story.

PART III

Christianity Invades the Graeco-Roman World

CHAPTER 11

The Graeco-Roman World

IT IS NOT possible to understand the world into which Christianity came except by going back to the results of the career of Alexander the Great. Alexander had not only dreamed of military conquest, he had also seen the possibility of a united world with a common civilization and culture, and had deliberately tried to promote it. Perhaps his most dramatic gesture in this direction was the mass marriage at Susa, where he himself took two wives from the royal house, married a number of his generals to oriental princesses, and encouraged some ten thousand of his soldiers to marry native women.

We need not follow the fortunes of the various states which arose after Alexander's death, nor the events by which, shortly before the beginning of the Christian era, Rome succeeded in bringing under its power a vast territory including Western Europe, the Mediterranean basin, Asia Minor, and the lands as far east as the Euphrates River. But some of the aspects of this process are of direct relevance for the story of the spread of Christianity.

THE HELLENISTIC AGE

In the first place, East and West came into fruitful contact. There was a tremendous expansion of horizons and cross-fertilization of different cultures. Commerce with the East was vigorous. Ambitious young men went out to seek their fortunes in trade or in government service. In the mixing of populations, the taking of large numbers of slaves was important. These slaves were usually of the same color as their masters, and had often been men of ability and refinement in their own country. Also contributing to the process of interchange were the movements of troops and the necessity of native soldiers for Rome's great military establishment.

When the development of commerce found full opportunity for expression, under the Roman peace which followed hundreds of years of war, the result was a period of hitherto unknown prosperity. However, the distribution of the new wealth was by no means equal; and extravagant luxury and degraded poverty existed side by side in the great cities like Alexandria, Rome, Antioch, Corinth, and Ephesus.

Most important was the spread of Greek as the language commonly spoken and understood everywhere around the edge of the Mediterranean basin. The extent to which this had taken place and its importance for the spread of Christianity is made plain when it is realized that even in Rome, Greek was the language of the Christian community, its liturgy,[1] and its theological writings, until about the year 200.

ART, LITERATURE, AND SCIENCE

In this fluid and stimulating atmosphere, art and literature flourished. Interest centered on man and nature. Romantic love was a common theme, as it had not been during the classical age.

---

[1] The *Kyrie Eleison* (which is Greek for "Lord, be merciful") in the Latin Mass is a survival from this period.

Individualism was dominant. Realistic treatment of themes was common, whether in art or in literature. In general, the restraints of the classical period were relaxed or abandoned, especially in the expression of emotion. The contrast is clearly brought out in a comparison of the Elgin marbles from the Parthenon with the Venus of Milo, the Apollo Belvedere, and the Laocoon.

These characteristics all find expression in the interest in and the writing of history, an interest which reached a peak in this period.

Equally characteristic of the age were its scientific achieve-ments, both theoretical and practical. Geometry was organized into a deductive system, conic sections were investigated, the calculus was almost anticipated. Astronomy made great progress. Star catalogs were constructed; the true form of the solar system was conjectured. Although it was not generally accepted, the earth was recognized to be a sphere and its size was known with some accuracy. Progress was made in understanding and ac-counting for the motions of the planets. In physics, both me-chanics and hydrostatics were developed to a high point by Archimedes.

Practical applications of great importance were the develop-ment of navigation and architecture. The foundation of cities like Alexandria and Antioch in this period gave rise to city plan-ning as a form of applied art and science. Navigation developed under the practical demands of the growth of commerce, but it also made possible the pursuit of exploration for its own sake.

In the tradition of Aristotle, who was primarily a biologist and who himself stood at the dividing line between classical and Hellenistic times, knowledge of botany and zoology increased. It is significant that Alexander's armies were accompanied by scientists detailed to study the plant and animal life of the re-gions they penetrated. Medicine also made great strides in this period, with the growing knowledge of anatomy and physiology as well as of the properties of drugs.

From many points of view this could be called a great age to be alive; but for all its achievements it was a difficult age too. Expansion of horizon, movement of population, prosperity, cross-fertilization of cultures, progress of knowledge—all led to the development of stresses which the established ways and institutions could not meet. Actually there are many analogies to our own times:

The resemblance of this world to our own is at first sight almost startling. There was the same complex of states, big and little, with different state-forms, some more advanced than others, working within the bounds of a common civilization; and, beside some of the phenomena noticed above, there were many others which look very modern. Such are the eternal trouble of prices and wages; Socialism and Communism, the strike and the revolution; the growth of ideas of humanity and brotherhood combined with savage quarrelling; the emancipation of woman and the restriction of population; questions of franchise and (possibly) representation, of emigration and the proletariat; exact learning and crass superstition side by side; a vast literature dealing with every sphere of human activity, often competent, but no longer producing writers equal to the great names of the past; the spread of education, resulting in the manufacture of masses of the half-educated; the more conscious emergence of propaganda; the growth of all the half-worlds that cling to the skirts of science, of history, and of religion.[2]

THE ROLE OF RELIGION

Even more significant was the widespread unrest due to the fact that established ways and beliefs were questioned and, in many cases, shattered. A society with clearly defined moral standards, upheld by the general opinion of the community and

[2] W. W. Tarn, *Hellenistic Civilization*, Arnold, 1947, pp. 3–4.

with accustomed ways of approaching the gods of the state, gave place to one in which moral codes were in doubt, and religion was reduced to a matter of civic custom, which was frequently discarded as outmoded superstition without a satisfactory substitute. But it should be stressed that this attitude toward religion was a symptom of a deeper malady, not the cause of it. The root of the trouble was what today might be called a loss of a sense of security, which is usually not felt directly, but which conditions all attitudes and behavior.

To say, however, that the ancestral forms of religion were proving inadequate is not to say that there was a vacuum in the area of religion. Here, too, there was a bewildering confusion of ideas and practices; and each man was faced with the necessity of making his own terms with it.

In approaching a more detailed consideration of the religious currents of the world into which Christianity came, it must first be recognized that ancient religion was thought of as the religion of the group, constituted by a relation between god and the group as a whole. This was true of the Hebrews as well as other peoples. Achan's transgression (Josh. 7) brings God's anger on the whole nation, and his anger can be appeased only by the execution of Achan's relatives as well as the culprit. Only with Jeremiah and Ezekiel was the principle recognized that God concerns himself with the individual as such. But even this recognition did not mean that God ceased to be the God of the nation. The principle of the separation of church and state would have been incomprehensible to ancient minds.

However, by the beginning of the Christian era there had come to be a radical difference between the state religion and the religion of many private individuals. The favor of the national gods was believed to be essential to the general welfare, in which all shared; and they were worshiped in the traditional way with public ceremonies on stated occasions, in which the citizens were expected to participate. But the god or goddess to whom a person turned in devotion or distress was likely to be an entirely different being.

THE WORSHIP OF THE EMPEROR

Unless this distinction between the religion of the state and of the individual is appreciated, the existence of emperor worship, the attitude of intelligent people toward it, and the conflict between Christianity and the Roman Empire cannot be understood. Also essential to comprehension of this phenomenon is a recognition of a different concept of divinity from ours. For us today, *God* and *man* are mutually exclusive terms. They represent different orders of being. But for the Greeks, gods and men were closely akin. Aristotle could say, "If, however, there be some one person, or more than one, although not enough to make up the full complement of a state, whose virtue is so preeminent that the virtues or the political capacity of all the rest admit of no comparison with his or theirs, he or they can no longer be regarded as part of a state. . . . Such a one may truly be deemed a God among men."[3]

The Egyptians had long held that their Pharaohs were descendants of the sun-god, and therefore themselves divine. Alexander and his successors deliberately laid claim to divinity. Their reasons were primarily political. The recognition of their divinity set them above those with whom they had been associated, above the rivalries and intrigues of which they had been a part, and at the same time it could serve as a center of unity for a heterogeneous collection of peoples. It follows that emperor worship was in many respects more akin to patriotism than to religion.

The first Roman to be called *divus* (divine) was Julius Caesar. Although he refused divine honors while alive, the Senate decreed that they should be paid to his spirit (*genius*), which

[3] Aristotle, "Politics," 1284ᵃ in *The Basic Works of Aristotle*, Random House, 1941, p. 1195.

surely, it was supposed, continued to concern itself with the fortunes of the empire after his death. When Octavian finally emerged as the heir to Caesar's power, he took the title Augustus, a word with religious connotations though not so strong as those

Caesar Augustus, first Roman ruler to hold the title of Emperor. His rule ushered in a period of general peace, security, and social welfare.
(Brown Brothers)

of *divus*. But even during his lifetime, in association with the goddess Roma, he received worship in the provinces. Later emperors varied in their attitude toward accepting such honors in Rome; but all accepted and encouraged them elsewhere—not always from vanity, but as providing a center of loyalty for the far-flung empire.

The ceremonies were simple. There was a temple with a priesthood whose function was to carry on an appointed ritual, but ordinarily there were no rites that presupposed the presence or participation of a congregation. Certain days, such as the emperor's birthday or the day of his accession, would be marked by public celebrations. All would enjoy the holiday, and probably the public exercises would be attended by about the same proportion of the population as now attend Memorial Day or Fourth of July celebrations in this country.

While this public veneration of the emperor never touched the hearts of people, it did not seem strange or unreasonable to them. They were generally polytheists. Many believed that ultimately there was only one god, but they still were ready to recognize a variety of manifestations of the one divinity. That the Roman emperor was one such seemed reasonable enough in view of the very tangible benefits derived from the peace, law, and order which centered in him. To most, he was as remote as any god in heaven. They never saw him in his obvious humanity on television, or received several bulletins daily on the progress of his surgical operation. All in all, within his sphere, he was worshiped with more reason than many gods that men have honored. Meanwhile, since no one supposed him to be the only god, it was possible to combine emperor worship with any form of polytheism.

TRADITIONAL RELIGION

The gods of the state played little or no part in the everyday life of men. In sorrow or rejoicing, in outward difficulties or inward struggle and longing, men turned to other deities. For some, the traditional religion sufficed. They sought healing from all sorts of ills at the shrine of Asclepius. They consulted the ancient oracles to learn the outcome of matters small and great. They made vows to whatever deity seemed likely to fulfill their petitions, and usually paid them when their wishes were gained. They recited charms to win the fair and to catch thieves. They feared the power of the spirits of the dead and tried to propitiate and control them. Some of the gods were concerned to uphold

A panel from the Altar of Peace, dedicated in 9 B.C., celebrating the era of peace inaugurated by Augustus. The figures represent the earth goddess and spirits of air and water. (The Bettmann Archive)

particular standards of conduct, as Zeus was especially concerned for hospitality to the stranger, or the punishment of perjury; but the belief that religion must express itself in moral conduct was generally lacking. After all, the moral standards of the gods themselves, as described in Homer, left much to be desired.

The traditional forms of religion, though still potent, were not without their critics. It was widely held that the old scandalous stories must be interpreted as allegories of edifying nature, just as Jews and Christians, borrowing the method, have interpreted the very secular love poetry of the Song of Songs as an allegory of God's love for Israel or of Christ's love for his Church. Superstition was ridiculed. While on the one hand, the effort was made to show that all supernatural beings were simply deified men, on the other hand there was wide recognition that God must be thought of as One. Often this was accomplished by asserting that the various gods were simply different names for the one true god. Thus Isis is made to say of herself:

> . . . My name, my divinity is adored throughout all the world, in divers manners, in variable customs, and by many names. For the Phrygians that are the first of all men call me the Mother of the gods at Pessinus; the Athenians, which are sprung from their own soil, Cecropian Minerva; the Cyprians, which are girt about by the sea, Paphian Venus; the Cretans which bear arrows, Dictynnian Diana; the Sicilians, which speak three tongues, infernal Prosperpine; the Eleusians their ancient goddess Ceres; some Juno, other Bellona, other Hecate, other Rhamnusia, and principally both sort of the Ethiopians which dwell in the Orient and are enlightened by the morning rays of the sun, and the Egyptians, which are excellent in all kind of ancient doctrine, and by their proper ceremonies accustomed to worship me, do call me by my true name, Queen Isis.[4]

ASTRALISM

One aspect of religion of great importance was the belief that men's lives were controlled by the stars. On the one hand, in the vast and intricate complexity of the Hellenistic age, men seemed to themselves to be pawns in some great game that they did not understand or control; while on the other hand, growing knowledge of astronomy revealed a fixed order in the motions of the planets. When, to the obvious fact that life and growth on earth

---

[4] Apuleius, *The Golden Ass*, William Adlington (trans.), Loeb Classical Library, Macmillan, 1915, p. 547.

were influenced by the sun, there was added the discovery that the moon was responsible for the mysterious ebb and flow of the tides, it was easy to suppose that the heavenly bodies had still

This ancient mechanism, found in 1901 by Greek sponge divers, dates from the first century B.C. (Actual size about 6.7 inches.) A system of complicated gearing and graduated dials enabled it to predict a variety of astronomical phenomena, perhaps for astrological use or as an exhibition piece. It is described and discussed by Derek J. de Solla Price in Scientific American, June, 1959, p. 60. *(Courtesy of Professor Price, the copyright owner, and* Scientific American*)*

other influences on human lives. As the seeming disorder of the movements of the heavenly bodies was seen to be the superficial observation of a real but complex order, so it was held that the seemingly meaningless course of human events was really the expression of a deeper order; and, indeed, that the order of the planets was the source of the course of human events.

The practical results of this belief were several. Because of its basis in astronomy, it could appeal to the intellect. It seemed to give some meaning to life, for even an unsatisfactory order is more bearable than a series of events which have no sense or connection whatever. Because the motions of the planets could be predicted, it was supposed that they formed the basis for predicting events. The configurations of the planets at the time of one's birth were supposed to determine the course of one's life. One might admire and feel genuine awe in the presence of laws, so simple in form and so complex in their results, which govern the motions of the heavenly bodies. One could find inner strength in submitting to the course of nature, refusing to be moved by misfortune or want. One could feel himself part of a great living whole, and at least, if life were not too hard, find security by accepting one's place in it.

But there were other aspects of this appeal of astrology. Because the planets bore the names of gods, it was easy in the popular mind to suppose that these might be influenced, or even that the gods themselves were subject to control by those who knew the proper spell. The result was a great accumulation of skulduggery and hocus-pocus which went under the name of astrology and magic and played upon the distress or the cupidity of men and women. But, on the other hand, these beliefs gave a great impetus to the worship of divinities claiming to be the sole god, having all power including the ability to deliver their worshipers from these astral gods. One such was Isis, already referred to—for such claims were made on behalf of other beings than the God preached by Jews and Christians. But when Paul referred to Christ as superior to "principalities and powers," and asserted that in Christ the Colossians had died to the "elemental spirits of the world," he was referring to these beings—

not to deny their existence, but to assert that the Christian was not subject to their power.

PERSONAL RELIGION: PRESUPPOSITIONS

A growing number of people found refuge from the emptiness of traditional religion and the sense of helplessness produced by astralism in newer forms of personal religion. These can be broadly classified as ritualistic, found in the Mystery religions; the quest for knowledge, offered by Gnosticism; and the individualistic ethics of Stoicism. The latter is comparatively well defined; the others each embrace a wide variety of attitudes and practices from exalted devotion to crass self-seeking, from penetrating thought to crude superstition. The range would probably be about the same as is found in the average American Protestant denomination. There is as little reason in the one case as in the other to try to distill some ideal essence representing the "true" form which never was embodied in actuality. In the writing of history we must take things as we find them.

In all these forms of personal religion, men were looking for deliverance, or, as they would have said, *soteria*, a word often translated "salvation." But though it might include cleansing from sin and guilt, the desired deliverance was by no means limited to this. Escape from poverty and insecurity, from the power of the heavenly bodies, self-realization through self-reliance, union with the divine being—any or all of these, as well as forgiveness of sin, could be called *soteria*.

Stoicism had its own philosophy; but the Mysteries and Gnosticism, for all their basic differences, shared certain presuppositions as to man's nature and destiny. Basic was a dualism between the higher and the lower world. How radically this was taken varied, but we can approach its meaning by starting from an idea of Plato's. Try to draw a circle. Even with the best compass you cannot produce a figure that exactly corresponds to the geometrical definition of a circle: "A curve such that every point on it is equally distant from another point called the center." The line you draw will have some width, and some points will therefore be nearer the center than others. If you look at your curve with a magnifying glass all sorts of irregularities will appear. The world of matter seems incapable of giving perfect expression to the idea of circularity. True circles exist only in the mental world. This, then, it was inferred, was the true world; and the material world was an inferior copy which by nature blocks the full expression of the higher realm. So with such things as justice or beauty: the world in which men lived was incapable of giving full expression to them. Man's mind or spirit seemed trapped in an alien world. Moreover, it was held that this entanglement of spirit in matter was not dissolved by death. When the spirit left one body, it entered into another. This situation was often believed to have come about by some kind of cosmic accident; and since it was thus not in the nature of things, there might be some hope of the soul escaping from its predicament and returning to the primeval realm of spirit from which it had fallen, to be lost in it as a raindrop is lost in the sea when it finally reaches the ocean again.

This Greek conception of immortality must be sharply distinguished from the Hebrew conception of resurrection. For the Hebrew, man is both body and spirit. Future life involves a reunion of the two. For the Greek, the spirit is deathless (i.e., immortal) and its connection with a body a hindrance. Paul offers a compromise in speaking of a "spiritual body" (I Cor. 15:44), but for many of the Corinthians this expression must have seemed as self-contradictory as "round square."

One corollary of the belief in the deathlessness of the soul was the belief in all sorts of invisible spirits, usually evil and eager to do harm to men. They caused sickness, mental disturbance, and misfortune in various forms. They might be controlled by spells which could drive them off, or turn their spite against an enemy, or force them to employ their powers for one's own benefit.

THE MYSTERY RELIGIONS

Operating within the limits of such presuppositions were the Mystery religions. They were originally vegetation cults, concerned with assuring the productivity of the fields and working by means of what is called *sympathetic magic*. By the beginning of the Christian era, their more objectionable features had been purged away or reinterpreted in a more spiritual fashion. Each had its myth, centering around a vegetation god who died with the coming of winter and rose again in the spring. Now, however, the god was thought of, by virtue of his experience, as able to confer on men the power to escape death and enter into the enjoyment of immortality unencumbered by a body. Instead of rebirth in a body, they were to be "reborn for eternity" in a realm of pure spirit.

The means by which this rebirth was to be brought about was the operation of ritual. For one who proposed to join a Mystery cult, there was a period of preparation, involving such rites as vows of secrecy, confession of sin, ritual washing, sacrifice, fasting, continence, pilgrimages, and self-mortification. The properly prepared candidate was then admitted to the initiation. These initiations were shrouded in a veil of secrecy; but we know that they must have been impressive ceremonies, involving things exhibited, things done, and things said. In some cases, there is reason to believe that a sort of "passion play" depicting the god's tragic death and glorious resurrection was enacted. Every resource of light and dark, sound and silence—even odor—was used to produce a lasting emotional experience, in which the devotee felt united with the god and assured of protection and the sharing of a blessed immortality. The meaning of the experience has been thus summed up: "The salvation imparted in the

Mysteries embraced deliverance from the physical ills of life, from bodily ailments, from the sense of alienation, from the galling power of Fate and the reckless caprice of Fortune, from the ubiquitous terrors of the demons, from the fears of superstition, and lastly from the gloom of death."[5]

In contrast to the traditional forms of religion, the Mystery religions were voluntary associations. A man took the steps leading to initiation by his own free choice. In this respect, they are analogous to the secret fraternal orders of the present day, though the Mysteries were in general open to all who applied. There was no provision for members passing on candidates and blackballing those who for one reason or another were deemed unsuitable.

The congregations of some of the Mysteries were widely spread throughout the Roman Empire. They were joined by bonds of a common fellowship; but there was no strong central control, such as the Christian movement developed. We know little about the details of variety within a given Mystery; but we do know what would have happened in Christianity without a strong organization, and analogy suggests that while the ritual was perhaps uniform, the interpretation of it in different congregations may have been very different.

Apart from the variety that might exist in a single Mystery religion, there was a wide variety among the different Mysteries. Egypt, Asia Minor, Syria, and Persia, each was a center for the diffusion of one or more of these religions.

In Egypt, the worship of Isis and Osiris goes far back in history. It centered on the story of how Osiris, a grain deity, was killed and dismembered by an enemy, how his body was found and brought to life by Isis. In the Ptolemaic period, the figure of Serapis was deliberately created and added, and related to Dionysus, to commend the religion to the Greek part of the population. Traders, slaves, and soldiers carried it everywhere in the Empire.

[5] S. Angus, *The Mystery Religions and Christianity,* Scribner's, 1925, p. 138.

Asia Minor was the original home of the worship of the Great
Mother, or Cybele. Associated with her was Attis, also a vegeta-

*Isis, like other deities of the mys-
tery religions, had a long history.
Here she is shown in an ancient
relief from Thebes. (The Bettmann Archive)*

tion god who died and came to life. Her principal rites were
celebrated in the springtime, when devotees worked themselves

into a frenzy, gashed themselves and sprinkled the blood on their altars, while her priests went so far as to emasculate themselves. This religion was officially introduced into Rome in 205 B.C., to ward off the Carthaginian threat; but native Romans were not permitted to take part in it until about the beginning of our era.

Representative of the Syrian religions was the worship of various Baals (the word means "Lord" or "Master") and especially of Astarte, a female figure who appears in the Old Testament as Ashtoreth. Here, too, flourished the worship of the sun as the lord of heaven.

Persia contributed the worship of Mithras, which, though old, did not begin its great period of growth and expansion until sometime after the end of our period. Then, however, it became Christianity's chief rival. It was a religion which appealed to the soldier. It taught universal brotherhood, a high standard of moral conduct, and, like all the others, promised deliverance from the ills of life and a blessed immortality.

Constantly recurring features of the rituals of these religions were rites of purification, including ceremonial washings, and cult meals in which the flesh of some animal sacred to the god was eaten, through which the participant believed he became identified with the god and shared in his substance and attributes. The Christian sacraments did not originate by borrowing from these religions, but undoubtedly the later development and understanding of the Christian rites was influenced by these ideas present in the minds of converts. But by the time this happened, the ideas of the Mysteries had been highly spiritualized.

If we choose to concentrate on the more primitive aspects of the Mysteries, it is hard to see how sensible people could have given them any credence. That they did not remain in this condition is clear from the prayer of Lucius to Isis after his initiation into her Mysteries:

O holy and blessed dame, the perpetual comfort of human kind, who by Thy bounty and grace nourishest all the world, and bearest a great affection to the adversities of the miserable as a loving mother, Thou takest no rest night or day, neither art Thou idle at any time in giving benefits and succouring all men as well on land as sea; Thou art she that puttest away all storms and dangers from men's life by stretching forth Thy right hand, whereby likewise Thou dost unweave even the inextricable and tangled web of fate, and appeasest the great tempests of fortune, and keepest back the harmful course of the stars. The gods supernal do honour Thee; the gods infernal have Thee in reverence; Thou dost make all the earth to turn, Thou givest light to the sun, Thou governest the world, Thou treadest down the power of hell. By Thy mean the stars give answer, the seasons return, the gods rejoice, the elements serve; at Thy commandment the winds do blow, the clouds nourish the earth, the seeds prosper, and the fruits do grow. The birds of the air, the beasts of the hill, the serpents of the den, and the fishes of the sea do tremble at Thy majesty; but my spirit is not able to give Thee sufficient praise, my patrimony is unable to satisfy Thy sacrifices; my voice hath no power to utter that which I think of Thy Majesty, no, not if I had a thousand mouths and so many tongues and were able to continue for ever. Howbeit as a good religious person, and according to my poor estate, I will do what I may; I will always keep Thy divine appearance in remembrance, and close the imagination of Thy most holy godhead within my breast.[6]

THE WAY OF KNOWLEDGE

The Mystery Religions offered men deliverance (*soteria*) by way of ritual. Another road to the same goal was offered in the name of knowledge. Here again, there was wide variety, from crude superstition to exalted devotion; but common to all was the idea that the saving knowledge (*gnosis*) was not information but insight. It was not facts stored in the memory, but a vision of man's nature and destiny. It was not something to be learned; it had to be seen.

[6] Apuleius, *op. cit.,* pp. 583, 585.

This movement is generally known as Gnosticism; and our knowledge of an important phase of it comes largely from the attacks on it made by Christians of the second and third centuries, who see it as a Christian heresy. The discovery of a Gnostic library in upper Egypt, only a small part of which has yet been published, has begun to throw further light on the matter. But this Christian phase of Gnosticism is not the whole story, even though some would like to keep the term to this historic usage. The attempt to find deliverance from life's miseries by illumination is much more widespread, and was a feature of the scene into which Christianity came. For this wider movement, a term is needed; and it is hard to find another. *Gnosticism* will therefore be used here in the broad sense.

This quest took in a radical way the dualism already described. Spirit and mind were good. Matter and body were evil. The contrast between light and darkness was central. The existence of matter was not a part of God's plan. How it had come into being, and how spirits had got entangled in it, were variously explained. But once the primitive tragedy had occurred, there was no escape except by the intervention of God, who sent a heavenly being to awaken the entrapped souls to their true destiny. Those who heeded would find release when death came, and they would ascend back to the realm of spirit whence they had fallen. In so doing, they would traverse the spheres on which the planets moved, and have to know the password for each if they were to be allowed to continue. In its degraded forms, the communication of these formulas came to be the main content of the saving knowledge; but when this happened, it represented a perversion of the Gnostic quest.

If we try to set down what the Gnostic claimed to know, we find ourselves in a dilemma; for we have to set down, in the form of items of information, what was held by the Gnostic in a different way. One of them describes this knowledge thus: *Gnosis* "is the knowledge of who we were, into what place we have been thrown; whither we are hastening, whence we have been redeemed; what is birth, what is rebirth."[7] But this knowledge could not be reduced to catechism form. The Gnostic believed it was a supernatural disclosure; but he did not receive it as information, to be accepted on authority or on argument. It "spoke to his condition." Confronted with the Gnostic message, his whole being responded. He seemed to himself to have awakened from sleep, or to have recovered from a drunken stupor. Only in subordination to this central experience would he accept other items as information he might need on his journey home. The essential thing was the awakening, and this itself was the deliverance.

Different forms of Gnosticism had different accounts of how man had come to his present plight and how it had become possible to escape this plight. In what was undoubtedly intended as figurative language, the fantastic story was told of how sparks from the world of light had come to be imprisoned in the world of matter. Part of the story would be a genealogy of spiritual powers, proceeding from the primeval One. Part of it would be the story of how the redeeming knowledge had been made available, either by the activity of a supernatural figure moving among men, or by a supernatural disclosure to a man. In the "Christian" forms of Gnosis, Jesus was the redeemer; but because of the assertion that matter was evil, it was usually felt necessary to deny that he had a real human body and was really crucified.

Because of its radical dualism between good spirit and evil body, two conclusions were possible as to the treatment of the body while the spirit was imprisoned in it. One procedure would be to punish the evil body, by denying it the satisfaction of its appetites and by inflicting on it various forms of self-torture. This is the way of asceticism. Equally logical, however, was the conclusion that, since body and spirit were utterly different, what

[7] Theodotus, quoted in Clement of Alexandria, *Excerpts from Theodotus*, 78.

the body did was of no concern to the spirit. The prisoner cannot be held responsible for the condition of the prison. So if the body wanted to enjoy itself, it was not for the spirit to try to stop it. This is libertinism. One of the reasons for the conflict between Gnosticism and Christianity was that the Church could not accept either of these extremes, any more than it could accept the position that Christ had no real human body.

The attempt to trace the origins of Gnosticism have led to no general agreement. The important thing, however, is that this movement was extremely hospitable to ideas from all kinds of sources. It borrowed indiscriminately whatever could be cut to fit its central conceptions of redemptive revelation. Such an attitude is called *syncretism*. It was characteristic of the age. Christianity was affected by it too, but within much narrower limits than Gnosticism.

At its best, the Gnostic way led to a mystical philosophy found in what is called the Hermetic literature and expressed, for example, in this statement: "Without philosophy it is impossible to be perfectly pious. But he who learns of what nature things are, and how they are ordered, and by whom, and to what end, will be thankful for all things to the Creator, as to a good father, a kindly fosterer, and a faithful guardian, and he who is thankful will be a pious man. . . . Let this, my child, be the end of piety, to which when you have attained, you will live nobly and die happily, because your soul knows where to fly aloft."[8] This is later than our period, but it was the outcome of tendencies already long at work.

THE INDIVIDUALISTIC ETHICS OF STOICISM

Whereas the forms of religion which we have been considering were dualistic, operating with a fundamental contrast be-

[8] *Excerpta apud Stobaeus*, Scott II B, 1, 3. Quoted in C. H. Dodd, *Interpretation of the Fourth Gospel*, Cambridge University Press, 1959, p. 15.

tween the realm of spirit and the realm of matter, Stoicism, to which we now turn, repudiates a dualistic view of reality in favor of a materialistic monism. In characterizing Stoicism as materialistic, it must be stressed that this adjective characterizes its theory of reality, not its theory of value. The values the Stoics sought were anything but materialistic. Christians who believe in a future life in which they will enjoy the kind of pleasure—however refined—which they enjoyed on earth, are much more materialistic than the Stoics.

The Stoics did not deny that man had a soul or that there was a God. God ruled the universe; but he did so because he was a form of matter finer than air, able to penetrate everything and operate it from within, in accordance with his purposes. To use the personal pronoun *his* is really, of course, an error; for the Stoic god was not a personal being somehow outside the world. God, they said, was within the world, its guiding principle and plan. As such, he is described as *Logos,* or "indwelling reason." There is a portion of this Logos in everything, and in man it constitutes his soul. It is plain, however, that man is not conscious of this fact; and herein, Stoicism maintains, lie the possibilities of his going astray.

But if God's purpose rules in everything, how can man go astray? The Stoic answer would be that, while events happen according to God's will, man is free to accept his lot or to rebel against it; but escape from it he cannot. The highest virtue, then, is to be content with one's lot, whether it be that of the slave Epictetus, or that of the Emperor Marcus Aurelius. To live simply and courageously is the ideal. Health, possessions, reputation, position, wife and children—these do not really belong to us, for a stroke of fate may deprive us of any or all of them. Therefore the Stoic will not depend on them, for if he does, he will not be free but a slave. What is always in his control is his reason and his attitude.

Because all men have within them a portion of Logos, all men are brothers, and all sons of God. It is the words of the Stoic poet Aratus which are quoted in Acts 17:28: "For we are indeed his offspring." The preceding words, "in him we live and move and have our being" may be from some other Stoic poet. Men should recognize their common kinship with God, claiming citizenship not in some city or nation, but in the world. To be a citizen of the world was, in Greek, to be *cosmopolitan*. Men should also recognize their sonship to God by trusting him, who has provided for their needs and ordered all things for the best. But it is to be remembered, that though God is spoken of in this way, it is just a manner of speaking. God is a personification, not a person— a personification of the immanent order and power of the universe. The popular gods were recognized as simply names for aspects of the divine power.

It is easy to see how the Stoic belief in a world order which could not be changed, but only accepted with more or less grace, could take up with the astralism described earlier. Not all Stoics did so, but those who did found it hard to keep clear of the superstition which tended to be associated with this position.

There was no general agreement about survival after death, but the tendency was to regard the dissolution of the union between spirit and body as the end. Death as well as life was part of the world process and should be accepted with equanimity, and anticipated neither with dread nor with hope. Stoicism, in contrast with the other forms of personal religion we have considered, found the meaning of life here, not in some hereafter.

It would be a mistake to suppose that Stoicism was simply philosophy or ethics. In contrast to the Mystery religions or the Gnostic illumination, it seems pale and without passion. Nevertheless, it was in its own way a true religion. It rested on the recognition by man of his relation to the deity; it called forth man's praises; it led him to prayer, not that the world order should be changed, but that he should accept in the proper spirit what it brought. It demanded self-examination. Only if religion be closely bound up with public ceremony would Stoicism fail to qualify.

The Stoic was often a vigorous progagandist. He was likely to be found on the ancient equivalent of a soap box, in the agora of any Greek city, challenging the hearers of his "diatribe" to abandon their foolish ways, mocking their superstition, ridiculing the popular conceptions of the gods. He made use of rhetorical questions and set phrases like, "Don't be fooled," "Do you want to know?", "See," "Look." He put and answered objections that would be in the minds of his hearers; appealed to analogy, common sense, and experience; used irony and stereotyped comparison. This style has left its mark on some of the New Testament books, especially Paul's letters and James.

Another favorite Stoic device was the use of allegory to make ancient and unedifying material, such as the stories told of the gods by Homer, the vehicle for up-to-date ideas and noble sentiments. This practice was quickly borrowed by the Jews and then by the Christians. Thus, Paul uses it, and doubtless it had come to him through Jewish channels.

HELLENISTIC JUDAISM

In many respects, the crucial transition of Christianity from its Palestinian origins to its eventual home in this Hellenistic world which has just been sketched, had been prepared for by the earlier contact with it by the Jews of the Dispersion.

Ancient population figures are at best reasonable guesses. The best estimates indicate that there were altogether probably four to five million Jews in the world, of whom perhaps a million lived in Palestine. Of those outside Palestine, approximately one million lived in Egypt, mostly in Alexandria. Strabo, a pagan writer who died early in the first century, speaks of the Jews as having penetrated every city so that it was difficult to find a place on earth free from them.

Despite their wide distribution, the Jews were able to maintain a basic unity. Jerusalem remained the central holy place, drawing pilgrims from all over the world. Josephus speaks of some three million attending one Passover, but this figure is generally considered to be much exaggerated. For the support of the Temple, every Jew twenty years old or more paid an annual tax. The right to collect this Temple tax was granted and protected by Roman law. Finally, all Jews, at least in theory, acknowledged the authority of the head of the Nation in Palestine. This also was recognized by the Roman state.

In its essential features this Judaism, therefore, was in agreement with the Judaism of Palestine. It was strictly monotheistic, worshiped without use of images, held a high standard of moral conduct, and observed circumcision, the Sabbath, and the kosher food laws, especially the abstinence from pork. The most striking difference from Palestinian Judaism was the lack of elaboration of the Law.

One reason for the failure to develop an interpretation of the Law along the lines followed in Palestine was lack of linguistic knowledge. Knowledge of Hebrew was rare and at best superficial. In the worship of the Hellenistic synagogues, even the Law was read directly in Greek, not first in Hebrew and then translated as was done in the synagogues of Palestine where the common language was Aramaic.

The universally accepted Greek translation of the Old Testament we know as the Septuagint, from the legend that it was translated by seventy-two translators brought from Palestine by Ptolemy II, Philadelphus (285–245 B.C.). Later the "seventy-two" was simplified to "seventy" and represented by the Roman numeral *LXX*. According to one form of the story, each translator translated independently and when all were finished they agreed exactly. Even for the purposes of a miracle, this seems a considerable waste of manpower, and actually the phenomena of the translation do not bear out the story.

If we take the Septuagint as a whole, the Greek varies greatly in different parts, from slavishly literal translation to Greek of literary quality. Some parts never had a Hebrew original, and there are often traces of what is known as Atticism—an attempt to write according to the standards of the classical age of Greek literature. It could be compared to the attempt to write English today according to the models provided by Shakespeare and the King James Version of the Bible.

This, then, was the Bible of Greek-speaking Judaism. It was not used alongside the Hebrew—it supplanted it. Doubtless one of the reasons for the growth of the legend about the miraculous character of the translation was the desire to justify the position that it was an adequate and equally authoritative substitute for the original.

The Septuagint, however, is important not only as the Bible of Hellenistic Judaism—it also became the Old Testament of Hellenistic Christianity. Most of the quotations from the Old Testament found in the New are taken directly from the Septuagint. Indeed, the Christians made such effective use of it in their propaganda that the Jews finally repudiated it altogether; and a later writer declared that the day on which the seventy elders wrote the Law in Greek for King Ptolemy was as bad for Israel as the day on which the golden calf was made.

One consequence of this fact that the Christian Church used the Old Testament in Greek was that its Old Testament contained books not in the Hebrew Old Testament. These are called by Protestants the Apocrypha, but from the early days of the Church down to the Reformation they were recognized and used without any such distinction.

Alexandria was the greatest center of Hellenistic Judaism. Not only the Septuagint was produced there, but also a considerable variety of other literature: history, Jewish propaganda purporting to be by Gentiles, epic poetry and drama, wisdom literature, and philosophy.

Among the writers of philosophy, Philo of Alexandria (about 20 B.C. to A.D. 50) is particularly significant, not for any permanent effect on Judaism, but for his influence on the development of Christian thought. Scholars argue whether Philo was or was not an original philosopher. In any case, it seems fair to say that his primary interest was religious, but that he could not be satisfied unless he could express his religious aspirations in philosophical terms. There is no doubt that Philo considered himself in every respect a loyal Jew, a devout worshiper of the One Lord God who had chosen the Jews to be his people and revealed to them his will and character in the Scriptures. He was highly critical of Jews who believed that God's revelation was to be understood in a purely symbolic sense, and that such things as the Sabbath law, the food laws, and circumcision did not need to be literally carried out, once their spiritual meaning was grasped. And yet it seems clear that for Philo himself these things were to be obeyed because God so commanded them, rather than because he found in them the core of his own religion. Here he seems to have been more deeply influenced by Greek ways than he ever realized.

The experience which for Philo is the crown of the religious life, that to which everything else leads up and is subsidiary, is the experience which is ordinarily described as "mystical" in the special sense of that word. As a matter of human psychology, it is beyond controversy—whatever value you may attach to the experience—that certain people under certain conditions do go through an experience which, they say, cannot be adequately described in words to those who have not themselves been through it. But they can tell us certain of its characteristics; and the accounts given of it by different people in different ages, and belonging to different races, so correspond, that we cannot take the mystical experience, as such, to be something peculiar to any one race or form of religion. One characteristic is that the individual seems to be lifted out of his ordinary life of successive thoughts and feelings; the flow of time ceases; the soul is absorbed into an eternal Now. Another characteristic is that the individual seems to come into direct contact with some tremendous Reality; he has a sense of extraordinary intellectual clarity, the Universe lies before him an open book. And the experience is accompanied by a wonderful expansive joy.[9]

Philo says:

Therefore, my soul, if thou feelest any yearning to inherit the good things of God, leave not only thy land, that is the body, thy kinsfolk, that is the senses, thy father's house (Gen. xii, 1), that is speech, but be a fugitive from thyself also and issue forth from thyself. Like persons possessed and corybants, be filled with inspired frenzy, even as the prophets are inspired. For it is the mind which is under the divine afflatus, and no longer in its own keeping, but is stirred to its depths and maddened by heavenward yearning, drawn by the truly existent and pulled upward thereto, with truth to lead the way and remove all obstacles before its feet, that its path may be smooth to tread —such is the mind, which has this inheritance.[10]

This mysticism is not native to Judaism—it is not found in the Old Testament—and although there is a mystical strand in later Judaism, it still is ultimately Hellenistic in origin.

With Philo's mysticism there went, as there often does, an attempt to understand the nature of things in such a way as to explain and justify the mystic quest. For the mystic, God is raised

[9] Edwyn Bevan, "Hellenistic Judaism," in *The Legacy of Israel*, Clarendon Press, 1948, p. 45.
[10] Philo, "Who is the Heir?" §§ 69, 70, F. H. Colson and G. H. Whittaker (trans.), *Philo, An English Translation*, Loeb Classical Library, Harvard University Press, 1949, vol. IV, p. 317.

above the world of matter and the senses. For this reason, he is said to be transcendent. Now Greek philosophy had developed the doctrine of the one transcendent God, reaching a climax in Aristotle's *Metaphysics,* which attempts to prove his existence. Aristotle goes on to assert that while God is the source of all the activity in the world, his relation to the activity is much like that of the light to the moth. The light simply shines, as is its nature; but it is not in the least aware of the moth, nor concerned with its struggles to reach the light. Philo obviously could not accept the Aristotelian conception of God; but he had somehow to bring the active, concerned God of the Old Testament, who had created the earth and men, chosen a people, guided their destinies according to his will, and revealed himself to them, into relation to the more remote deity of Greek speculation.

Some kind of a bridge was needed, and Philo found it in the conception of the *Logos* ("Word" or "Reason").

This was not a new concept in Greek philosophy; and we have already seen that it was used by the Stoics, although Philo adapted it to his own purposes. *Logos* was a noun of many uses (the best Greek-English lexicon devotes about two and a half large pages to it), but they have in common some idea of connection or relation. If we translate it "Word" it is not a word as a sound or printed symbol, but a word as the vehicle of thought. So a distinction could be made between the Logos as reason in the divine mind, and Logos as the expression or utterance of what is in God's mind. In this way, the Logos in its twofold nature could serve to bridge the gap between God and the world. On the one side, it was inner thought; on the other, it was outer expression. The first expression of God's mind was the creation of a world. Philo found support for this in the Old Testament; for according to Genesis, creation took place as a result of the divine utterance, while according to Proverbs, Wisdom was God's agent from the beginning. In the Psalms he read, "By the word (*LXX logos*) of the Lord were the heavens made." (Ps. 33:6.)

Philo recognized a further complexity in the concept of the Logos, distinguishing in it creative power and ruling power; from the creative power flowed mercy, and from the ruling power flowed law and justice. The Logos is thus the means of creation, the channel of revelation, and the instrument through which God exercises control over events. From another point of view, the Logos is the pre-existent divine pattern of man, the "idea" of man in Plato's sense. Nevertheless, Philo did not conceive of the Logos as a personal being. He sometimes speaks of it as a "second God" and in personal terms. But it is clear that he is not serious about this, any more than the person is who refers to his native state as *she*. Indeed, if it were not for its Old Testament background, it would be fair to say that Philo's basic idea of God is not personal. We cannot know, he says, what God is, only that he is.

The goal of human life, the highest blessedness, is to know God. We rise to this knowledge by ascetic practices, by which the spirit is set free from its bondage to matter; by inference from the existence of the world to the existence of its creator; by contemplation of the "ideas" which Philo, differing from Plato, considered to be ideas in the mind of God. The consummation of the quest is found in the vision of God.

> Those, if such there be, who have had the power to appre-
> hend Him through Himself without the co-operation of any
> reasoning process to lead them to the sight, must be recorded
> as holy and genuine worshipers and friends of God in very
> truth. In their company is he who in the Hebrew is called
> Israel but in our tongue the God-seer, who sees not His real
> nature, for that, as I said, is impossible—but that He is. And
> this knowledge he has gained not from any other source, not
> from things on earth or things in Heaven, not from the elements

or combinations of elements mortal or immortal, but at the summons of Him alone who has willed to reveal His existence as a person to the suppliant. How this access has been obtained may be well seen through an illustration. Do we behold the sun which sense perceives by any other thing than the sun, or the stars by any other than the stars, and in general is not light seen by light? In the same way God too is His own brightness and is discerned through Himself alone, without anything co-operating or being able to co-operate in giving a perfect apprehension of His existence.[11]

It might be supposed that this attempt, utterly sincere as it was, to impose a basically Greek view of God and religion, resting on a dualism between mind and matter, on the radically different view of the Old Testament, would have been impossible to carry out. Here Philo helped himself by means of allegory, using this device to read into the Old Testament his Greek philosophy, just as the Stoics used it to find edifying material in the scandalous stories of the doings of the gods in Homer.

Philo apparently left no followers in Judaism; but when the Christian movement began to feel the necessity of making an originally Jewish form of religion intelligible and attractive to educated Greeks, its thinkers, especially in Alexandria, found that Philo had broken the ground for them. It is no accident that during the fifteen hundred years during which the survival of books depended on someone's being sufficiently interested to copy them by hand, it was Christians and not Jews who preserved most of Philo's voluminous work for posterity.

---

[11] Philo, "On Rewards and Punishments," §§ 43–45, in *Philo, An English Translation*, by F. H. Colson, Loeb Classical Library, Harvard University Press, 1954, vol. VIII, pp. 337, 339.

CHAPTER 12

Paul: Sources

There are two possible sources for a knowledge of the career and the ideas of Paul of Tarsus. These are the later chapters of the book of Acts and his own letters. There is also a book called the Acts of Paul, composed in the second half of the second century, which has a supposed description of his appearance and, among other stories, the tale of a lion whom Paul encountered in the arena at Ephesus that refused to eat him. The lion explained that Paul had once baptized him! Further discussion of the value of this book as a source seems hardly necessary.

The book of Acts introduces Paul first as an official witness to the execution of Stephen (Chapter 7). The story of his conversion is told in Chapter 9. In Chapter 11 he is presented as a member of a mission taking money for famine relief from Antioch to Jerusalem. Then, sponsored by the Church at Antioch, he sets out on a missionary tour. The rest of the book (Chapters 13–28) tells of this and later missionary journeys, his arrest at Jerusalem, and his final journey to Rome, in custody. What his fate was we are not informed.

Something over half of the book thus deals with Paul. The

A page from the Chester Beatty Papyrus of Paul's Epistles, designated P46, the oldest known codex of Pauline writings. Reproduced is the opening page of Ephesians, though the word does not here occur in the body of the letter. (Courtesy of the University of Michigan, Kelsey Museum of Archeology) question the historian must ask is: How reliable is the information it gives? This question must always be asked, on general principles; but in this case, it must be asked because there appear to be discrepancies at certain points between Acts and Paul's own letters. These are chiefly that the Acts' representation of Paul's teaching seems to miss the real force of Paul's ideas; and that Acts presents the Council meeting in Jerusalem, where the matter of the acceptance of uncircumcised Gentiles was dealt with, as Paul's third visit to Jerusalem, while Paul tells of such a meeting but solemnly asserts that it was on his second trip. Much thought and ingenuity have been expended on these matters, which turn out to have wide ramifications; but no one has offered a solution which has gained general acceptance. We are left with a serious question as to just how much of the information about Paul, given us by Acts, is accurate. Or perhaps better, even though we may justly believe that much of the information is accurate, we are not in a position to know surely of any specific piece whether it belongs in the accurate or the inaccurate class.

It might increase our confidence in all the details of Acts if we could be sure it was written, as tradition affirms, by the physician Luke, the companion of Paul on at least some of his journeys. But here again, the evidence is far from decisive. It anyone is eager to believe that Luke wrote the book, there is nothing to stop him; and if one prefers to believe Luke did not write the book, he cannot be decisively refuted either. Some of the considerations involved have been already suggested in discussing the authorship of the Gospel.

Of special interest, if we could be sure of their substantial accuracy, are the reports of Paul's speeches. But, as has been pointed out, here again we are on dubious ground because of the practice of ancient historians in composing speeches rather freely.

One of the striking phenomena in Acts which may be of help in connecting at least part of the content with eyewitnesses is the occurrence of the so-called "we passages." Beginning at

16:10 there is an abrupt shift from the third person—*he* or *they*
did—to the first person plural—*we*. But after verse 17, the first
person disappears, to be suddenly resumed at 20:5, continuing
through verse 15, at which point a speech is introduced. After the
speech the *we* returns at 21:1 and continues through 21:18. The
last "we passage" is the account of Paul's journey to Rome in
27:1 to 28:16. It is to be noted that each such passage begins
where the party is about to get on a boat, and ceases shortly after
they get to land. Now, strange as the abrupt transition from
third to first person seems, this connection with voyaging seems
to explain it; for travel stories of the period frequently included
such narratives of coastal voyages, called *periplus,* written in the
first person. It would then have been natural for the author,
whoever he was, to use a travel diary if he had one available;
and this seems to have been what was done. What we do not
know is, whose diary it was—the author's or someone else's—
and whether the diary was more extensive, and really lies behind
the intervening story of what happened on land, where, after
all, the more significant occurrences take place. But even though
we cannot settle finally the question of author or sources, there
seems to be ground for thinking that the latter part of the book
is in rather close touch with the actual events.

These questions about Acts, important for a full-scale study of
Paul, are actually secondary for the present purpose—to give a
sketch of the personality of the man and a statement of his main
ideas. For this, we can learn what we need to know from Paul's
own letters.

Traditionally, fourteen letters have been ascribed to Paul.
They are Romans, I and II Corinthians, Galatians, Ephesians,
Philippians, Colossians, I and II Thessalonians, the Pastoral
Epistles, Philemon, and Hebrews.

Four of these—Hebrews and the three Pastoral Epistles—
were certainly not written by Paul. The reasons for saying this
can be more clearly stated later when these books are discussed

in the context of their times, for the most convincing evidence of their non-Pauline origin is the fact that they fit so exactly into the later situation, while they have no clear point of attachment to the Pauline environment. Weighty also are considerations of style. Such matters as choice of words, especially words expressing connections and relations (nouns and verbs are more directly affected by subject matter), use of participles and infinitives, balance and rhythm, are characteristic of a person who is in the habit of expressing himself in writing. These differences, especially in the case of very distinctive styles, can often be felt directly; but they can also be made the subject of analysis and statistics. The difference between the styles of Romans, say, and Hebrews, takes very little skill to recognize, even in English translation. The Pastorals are not as immediately seen to be non-Pauline, because these were deliberate imitations of Paul; but the difference shines clearly through the imitation in most places if attention is turned to it.

The case of two or perhaps three other letters is more difficult. These are II Thessalonians, Colossians, and Ephesians.

II THESSALONIANS

Probably no one would raise any questions about II Thessalonians if it stood by itself. The style is not un-Pauline; but it is noticeably stiffer and more formal, in contrast to the overflowing warmth and gratitude of I Thessalonians, without there being anything in the content that would suggest that something had happened to cause a cooling off in their relationship. Another difficulty lies in the great similarity of the two in certain parts, so great that the obvious explanation would be that Paul, if he wrote it, got out his file copy of the first letter, reread it, and deliberately repeated himself—not in re-emphasizing main points, but in minor turns of expression. Each of the letters deals principally with a misunderstanding of Paul's teaching about the coming day of the Lord, but they deal with it in quite different terms.

A number of solutions to these difficulties have been proposed. It has been suggested that II Thessalonians was really the first written, and this might obviate the first objection—though Paul's account of how he came to write (I Thess. 3:1–6) certainly does not suggest, even though it does not completely exclude, a previous letter. Another suggestion is that there may have been two congregations in Thessalonica, to one of which Paul felt closer than he did to the other. This is, of course, sheer conjecture. Others have thought that one of the letters might originally have been sent to another near-by church—perhaps Berea.

All these hypotheses recognize the letter as a genuine letter of Paul. It is possible, however, to deal with the problems raised by this letter in more radical fashion—by the hypothesis that it is not by Paul at all, but an imitation by someone else, at a later time, who wished to claim Paul's authority for his own ideas. Each of these hypotheses has been urged with subtle argument and considerable ingenuity. But when all is said and done, it can hardly be stated that any of them stands out in clear superiority to the rest. Each of them has its own difficulties; and it seems fair to say that, in each case, the difficulties are at least as great as those presented by simply taking the letter as a second letter of Paul's to the Church at Thessalonica. In any case, our understanding of Paul and his thought will not be seriously distorted by accepting the traditional ascription.

COLOSSIANS

The problem of Colossians is more serious, because here the ground for the objection is basically that its author goes much farther than Paul does anywhere else in his doctrine of the nature of Christ and his relation to the divine being. If the author was Paul, Colossians offers material of prime importance for his thought. If not, we may introduce a serious distortion by taking it as genuine.

In the consideration of this problem, style does not help us much. The style is somewhat more flowing, more diffuse, more rhetorical; but these characteristics may well be due to the exalted nature of the subject matter. The vocabulary used includes a number of words not otherwise used by Paul, or used only rarely, while other much-used words are absent. But the letter professes to be an answer to certain erroneous ideas which, the author has learned, are being taught in Colossae, so the language used would have been determined not by Paul's habits but by the ideas he was trying to combat.

Nor is there any inherent improbability in the belief that confrontation with a rival view caused Paul to develop his own ideas on certain points much more fully than he had previously done. This is the more plausible because the ideas fully developed here do already exist in germ elsewhere. Christ's pre-existence and participation in creation are clearly suggested in I Corinthians 8:6: "There is . . . one Lord, Jesus Christ, through whom are all things and through whom we exist," while his triumph over hostile spirits is presupposed by Philippians 2:10: "at the name of Jesus every knee should bow, in heaven and on earth and under the earth."

It would, of course, be reassuring if we found these ideas fully developed in several of Paul's undoubted letters; but even without this, it is certainly arbitrary to hold that we know Paul's mind so well that we can say that he could not have written what is at most a development of ideas he certainly did have. We may reasonably suppose, therefore, that Colossians is genuine.

EPHESIANS

Ephesians presents the most difficult problem of all. The difficulties begin with the fact that our oldest and best manuscripts did not originally contain the words "at Ephesus" in 1:1, though they have been inserted between the lines by a later hand. Second, if it is a letter of Paul's, it is the only one written in such broad terms. All Paul's other letters have a clear, identifiable, specific occasion which led to their writing and which determines the content of the letter. This one does not; and while this fits in with the textual evidence that it was not originally addressed to any church, it does not agree with what we otherwise know of Paul's habits.

Even in English translation, the style is noticeably different from Paul's other writings. E. F. Scott, who believes that it is a genuine letter of Paul, admits that the style is "involved and monotonous, instead of concise and forcible and full of variety. The whole epistle is made up of a few interminable sentences, in which clauses are all tangled with each other."[1]

Strange is the reference to the writer in 3:4: "When you read this you can perceive my insight into the mystery of Christ." Paul had a strong ego, but did he have this much? It would be easier, as it would be more charitable, to suppose that someone else was writing this way about him, than that he patted himself on the back in this crude fashion.

Then there are the cases where the author uses certain undoubtedly Pauline expressions, but with a different meaning. Ephesians 4:15–16, should be compared with Colossians 2:19, where "the whole body, joined and knit together by every joint with which it is supplied" means the Church in the first case and the cosmos and its powers in the second.

This comparison brings out one of the most puzzling phenomena of all—the close relationship between Ephesians and Colossians. Again Scott[2] may be quoted: "It is based on Colossians and continually repeats its very language. Would Paul, whose mind was so fertile in ideas, be thus content to copy from

[1] E. F. Scott, *The Epistles of Paul to the Colossians, to Philemon and to the Ephesians,* Moffatt New Testament Commentary, Harper, n.d., p. 120.
[2] *Ibid.*

himself? The natural answer is that he wrote the two epistles together, and while the thoughts of Colossians were still in his mind he could not help reproducing them. But the difficulty is that he does not reproduce them." As we have just seen, we have the same language used to express different thoughts. The more closely we associate the two letters in time the stranger this becomes.

The German scholar, Martin Dibelius, is particularly struck with the "wealth of abstract expressions, especially such as appear to belong to the world of Hellenistic mysticism, viz. secret, the perfect, knowledge, breadth, length, height, depth"[3] and sees an effort to introduce such mysticism into the Church.

One very ingenious attempt to solve the problem has been proposed by E. J. Goodspeed. He attacks it at the central point, the lack of a situation to which the letter applies, and suggests that it was composed by the man who, inspired by the publication of Acts, first collected Paul's letters and issued them as a whole. The "letter" was intended as a covering letter, introducing the others. This explains its generality and its partly Pauline, partly un-Pauline character; while its relationship to Colossians springs from the fact that the composer was a Colossian intimately acquainted with that letter. This is supported with much acute observation and plausible speculation, but it can hardly be said to have been demonstrated.

It cannot be said that more recent discussion has brought the problem much nearer solution. The Swedish scholar, Ernst Percy, in a detailed study of the style and ideas of both Colossians and Ephesians, has concluded that in both these respects the apparent peculiarities of these Epistles are anticipated in the unquestionably genuine Epistles. This important contribution seems to have been generally neglected in England and America. In England, C. L. Mitton has sought to break out of the impasse

[3] M. Dibelius, *A Fresh Approach to the New Testament and Early Christian Literature*, Scribner's, 1936, p. 186.

by a detailed consideration of the relationship between Ephesians and the other Pauline Epistles, and reaches the conclusion that the weight of evidence is clearly against Paul's authorship.

The most telling argument for the position that—in spite of the objections, none of which is quite conclusive—Paul himself did write the letter, is perhaps the fact that, when all is said and done, the letter shows deep and original insight. The point is not that we know Paul to be the only such thinker of the period, but that the combination of original and creative thought cast in a style which is borrowed from another man is a most improbable combination.

Still, we can hardly say that it is utterly impossible. Perhaps the question is insoluble. But as a source for the teaching of Paul, Ephesians will have to be used with great caution. In using it we must not get too far from what we can check by the other unquestionably genuine Epistles.

PROBLEMS IN THE GENUINE LETTERS

The remaining letters—Romans, I and II Corinthians, Galatians, Philippians, I Thessalonians, and Philemon—are surely Pauline, though it may be that some of them were not put in their present form by Paul. They all, however, bear the imprint of the same powerful personality, with no more inconsistency than is normal for human beings. They are homogeneous in style and in point of view. No attempt to deny any or all of them to the great apostle to the Gentiles has ever been successful in convincing most of those who have studied them carefully.

Still, there are some problems about parts of some of them. In regard to Romans, the chief problem has to do with the latter chapters. There is a grace which, in the King James Version, following late manuscripts, occurs twice, at Romans 16:20 and 16:24. Earlier manuscripts have it only at one place or the other.

The concluding doxology appears at the end of Chapter 14 in some manuscripts. There are indications that some early writers had a form lacking chapters 15 and 16. Some modern scholars have been struck by the fact that the list of those to whom Paul sends greetings in Chapter 16 is much the longest such list in any of his Epistles, and they are surprised that he seemingly knows more people in this church—which he has never visited —than in those where he has worked; and it is suggested that this is really a short note of introduction to another church, somehow incorporated with Romans. These scholars feel that the other problems are in some way connected with this addition. Other scholars, however, suggest that just because Paul was not known to most people in the Roman church, he called the full roll of all those he had ever met. There is no generally accepted solution to these questions; and, fortunately, nothing vital to our understanding of Paul seems at stake.

The Corinthian correspondence is more complex. In its present form it bears witness to the existence of at least four letters from Paul to this Church. I Corinthians 5:9 refers to a prior letter, dealing with the treatment of immoral persons, which was misunderstood. II Corinthians 6:14 to 7:1 could be part of such a letter. II Corinthians 2:3–4 refers to a letter written out of "affliction and anguish of heart and with many tears," which caused pain to the recipients (cf. 7:8–9). Unless we accuse Paul of gross exaggeration, he can hardly be referring in this way to I Corinthians, and 7:12 alludes to a situation with which this "painful letter" dealt, that it would be hard to identify with anything in I Corinthians. We must therefore suppose a letter which was written between our I Corinthians and II Corinthians. With considerable plausibility, a part of this "painful letter" has been identified with II Corinthians 10 to 13. The sudden change from the note of thanksgiving and reconciliation which has marked II Corinthians 1 to 9, to the sarcastic self-defense and rebuke in the latter chapters is hard to understand as the con- clusion of the earlier chapters. Certainly their effect would have been to undo all the good which had been done and put the situation back where it had been prior to the reconciliation. But if II Corinthians 10 to 13 were part of the "painful letter," which, by the kind of accident which only too frequently hap- pened to ancient manuscripts, got attached to the end of the later letter, then we could understand things much better. Cer- tainly these chapters were written out of affliction and anguish of heart, and they must have caused pain to those who heard them.

It is not impossible that the actual situation is even more complicated. There are a number of rough spots in I Corinthians. Chapter 9 certainly interrupts the discussion begun in Chapter 8 and continued in 10. The direction that women should keep silent in church and ask their husbands at home if they want to know anything (I Cor. 14:34–35) is puzzling after 11:5 which presupposes their actual participation in the worship of the church, subject to the limitation that they must not pray or prophesy unless their heads are veiled. To solve or help solve such problems, various theories breaking up I Corinthians have been propounded; but none has had much success.

The problems of Galatians are problems of interpretation, not problems of literary structure. The same is true of I Thessalo- nians and Philemon.

Philippians, on the other hand, has frequently been suspected of being composite. Certainly the warning against the Jews comes very harshly at 3:2, while, if 3:1 were originally con- tinued at 4:1, the progress of thought would be much smoother. Is it possible that 3:2–21 is another case of a misplaced portion of another letter? The first verse of chapter three, which apolo- gizes for repetition in his writing to Philippi (which is not ap- parent in the present letter) presupposes other letters to this Church. We can hardly be sure, though, that these verses belong to one of them, for while the material comes in awkwardly, it is not quite impossible. But in any case, there is no reason to question that it is all genuinely Pauline.

ORDER

The order in which the Pauline epistles have been discussed is that in which they occur in the English Bible; but this cannot possibly be the order in which they were written, even though we cannot be certain at all points just what the true order was. However, Romans must have been written considerably after I Thessalonians, for the latter indicates that it was written shortly after Paul's first visit, just after he had first crossed over to Europe; while Romans was written on the eve of his departure for Jerusalem, on the visit which led to his arrest and voyage to Rome. Actually, I Thessalonians seems to be the first of Paul's surviving letters.

Unless the traditional order is reversed, II Thessalonians, if it is by Paul, must have been written shortly after I Thessalonians. The correspondence with Corinth refers to the collection Paul is sponsoring (I Cor. 16:1 ff., II Cor. 9:1 ff.) which gave the occasion for the last trip to Jerusalem, but he does not speak of being on the point of taking it to Jerusalem. I Corinthians 16:8 locates Paul in Ephesus. Perhaps all of his correspondence with Corinth was conducted from Ephesus. Apart from four letters which presuppose that Paul was writing in prison, this leaves only Galatians to be fitted in. At a number of points, the argument of Galatians resembles that of Romans, so that it is natural to suppose that they were written about the same time. Since the argument of Romans as a whole is more highly developed, it is assumed that Galatians preceded Romans. It is true, however, that some scholars have been of the opinion that Galatians was the first of all Paul's letters—not because of any direct evidence, but because they believed that this hypothesis would relieve some chronological problems in relating Acts 15 to Galatians 2. But this makes the relation to Romans very hard to understand, and there are other reasons for doubting that this is the true solution to a most difficult and complex problem.

THE LETTERS FROM PRISON

Four letters—Colossians, Philemon, Philippians, and Ephesians (assuming it is by Paul)—indicate they were written from prison.[4] Paul was imprisoned several times,[5] but the only extensive periods of confinement of which we have any knowledge are those in Caesarea and Rome. Caesarea seems excluded, since Philemon, verse 22, asks that a guest room be prepared for him, as he expects soon to visit. It seems unlikely that he had while in Caesarea either the purpose of returning to Asia Minor (in view of his stated intention of going to Rome after his visit to Palestine) or a sufficiently lively prospect of coming release, for him to ask his friends to get a room ready for him. Then, too, the letters imply more activity in preaching than would seem to have been available to him in Caesarea. If we must choose between Rome and Caesarea, Rome is doubtless to be preferred.

More recently, the theory has been proposed that these letters come from a conjectured imprisonment in Ephesus. In the letters, Paul seems in close touch with the churches in Asia Minor; and it would certainly be easier for the runaway slave, Onesimus, to reach Ephesus from Laodicea than to get to Rome. The easy communication with Philippi which is implied in the letter to that Church would be more natural from Ephesus than from Rome. Of Paul's associates mentioned in the letters, most

---

[4] See Col. 4:3, 10, 18; Philemon, v. 1; Philippians 1:13, 14, 16; Ephesians 3:1, 4:1; 6:20.

[5] It must be remembered that in the ancient world people were held in prison simply while waiting trial. Sentence to prison was not commonly used as a means of punishment. We might better get the sense of Paul's *far more imprisonments* if we translated it "locked up" or "arrested far more often." The beatings to which he refers would be the result of the sentences. Sometimes he was acquitted, as at Philippi and Corinth.

of them appear elsewhere in connection with Ephesus. When Paul wrote Romans he was planning to go on from Rome to Spain. There is no known reason for supposing that he had abandoned these plans, even though his voyage to Rome was

Ruins of Caesarea, the seat of the Roman occupation government of Palestine. To build a port on an open coast, with no natural harbor, was a tremendous engineering feat. (Courtesy of the Israel Government Tourist Office)

made in custody. Yet both Philemon and Philippians refer to his intention of visiting Laodicea and Macedonia when he is at liberty.

These objections are not unanswerable, however. Communication between Rome and the provinces was, for that day and age, relatively easy. Certainly runaway slaves frequently headed for Rome, where it would be simple to disappear. Then there is the reference to the fact that Timothy is the only one present Paul can count on (Phil. 2:19–23) and this certainly tells against Ephesus. As for plans, it is not impossible that they had changed, though we have no direct indication of this.

If we try to balance these arguments, neither side has an overwhelming superiority; but the balance seems slightly in favor of Rome.

This group of letters, then, will come from the latter part of Paul's life, while he was in Rome awaiting trial. Colossians and Philemon seem to have been written together, as shown by the lists of Paul's companions, and by the fact that Archippus of Laodicea is addressed in both. Paul seems to feel, at this time, that his prospects of release are good. There is no clear indication of where Ephesians fits in (if it does), though both it and Colossians refer to the fact that Tychicus will bring them up to date when he comes. This suggests that, if Ephesians is genuine, the two letters may have been sent at the same time; and perhaps it supports a conjecture that "Ephesians" was really the letter to Laodicea referred to in Colossians and in Marcion's list. Philippians seems later, for Paul's prospects are more dubious and he seems now to be almost alone.

Assuming the doubtful letters to be all really by Paul, the order of writing is then most probably I and II Thessalonians, the Corinthian correspondence, Galatians, Romans, Colossians, Philemon, Ephesians, and Philippians. But though this is a plausible order, it needs to be recognized that the data on which it is based are really very slim, so that the degree of probability for this order is not the highest.

CHAPTER 13

Paul's Career and Letters

W̲E TURN now to the utilization of our sources for the purpose
of drawing a sketch of the career of the man who played such a
vital part in the expansion of Christianity, in the determination
of its relation to Judaism—especially with regard to the observance of the Law—and who gave powerful statement to a
way of interpreting the significance of the life, and especially
the death, of Jesus—an interpretation which has had a dominant
role in Christian thought and inspired such men as Augustine
and Luther, and a host of lesser figures as well.

THE SCENE

The scene of Paul's career coincides with the scene of the
New Testament in general: the eastern end of the Mediterranean basin. On the map this is a rectangular area, with the
broad but tapering Balkan peninsula at the center, projecting
well into the sea from the north. To the west is the Italian
boot, poised to kick Sicily out of the picture. The large rectangle
of Asia Minor sticks well out above the middle of the eastern
end, with the narrow strip including Syria and Palestine ex-

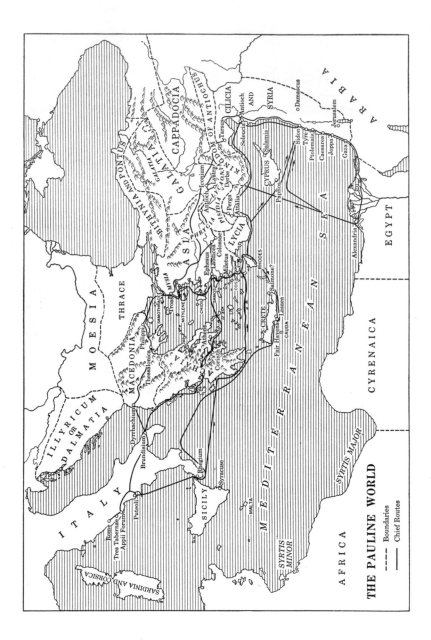

THE PAULINE WORLD

---- Boundaries

—— Chief Routes

tending below it. At the bottom is the sprawling coast of northern Africa.

The topography of these several land masses shows considerable variety. Northern Africa is largely barren desert, except for the fertile valley of the Nile and its delta, with the great metropolis of Alexandria at its mouth. Syria, including Palestine, is mountainous or hilly except for a coastal plain, never very wide and sometimes vanishing. Asia Minor is bordered by lowland but soon rises to high mountains and an elevated central plateau. The Balkan peninsula is also mountainous, with ranges running predominantly north and south, though in the lower part other ranges run almost east and west, with complicated watersheds, and that division into the series of independent shut-in valleys which played such an important role in the history of ancient Hellas. In general, the land slopes away toward the east, with considerable areas on the Aegean side which do not rise over 500 feet above sea level. This general tilt has laid the richest lowlands open to Asia. The Italian peninsula is dominated by the Apennines, running the entire length of it.

This region shows a general similarity of climate. Winter is the season of rain; summer is a time of drought. The range of temperature is comparatively small. In the winter the winds are from the west and carry moisture which they deposit chiefly on the windward side of the mountain ranges. The eastern coast of Greece, for example, receives only half as much rain as the western coast.

It is difficult for the modern man, living in a world where distances, for practical purposes, are almost annihilated, and in which communication takes place at the speed of light, to realize the difficulty of travel in this ancient world. The various areas were linked together by established routes both by land and by sea, but a journey, whether for public or private business, or in the service of the Gospel, was a slow and dangerous undertaking.

Between Syria, which includes Palestine, where Christianity

originated, and Rome, the capital city, which is the goal of the story in Acts, there were four regular routes. The New Testament story of the spread of the new movement keeps within the limits marked out by these lines of communication.

One way was wholly by sea, with slightly different routes for the eastward and westward voyages to take advantage of the prevailing winds. Going west from Antioch, say, the ship kept fairly close to the southern coast of Asia Minor, with various stops along the way, turning southward at Rhodes and making Crete. Passing along the southern coast of Crete, the course was then north and west, keeping near land where possible, and arriving off the Italian coast at the ball of the foot. The Italian coast was followed then, through the Straits of Messina and along the western shore to Puteoli[1] on the Bay of Naples. For the traveler, eager now to reach his destination after two months or more on ship, the final stage of his journey would probably be up the Appian Way to Rome. Freight, especially grain, would probably be loaded on wagons, or might be transshipped in coasting vessels to Rome (or Ostia, its port) and other Italian cities.

Another route, again mostly by water, was by way of Corinth, then across the narrow Isthmus, down the Corinthian Gulf, up the coast to a point from which Brundisium (Brindisi) could be directly reached. The journey would be completed by land up the Italian peninsula.

A route much favored by those who, either for business or pleasure, intended to make stops along the way, led across Asia Minor to Ephesus, across the Aegean to Corinth, with the journey completed from that point as in the previous route.

The fourth great route was largely a land route, across Asia Minor to Troas and thence by water to Philippi. It was also possible to keep to land and cross into Europe by way of the Hellespont, proceeding thence to Philippi. From Philippi the

[1] The modern Pozzuoli.

way led through Thessalonica by the Egnatian Way across Macedonia to Dyrrhachium (Durazzo), with a short run then across the Adriatic Sea to Brindisi.[2]

All of these routes, whether by land or water, were impracticable during part of the year. The Mediterranean was considered closed from November 10 to March 10 each year, and really safe only from May 26 to September 14. The mountain roads in Asia Minor were blocked by snow and ice during a similar period.

We know Paul first of all as a traveler and a letter writer, so it is well to have in mind the fact that communication over such routes was slow. News of first importance, such as the accession of a new emperor, might take two months to reach Egypt from Rome. Under very favorable conditions, a month might suffice. Private letters from Syria to Rome would take from two to three months. Because prevailing winds were from the west, sea voyages were slower from east to west than in the other direction.

CHRONOLOGY

The chronology of Paul's life is a most discouraging subject, for we do not know with certainty a single date in his career— not even birth, conversion, or death. His letters, which we have seen are the most reliable sources, make only one reference to a contemporary figure (King Aretas, II Cor. 11:32), but even this cannot be tied down, beyond the fact that Aretas died A.D. 40, so that Paul must have been converted before that. Since estimates of the date of this turning point in Paul's life have varied from A.D. 31 to A.D. 40, this is of no great help.

Acts offers us a number of other references; but apart from the problems of relating Acts and Epistles, and any question as to

[2] It is obvious, of course, how much the scenes of Paul's work were determined by these established routes. On the basis of our knowledge of these established routes the student can draw his own map of Paul's missionary journeys as accurately as anyone can.

whether the author of Acts was in possession of an accurate chronology, each of the references is subject to uncertainties of its own. The events referred to are as follows: the death of Herod (Acts 12:23); the famine during the time of Claudius (11:28); the proconsulship of Sergius Paulus in Cyprus (13:7); the edict of Claudius banishing the Jews from Rome (18:2); Gallio's proconsulship in Achaia (18:12); and the accession of Festus as procurator of Judea (24:27). All of these are referred to in Josephus or by the Roman historians such as Tacitus and Suetonius, or witnessed to by contemporary inscriptions; but in every case there are problems of interpretation or reconciliation, and the best dates are still uncertain by at least a year or two.

Even if we could attain certainty about these dates, the problem would still remain of relating these incidents to the data provided in Paul's letters. Central is the problem of his visits to Jerusalem. Acts mentions five, although only three are referred to in the letters either as having taken place or as being in prospect. These have been described as being for acquaintance, for a conference, and for presenting an offering. Acts only mentions the purpose for three of those to which it refers and the purposes of these three do coincide with the purposes stated in the letters, though they are in a different order. It is also a little hard to see from the letters how there could be any room for two more visits to Jerusalem. If we conclude that the author of Acts did not have available an accurate chronology of Paul's life, then we derive from the letters the following data.

Paul says that three years after his conversion he went up for the first time to make the acquaintance of the leaders in Jerusalem. Meanwhile he had been in "Arabia" and Damascus. After fourteen years he went to Jerusalem again, this time for a conference as to whether circumcision should be required of Gentile converts. It was agreed that it should not be, the only requirement being that they should "remember the poor." The most natural interpretation of this requirement would be that it led directly to the taking of the collection referred to in I Corinthians 16:1, II Corinthians 9:1, and Romans 15:25. The letters indicate that gathering this took at least two years. It was to take this offering that Paul made his dangerous last trip to Jerusalem where he was set upon by riotous Jews and taken into custody. Being transferred to Caesarea, he was held there until he appealed to Caesar as his case was being heard by the new procurator, Festus.

If we could date the arrival of Festus, we would have a point to reckon back from. The literary sources for this event are not in agreement, and dates from A.D. 55 to A.D. 60 are given. It has recently been pointed out, however, that a new coinage was issued in Palestine in A.D. 59, an event which seems most naturally to be associated with the coming of a new procurator. If this is so, Paul presumably was arrested about two years before (this interval depends on Acts), which would bring him to Jerusalem with the collection in A.D. 57. If he had been there three years previously (allowing for returning, taking, and bringing the collection) at the conference, that would have been in A.D. 54. Fourteen years prior to that, when he made his first visit as a Christian, would be A.D. 40, putting his conversion about A.D. 37. This would make the fourteen years between his first and second visits the great productive years of his life when he worked in Asia Minor and Europe, instead of being "silent years" as they are commonly called.[3]

No clues as to the dates of Paul's birth and death are to be found in his letters.[4] Nor are there clues elsewhere as to his age at any point in his career. We simply infer that he must have

---

[3] This scheme is basically that proposed by John Knox in *Chapters in the Life of Paul*, Abingdon, 1950, modified—perhaps unwisely—to accommodate the assignment of the beginning of the procuratorship of Festus to A.D. 59, on which see H. J. Cadbury, *The Book of Acts in History*, Harper, 1955, p. 10. It assumes that the three years and the fourteen years are full periods, and that they do not overlap.

[4] The word usually translated "old man" in Philemon, verse 9, probably should be *ambassador*.

been grown up by the middle thirties of the first century, so that he may have been born a short while before, but certainly not much after, the beginning of the Christian era. As for his death, we do not even know the circumstances of it, though Acts certainly seems to presuppose that his journey to Jerusalem had an eventual fatal outcome (Acts 20:38, cf. 21:4, 10–14). Clement of Rome, about the end of the first century, tells us that after Paul "had reached the limits of the west [i.e., Spain] he gave his testimony before the rulers, and thus passed from the world."[5] The question here is whether Clement had direct knowledge of a voyage to Spain, or simply inferred it from Romans 15:24. It seems a little strange that if Paul spent several active years in the west it has left no clear traces. It is generally supposed that he was martyred during the Neronian persecution in A.D. 64. This is the later tradition of the Roman Church, but we cannot find early confirmatory evidence.

CHILDHOOD AND EDUCATION

The obscurities in Paul's life persist when we come to consider his childhood and education. There seems to be no reason to doubt the statement of Acts that he was born in Tarsus, the chief city of Cilicia, the seat of a university and a center of Hellenistic culture. It does not follow, however, that he was exposed either to Greek learning or religion. The Jewish communities kept pretty much to themselves, deliberately guarding themselves from the enticements of the Gentile way of life. His letters show no evidence of knowledge of or interest in such things. If he quoted the poet Aratus in Athens, this no more proves his classical education than quotation of "The quality of mercy is not strained" proves that a preacher is a regular and diligent reader of Shakespeare.

[5] I Clem. 5:7 in *The Apostolic Fathers*, K. Lake (trans.), Loeb Classical Library, Putnam's, 1925, vol. I, p. 17.

What education Paul had was therefore undoubtedly Jewish, but as to its extent we are largely in the dark. According to Acts, he studied in Jerusalem under Gamaliel; but even if true, this gives little knowledge of how long or with what profit. The opinion that Paul had spent much time in Jerusalem and there became a persecutor of the Christians is difficult to square with Paul's own statement (Gal. 1:22) that even after his first visit to Jerusalem, following his conversion, he was still unknown by sight to the churches of Judea. Certainly Paul does not give evidence of any profound rabbinic scholarship. It is clear that he read, studied, and quoted the Bible in Greek. He knows many bits of rabbinic lore, but that these go beyond what he could have acquired in Hellenistic synagogues would be hard to demonstrate. Most surprising is his failure to take account of the rabbinic doctrine of the efficacy of repentance. Paul assumes that, apart from Christ, once the Law was transgressed, a man's case was hopeless. It is not enough to say that Paul came to believe that the Jewish doctrine of repentance was not sound. If so, he ought to have shown why this was so; for to those who held that repentance was available for the transgressor, Paul was offering a cure for a condition that they did not believe existed. Paul speaks in Galatians (1:14) of having made much progress in Judaism, but this is not necessarily progress in rabbinic learning. It may quite as well mean progress in ordering his life according to his understanding of the Law.

PERSECUTION OF THE CHURCH

We begin to get on solid ground when we turn to Paul's persecution of the Church. We have his own statement for this (I Cor. 15:9, Gal. 1:13, 23, Phil. 3:6). He does not tell us what the persecution consisted in, except that it was violent and intended to destroy the new movement. Neither does he tell us exactly what he and others saw in the movement so dangerous to Judaism that it ought to be stamped out. The recognition of Jesus as Messiah was hardly sufficient ground. Was it because of the presence in the movement of "Hellenists" who were proposing to abolish the Law, or at least some of it? Whether we can specify it or not, this zealous, devoted Jew certainly found something in the activities of these followers of Jesus which called for vigorous action against it. Later, Paul was to look back on this activity with profound regret.

CONVERSION

Somewhere in the vicinity of Damascus, Paul had a vision which changed his whole career. God "was pleased to reveal his Son" to him, in order that he might "preach him among the Gentiles." Efforts are often made to explain this sudden change in psychological terms. Doubtless it had psychological roots, but we hardly have sufficient knowledge to uncover them. The interpretation frequently given of a young man struggling vainly to conform his conduct to the demands of the Law is in flat contradiction to the general tenor of his references to the Law and in explicit contradition to his statement in Phil. 3:6 that he was "as to righteousness under the law blameless." The suggestion that he had guilt feelings as a result of his part in the execution of Stephen, or that he was haunted by the courage of the martyr, rests on nothing more substantial than imagination. Except for the unquestioned hostility, we do not know what was in Paul's mind before he was called to be an apostle to the Gentiles. But that he felt himself called to this mission is one of the central facts of history.

What, then, did being "converted" mean to Paul? He did not think of himself as ceasing to be a Jew, though he surely thought of himself as having come to the true understanding of what Judaism really meant. Nor was his conversion simply a reorientation in his thinking about Jesus of Nazareth. It did involve a conviction that Jesus was the Son of God, but the importance of this to him was that it threw new light on God. It meant that man's relation to God rested on God's overflowing goodness, not on man's success in conforming to the rules God had laid down. It followed that Gentiles who did not observe the Law were not thereby excluded from God's favor; and central in Paul's conversion was the call to be the messenger of this "good news" to them. As Paul looked back on his early life, he saw himself as having then been a miserable sinner, especially because of his activities as a persecutor; but he did not come to this crucial encounter with the risen Jesus borne down by an acute consciousness of sin. His conversion was not the throwing off of a huge weight of felt sin, but a profound reorientation which made a persecutor into an apostle of the very thing he had persecuted.

EARLY MISSIONARY WORK

Paul stresses the fact that after his conversion he was not instructed in his new faith, and specifically that it was only some three years later that he went to Jerusalem to see the leaders there. Instead, Paul tells us, he went off to Arabia, returning eventually to Damascus. What he did during this period he does not tell us, but the obvious conclusion would be that he spent it in carrying out the mission to which he had been called. Then, after his first visit to Jerusalem, he tells us that he went into Syria and Cilicia. Here he came into contact with the Church at Antioch; and if the chronology suggested above is right, it would be the next fourteen years that were spent in the work which Acts describes as the first and second missionary journeys.

It was during this period that Paul made the momentous decision to cross over from Asia to Europe. Acts, in a "we passage," tells us that this decision was the result of a vision; and we are doubtless justified in accepting this account even though Paul does not refer to it in any extant letter.

In Macedonia he found hearers in Philippi and Thessalonica and doubtless other places, but in each case encountered Jewish hostility and was forced to flee. After leaving Thessalonica he

went to Athens, and perhaps from there wrote the first of the letters which have come down to us. The hostility which forced him to leave continued after his departure. From Athens he sent back Timothy to encourage and instruct the Thessalonians. When Timothy brought the good news of their faithfulness and continued regard for Paul, he dictated the letter known as I Thessalonians.

After a formal address, he turns to personal concern for them, recalling his visit and its results, how they had "turned to God from idols, to serve a living and true God, and to wait for his Son from heaven, whom he raised from the dead, Jesus who delivers us from the wrath to come" (1:9, 10). He reminds them of the circumstances of his visit—the opposition he had met, the purity and sincerity of his own motives, and his strenuous efforts. Calling for special mention was the hostility shown by "their fellow countrymen," the Jews, and his anxiety after he had left, with consequent relief when he learned of their continued steadfastness. This part of the Epistle closes with a benediction.

Paul then turns to certain points where he feels—perhaps on the basis of Timothy's report—that they need instruction and reminder. He warns them against the ever-present danger of immortality, and enjoins them so to live that they command the respect of outsiders. Especially does he find it necessary to clarify a misunderstanding about the coming resurrection. Paul is thoroughly convinced that the last day is at hand, and that he and most of his fellow Christians will see it. But somehow the Thessalonians had assumed that no follower of Jesus would die in the interim. When some did die, they were disturbed, supposing that these would miss the great day. This is a misunderstanding, Paul says. When the day comes "the dead in Christ" will rise first, and all, together, will be caught up to meet the Lord "in the air." He exhorts them to be on the alert, to be prepared when the great day comes. They should respect their leaders, and do well. The letter closes with prayer and benediction.

If we accept II Thessalonians as Pauline, it presumably was written shortly after this. At two points it goes beyond I Thessalonians. Paul warns the Thessalonians not to pay any attention to letters purporting to be by him which assert that the day of the Lord has already come. This cannot happen until "the man of

Athens, the intellectual center of the Graeco-Roman world. Paul saw the Acropolis with its cluster of buildings, old even in his day. (Ewing Galloway)

lawlessness" has been revealed, but he is now being restrained. It is generally agreed that this is a reference to the figure known as the Antichrist, who is expected to appear in the last days and claim to be the Messiah. The problem as to what was supposed to restrain him from an immediate appearance is a difficult one. Most frequently it is believed to be Rome, the instrument of law and order; but if so, this realistic political reference is unique in an area where otherwise thought moves in a highly supernaturalistic atmosphere. Others therefore seek for some supernatural figure. Perhaps Augustine says all that can be said: Paul's statements "show that he was unwilling to make an explicit statement, because he said they knew. And thus we who have not their knowledge wish and are not able even with pains to understand what the apostle referred to, especially as his meaning is made still more obscure by what he adds. . . . I frankly confess I do not know what he means."[6]

The other chief point in II Thessalonians is the command to keep entirely away from those who live in idleness. It is generally supposed that some of the Thessalonians had stopped work because of their vivid expectation of the imminent coming of Christ. This is a possibility; but it is not the only one, for people have been known to be idle for other reasons. Paul gives no indication as to why they were idle, but he is very certain that Christians should not be, for any reason.

CORINTH

Paul made no lasting impression at Athens. The speech before the court of the Areopagus which Acts attributes to him is probably one of Luke's compositions. In proceeding to Corinth he may have had the intention of taking ship there and returning to Asia, or he may have gone with the deliberate intention of

[6] Augustine, *The City of God*, xx, 19, Marcus Dods (trans. and ed.), Hafner, 1948, vol. II, pp. 381–382.

working there. At any rate, he found there one of his most important spheres of activity.

Corinth, at one end of the isthmus connecting the Peloponnesus with the rest of Greece, was at this time the capital of the Roman province of Achaia, that is, Greece south of Macedonia.

Columns of the ancient temple of Apollo in Corinth. The temple was standing in Paul's day. (Ewing Galloway)

Here was the seat of the Roman proconsul who was the governor of the province. It was before the proconsul Gallio that Paul was brought on Jewish charges of teaching men to worship contrary to "the law." (Whether this was the Roman law or the Jewish is not quite certain. At any rate, the proceedings turned into an anti-Jewish demonstration.)

The old city of Corinth had been burned in 146 B.C. and refounded about a century later by Julius Caesar, who made it a Roman "colony," settling a Roman population there and organizing its civic life on Roman rather than Greek models. Two of the main east-west routes passed through the city. Small boats were regularly hauled across the eight-mile isthmus to Cenchreae. Goods arriving in heavier vessels were transshipped.

In addition to being a thriving commercial metropolis and the seat of government, Corinth was famous as a resort. It was a wide-open town, and "Corinthian girl" had about the same connotation as "Geisha girl" has nowadays. Stoic preachers, as well as Paul, found Corinth a fruitful ground for their demands for moral reformation.

Acts, in its account of Paul's work in Corinth, confines itself as usual to the external features. For a look behind the scenes we have Paul's correspondence. Paul worked in Corinth for some time (Acts says a year and a half). Why he left we do not know, although if the chronological scheme followed here is right, it is quite possible that it was to go to Jerusalem for the conference on Gentile inclusion.

THE JERUSALEM CONFERENCE

It is clear from Paul's letters to Corinth that he ran into formidable opposition on the part of those who had a different conception of the nature of the Christian gospel. It would not be strange if it was this opposition which sent him to Jerusalem for a conference on the subject of the conditions under which Gentiles could be received, and to what extent it was necessary for them to practice the Jewish Law. Paul insisted that it was not necessary to practice it at all as a condition of God's favor, and he reports (in a letter to churches in Galatia) that his position was fully accepted by the leaders, in spite of the opposition of a third party composed of "false brethren." There seems every reason to suppose that Acts 15 gives an account of the same meeting from a different point of view; but while the two agree on the general point that Paul's work with the Gentiles was accepted,

Acts states that minimum requirements of observance were agreed on. If so, then Paul's statement that the only condition was that the Gentile churches should "remember the poor" (in Jerusalem) involved the deliberate suppression of an essential part of the real decision. It is easier to suppose that Acts, written a generation later, was honestly mistaken.

PAUL IN EPHESUS: CORRESPONDENCE WITH CORINTH

Paul returned from Jerusalem with the intention of fulfilling his promise by taking a great collection which would demonstrate the solidarity of his Gentile converts with the Church at Jerusalem, and it occupied a place in most of his letters from then on till his imprisonment. Meanwhile, he had arrived in Ephesus, which was to be the other great center of his work.

The main mass of Asia Minor is a high plateau, into which four narrow clefts stretch upward and eastward, through which descend four rivers providing an outlet from the central highland to the seacoast. Of these rivers the Cayster, the third from the north, afforded the easiest access to all parts of Asia; and at its mouth was located the important city of Ephesus. Ephesus in ancient times was the western terminus of a system of Roman roads, connecting via Colossae and Laodicea with Mesopotamia, with Galatia by way of Sardis, and with the south by means of the valley of the Meander River. In the intervening centuries, the harbor has silted up; and the site now stands deserted.

The main part of the city was on the hills overlooking the valley and the harbor. Modern excavations have revealed the most conspicuous monuments—the large theater with a seating capacity of about twenty-five thousand; the market place, the quay, a beautiful public library, well-paved and lighted streets with porticoes along both sides to protect from sun and rain.

The city was a center for the Roman administration of the

province of Asia (roughly the area we call western Asia Minor) and the proconsul who was its head was required by law to land and assume office at Ephesus. According to Strabo, the ancient geographer, it was the greatest trading center in the province, especially noted for the production and exportation of woolen

The theatre of Ephesus, scene of the riot described in Acts 19.
(Ewing Galloway)

fabrics. People came not only to trade but to participate in the great Roman festivals and to worship the ancient deity whom the Greeks identified with Artemis and the Romans with Diana, whose magnificent temple stood on a low hill in the plain two miles above the city. A substantial income was derived from what we would call the tourist trade. Acts tells us that the threat offered to these commercial interests by Paul's preaching led to a riot involving two of Paul's companions, and that Paul was advised by friends in the provincial council not to go to the theater where the mob had assembled.

There were schools of philosophy in Ephesus, and Paul was able to obtain the use of a lecture hall "after hours"; but at the beginning of the Christian era, Ephesus' reputation was rather

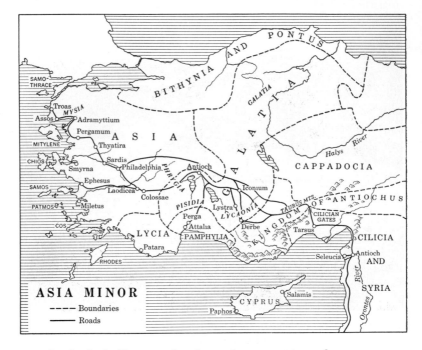

as a hotbed of all sorts of cults and superstitions than as a seat of learning. As a center for the compilation and publication of works of magic it was notorious throughout the ancient world. This interest in magic is the background for the narrative of the burning of the magic books as a result of Paul's encounter with some Jewish exorcists.

While in Ephesus, Paul heard disturbing reports as to conditions in Corinth, and wrote a letter, now lost. What else was in the letter we do not know, but he indicates that among other things it dealt with the treatment of immoral people, and that it was misunderstood. His advice to have nothing to do with immoral people who claimed to be Christians was taken as advising them to have nothing to do with any immoral people at all. If, as seems probable, a bit of this letter has been preserved in II Corinthians 6:14 to 7:1, the misunderstanding was natural, if not inevitable.

Somewhat later Paul wrote the letter which we now call First Corinthians. This is a discussion of matters about which Paul learned from "Chloe's people" (who Chloe was we do not know), and an answer to certain questions on which the Church had asked Paul's opinion. Most distressing was the fact that the Church had divided into parties, each professing to teach the true gospel, as proclaimed by Paul, or by Peter, or by Apollos, an Alexandrian teacher who had come to Corinth after Paul. One group claimed to be the party of Christ. Paul rebukes them all. The gospel has no room for party spirit. Christ is not divided. It was Christ, not Paul, who was crucified for them. Apparently Paul is not sure that his words will have the desired effect and looks forward to a visit to them, asking, "Shall I come to you with a rod, or with love in a spirit of gentleness?"

Another item in the report to Paul has to do with a case of what to Paul is flagrant immorality, which the congregation has done nothing about. Paul demands action in the matter. In general, the members of the Corinthian Church seem to take morality rather lightly, doubtless justifying themselves by Paul's assertion that man's relation to God is not determined by his success in conforming himself to the standard of the Law. They are to remember that their bodies are temples of the Holy Spirit. The realization of that should regulate their conduct.

Also disturbing is the news that the Corinthians are invoking the ordinary law courts in their disputes with one another. It is bad enough that they have such quarrels, but at least they ought to be able to settle them themselves. When the Judgment

Day comes they will be expected to judge the world! Surely they ought to be able to work things out among themselves without lawsuits.

Paul then turns to the questions raised by the Corinthians. The first of these is about marriage. In his mind, celibacy is definitely preferable to marriage. He believes in the permanence of

Façade of the ancient library in Ephesus. (Ewing Galloway)

the tie once entered on, even though only one of the parties is a Christian; but he believes that the unmarried would do well to stay as they are. He explains his position with reference to the soon-expected day of the Lord. This will be accompanied by a period of distress which marriage will complicate. He also sees in marriage a distraction from the fullest service of the Lord; but here, too, the ruling thought is the imminent end of the present order of things.

The next question has to do with whether Christians can eat

"meat sacrificed to idols." The slaughter of meat was usually, in form at least, an act of sacrifice; so the question was practically the question of whether to eat meat or not. Paul's expression of his thought is not altogether clear here, but the general conclusions are not in doubt. He agrees that idols are nothing, and that sacrificing meat to them as a matter of form does nothing to the meat. When you buy meat in the market, you do not need to inquire as to its past history. If you go to dinner at a friend's house, you need ask no questions about what you are served. If, however, someone calls your attention to the fact that this is sacrificial meat, you should refuse it; because otherwise you may seem to take lightly what is a matter of conscience to someone else. Paul recognizes that there are such people, and holds that it is better to forego your privileges than to offend someone else's conscience.[7]

Paul turns then to the discussion of various matters in connection with the Church, directing that women who take part in the ministry should veil their heads. For a woman not to do so would be as bad as for her to have her hair bobbed, and everyone knows that is utterly disgraceful.

The next problem seems, at least to us, a much more serious matter: abuse in the holding of the Lord's Supper. It was certainly not the staid sacrament that it is in Christian churches today. It was a real meal, and people brought and ate and drank their own provisions. People divided into groups and started when they got ready. Some overate, others became drunk, while others who were not so well off did not have enough to satisfy their hunger. Paul, in solemn words, which he is hardly the originator of, recalls the Lord's Last Supper with his disciples and warns the Corinthians that whoever "eats the bread or drinks the cup of the Lord in an unworthy manner will be guilty of profaning the body and blood of the Lord." (I Cor. 11:27.)

[7] One might argue that when a man's conscience is plagued by unessential matters, what he needs is to be enlightened, not left undisturbed.

Central in the experience of the Corinthian Church was the possession of what Paul called "spiritual gifts." The ministry and work of the Church were supposed to be under the control of the Spirit of God (or of Christ). This included not only preaching and exhortation, but healing, ecstatic speech, and administration. No one should pride himself on his particular gift, or suppose it sets him higher than others. The harmonious working together of all is necessary for the health of the Church. What is higher than any of these things is love.

One activity, much prized, Paul lays claim to himself; but he sees little room for it in public worship. Ecstatic speech ("speaking in tongues"), he says, is a divine gift; but because it is intelligible only to God, it does not contribute to the edification of the rest of the worshipers, and therefore it should be severely restricted. It is better to speak five words which are intelligible than ten thousand words in a tongue. Only one person should speak at a time. "All things should be done decently and in order." (I Cor. 14:40.)

Apparently some at Corinth, holding the Greek idea of immortality of the spirit, denied that there was to be a bodily resurrection. Paul asserts that this cuts the ground from under his message. If there is no such thing, then Jesus was not resurrected and Paul has been talking nonsense. He offers an impressive list of witnesses to the Resurrection of Jesus. This is the ground for the assurance that all are to rise. As to how the dead are raised, it will not be with a physical body but with a spiritual body. Thus the mortal will put on immortality.

In closing the letter, Paul gives directions for the collection in which he is so interested.

Shortly after this letter was received, a crisis developed in Corinth which seemed to call for Paul's own presence; and he made a visit to Corinth. We do not know the exact nature of the trouble. We only know that Paul's attempt to deal with the matter, whatever it was, was not well received. His efforts were re-

jected, and he departed in defeat and humiliation. Being unwilling to accept the situation which had developed, he wrote to the
Corinthians a letter, which he later admits was written out of
pain and anguish. We seem to have a portion of this in II Cor.
10–13.

What we have in these chapters is primarily a vindication of
Paul's authority. No summary can convey the intense feeling
that lies behind these chapters and leads Paul to cutting irony
(e.g., 11:21 and 12:13) and boasting of his own accomplish-
ments and hardships which he admits really goes too far (10:8,
11:21b). He defends himself against the charge that he talks
beyond what he can perform; that he is eloquent in letters but
ineffective in person. He reminds them that it was he, after all,
who brought them the gospel; he did not appropriate someone
else's work, as his opponents have done.

Especially he replies to the charge that he accepted no fees
from the Corinthians. Apparently this was made the basis of an
accusation that he really had no warm feeling for them, or he
would not have turned elsewhere when he was in need. This
he vehemently denies.

He goes on to assert that his Hebrew ancestry is as good as
anyone's and his sufferings greater. He tells of a vision in which
he was caught up into the third heaven and says that to counter-
balance it he was given a "thorn in the flesh," generally taken to
be a chronic illness.[8] But really, he says, he has not been concerned to defend himself; it is all for their upbuilding. What is
important is their improvement—that they may do right—not
that he may be vindicated.

This letter, perhaps with some help from Titus who carried
it, accomplished its purpose. Titus brought him the good news of
the Corinthians' submission to Paul's authority; and he wrote the

---

[8] What this was we simply do not know. Epilepsy, trachoma, malaria, and
migraine headaches have been suggested; but any modern physician who
ventured a diagnosis on the basis of such slim and ambiguous data as we have
for Paul would soon lose his license to practice.

warmhearted letter of thanksgiving and reconciliation which we have in II Cor. 1–9. No simple, coherent plan appears on the surface of the letter. It seems to move from one topic to another by a chain of association.

Paul begins with the customary formal address and proceeds to speak of God's comfort in affliction, having in mind his own recent escape from seeming certain death. He goes on to explain that he had not made his proposed visit to Corinth because he was afraid that it would have made the situation worse. Now the crisis is past and all is forgiven. This leads Paul to express his conviction that the Corinthians, like letters written not on stone but on human hearts, express the true splendor of the new covenant in the Spirit. This treasure, however, resides in human beings who, with all their frailties, are not free from affliction and persecution. The body, our "earthly tent," through which these things come on us, is to be destroyed and replaced by a building from God (cf. the "spiritual body," I Cor. 15:44). Meanwhile, he is the ambassador of Christ. In Christ, God was at work reconciling the world unto himself; and Paul accepts whatever hardships this proclamation may involve. But, with all his affliction, he is overjoyed at the news of the outcome in Corinth brought by Titus. He concludes with an appeal to the Corinthians to do their full share in putting aside money for the collection which is to go to Jerusalem. The original close of the letter seems to have been lost in the process by which the painful letter became attached to the end of this later letter.

GALATIANS

Somewhere about this time, the churches in Galatia were being invaded by missionaries from Jerusalem who undertook to convince the Galatians that Paul had told them only part of the story of what Christianity demanded; and declared that, if they wanted to be heirs of the promises made to Abraham, they must be incorporated into the community of his descendants by circumcision. To them Paul wrote a letter upholding the freedom of a Christian from any obligation to conform to the Law.

After a brief greeting, Paul turns to a vigorous defense of his authority as an apostle, in opposition to some who are preaching a different gospel. In the first place, his gospel was given to him by revelation, not by the leaders in Jerusalem. Though he was in contact with them, he worked independently. However, at a conference in Jerusalem, his call to preach to the Gentiles had been recognized; and it was agreed that they need not be circumcised. When, later in Antioch, Cephas shifted ground, Paul publicly rebuked him.

His message is that a Christian is not justified by obeying the Jewish Law but through faith in Jesus Christ. Such a person had died to the Law and been crucified with Christ; and it is no longer he who lives, but Christ who lives in him.

Paul reminds the Galatians that by his preaching they had received the Spirit—what more could they want? Abraham had been justified by his faith, and his real descendants are the men of faith. The Law was given later and had a place in God's plan, but now all are sons of God through faith. So he cannot understand the Galatians' wavering. Abraham had descendants by Hagar who were slaves and by a free woman whose children were free. Thus Christ, who belongs in the latter succession, has set men free from the Law; but this freedom is not an opportunity for the flesh. Those who really have the Spirit will inevitably be led by the Spirit, whose fruit is love, joy, peace, patience, kindness, goodness, faithfulness, gentleness, self-control.

Those who are spiritual have a special obligation to those who are weaker. What a man sows, that he will reap. Therefore, they should not lose heart.

In a postscript in his own handwriting, Paul insists that outward rites are unimportant. A new creation must take place in man.

The letter closes with a benediction.

ROMANS

As the taking of the collection which Paul recognized as such a pressing obligation progressed, Paul began to look ahead to his work after he had delivered the collection in Jerusalem. For some reason, he felt that he had done all he could in Asia Minor, Macedonia, and Achaia, and turned his eyes to the west, proposing eventually to go to Spain. For the successful accomplishment of this plan, it was essential that he have the support of the Roman Church. He felt, too, that he had something to contribute to the Roman understanding of the gospel. As far as we know, the Roman Church was not founded by any outstanding leader, but was simply the result of people who had become Christians elsewhere settling in the capital and bringing their religion with them. What Paul was planning did not involve any breach with his principle of not "building on another's foundations."

In anticipation, then, of a coming visit, Paul set out to write a letter to the Roman Church that would prepare the way. He would disarm criticism, if there were any, and explain his profound concept of the human situation and how man stood with God.

The letter has two main divisions: a sustained argument for the proposition that the only way man can satisfy God's demand for righteousness is by faith, and a substantial section explaining in specific terms some of the requirements of the Christian life. The part containing the argument has two subdivisions: the first, the assertion, defense, and explanation of his main proposition; the second, a discussion of a question that inevitably grew out of this—the question why, if Paul's gospel were really the fulfillment of the promises which God had made to his chosen people, the chosen people seemed to be particularly unable to recognize the fact.

Paul begins this letter with the usual formal greeting, elaborated to an unusual degree, to bring out the fact from the very first that Paul considers himself the divinely commissioned herald of the gospel of Jesus Christ, who is the fulfillment of God's ancient promise.

He speaks particularly of his interest in Rome, and his long-standing desire to visit the Church there, as well as his sense of obligation to proclaim there the fact that the only source of human righteousness is faith.

Failure to recognize this can only lead to the manifestation of the wrath of the righteous God. It is true that the Gentiles have not had the detailed description of God's will which the Jews had in the Law, but creation itself was enough to show men their obligation to God. Because they had ignored their true relation to him, turning instead to "religion" as the means of using the divine for their own purposes, through worship of idols, God had allowed them to sink into all kinds of degradation and perversion.

Nor was the Jew really any better off, in spite of his possessing the Law. To possess the Law was not enough. It was to be obeyed, and obeyed in a much more radical way than anyone obeyed it. Not that there is no advantage at all in being a Jew; the Jew does have God's self-revelation in Scripture, and man's unfaithfulness only serves to set off God's faithfulness. But of course this does not mean (as Paul's critics accuse him of saying) that God has no right to condemn those who thus give him opportunity to exhibit his righteousness.

All, then, Jews as well as Gentiles, have sinned, falling short of the glory of God. God's righteousness, now about to be fully manifested in the coming judgment, can only result in utter condemnation for all, except there be some new basis for attributing righteousness to men. This God has made available in Jesus Christ.

This new basis for human righteousness is God's grace, his love, by which he freely forgives man his wrongdoing and acquits him of the charges against him, solely on the basis of his faith. This faith is, positively, trust in God and his goodness, and negatively, a humble recognition of one's lack of righteousness, and renunciation of the effort to achieve righteousness by one's own efforts.

After all, Paul says, Christians claim to be heirs of the promises to Abraham. Just what, then, was it that gained Abraham God's favor? It was surely not circumcision, or any other "works of the Law," for at the time Abraham had not been circumcised nor the Law given. No, it was simply Abraham's willingness to place himself in God's hands. It was his faith that was counted to him for righteousness, and through his faith he became the spiritual ancestor of God's true children.

This faith by which men may be acquitted at the day of judgment is faith in God, but they gain access to this grace of God through Jesus Christ. Jesus' death involved the shedding of blood and could thus, in the way God had decreed of old, expiate man's sin. It gives men also a more profound insight into the meaning of suffering. It expresses God's love for men, and teaches them to find a basis for growth in their own suffering. This their hope, however, is not the hope that thus they can achieve anything themselves, but that God has acted for them.

Paul has been arguing that, for those who have faith, God has revealed his willingness to acquit them in the day of judgment. Through Christ we are thus "justified," and through him we are also reconciled to God. Now Paul approaches the same conclusion by a different route: by an analogy between Adam and Christ. Adam transgressed God's commandment and became subject to death, and all men have followed him. In some sense

Adam was the prototype of the race, and his deed had dire results. But in contrast with the first Adam (whose name is a Hebrew word for *man*), the prototype of the new humanity is Christ. Just as the disobedience of Adam was the source of disaster, in which all shared, so the righteousness of Christ is the source of blessing in which all may share.

Paul turns now to a question which must inevitably arise: Is there any longer an obligation on men to refrain from sinning? If God's mercy freely pardons their sin, then will it not be true that the greater the sin, the greater the mercy? Paul emphatically repudiates any such notion. Christians have been baptized. This means they have really shared in Christ's death, sharing now by anticipation in Christ's Resurrection, and sharing fully in it on the day of judgment. How can those who have died with Christ take sin lightly?

This is an important point; once again Paul tries to make it in another way, this time by another analogy, though he is really not at his best in using illustrations. The Law provides that a woman must be faithful to her husband as long as he lives. When he dies she is free to enter a new relationship. Well, man's obligation to the Law died with Christ, so that man is free now to take on a new relationship, this time to God. And whereas the old relationship brought forth only sin, the new relationship is expressed in a new life marked by the gift of the Spirit.

But what does this imply about the Law—that it was bad? No, not at all. It is true that it brought sin to self-consciousness, and even aroused sinful desires; but this was not because it was basically wrong, but because in man's warped condition he tried to use it as the basis of a claim against God. However, man is aware of a division within himself—he finds himself breaking the Law when he really wants to keep it. He thereby acknowledges the true goodness of the standards of conduct the Law lays down, and also that he is really in the grip of an alien power. Paul puts this in the first person and in the present tense. He is speaking not of his state of mind in the past, before he became a Christian, but of his present experience, as representative of the common Christian experience. Sin has been decisively defeated, but the consequences of the defeat have still to be worked out fully. Deliverance from this impasse has been won for men through Christ; it has already begun to be effective; but it will not be fully effective until the day of judgment, when men's bodies of "sinful flesh" will be changed into spiritual bodies.

Meanwhile those who are "in Christ," who belong to the new spiritual organism of which Christ is the head, the new order which is shortly to dawn, have at work in them a new life-giving spirit. God, who raised Jesus Christ from the dead by his Spirit, will give life to their mortal bodies. By this Spirit their bodies may be brought under control. Those who live by the Spirit are the sons of God, joint heirs with Christ.

This does not mean that men escape suffering, any more than Christ did. But the sufferings are insignificant in comparison with the glory which lies beyond. The whole creation, now in God's purpose under the dominion of inferior spiritual powers, is eagerly awaiting the great day. Men look forward to it with hope. Meanwhile, the Spirit helps them in their weakness.

As a Jew, Paul is conscious of belonging to a chosen people; nonetheless, he has come to see that physical descent from Abraham is not the mark of that choice. As a Christian, he owes his hope to God's purpose and choice; but God's chosen people are really those whom he has predestined to share in the glory of his Son. To them God will give all things. Paul is sure that neither death nor life nor spiritual powers nor anything else will be able to separate men from Christ Jesus their Lord.

But what of God's "chosen people" in the ordinary sense? The Jews have been signally unresponsive to this message, in spite of the fact that to Paul it is precisely the fulfillment of all God's promises to them. Well, he says, not all of Abraham's descendants were included in the promise in any case, nor can anyone accuse

God of injustice at this point. Men simply cannot apply their standards to him.

Paul is deeply concerned, however, about this failure of his fellow Jews to respond to the gospel. He sees it as a failure to understand what was really set before them in the Scriptures, finds their hardness of heart a persistent feature of their relation-

The Appian Way, along which many travelers from the Near East, including Paul, approached Rome. (Brown Brothers)

ship with God, and takes refuge finally in the thought that it is all part of God's purpose. There is no reason for the Gentiles to feel superior. The Jewish opposition has made it easier for the Gentiles to hear the message; but in the end, Paul is sure, God will bring his chosen people to a true knowledge of himself.

In the concluding section of his letter, Paul turns to the consideration of certain matters of practical conduct. Man's salvation does not rest on his good works; but men must nevertheless present themselves to God, that his will may be done through them. Let them remember the Body of which they are members and find their proper place in it. They are to live in harmony with one another, never repaying evil for evil. The authority of the government must be recognized, for it was set up by God.

The primary principle in human relationships is love, for love is the fulfilling of the law. Christians must always remember that they live in the last times and act accordingly.

Paul now devotes a special section to the problem of dealing with conscientious differences of opinion in matters of religious practice. Here, as in Corinth, were those who had questions about the proper use of food, as well as others who felt that certain days were peculiarly sacred. Paul agrees in principle with the liberal attitude, but holds, as on the previous occasion, that it is more important not to disturb the tender conscience than to assert one's rights. The essential thing is that they all live in harmony with one another.

In closing, Paul undertakes to turn aside any feeling that might arise that he has overstepped in writing thus to the Romans; and he goes on to speak of the mission he has been given and his present plans to come to Rome on the way to Spain. He asks for their prayers as he proceeds meanwhile with his dangerous mission to Jerusalem.

In the final chapter of this letter as we have it, there is a brief note of introduction for Phoebe, a deaconess of Cenchreae, and greetings to a long list of friends and co-workers. After a final appeal for unity, the letter closes with greetings from Paul's companions and an ascription of glory to God.

COLOSSIANS AND PHILEMON

When Paul wrote these two related letters, he was in prison. We have assumed that this was in Rome. Wherever he was,

word of a serious distortion of Christian teaching, and the conversion of a runaway slave, caused him to write them.

The false teaching at Colossae is not immediately identifiable
with anything we can point to elsewhere. We have to reconstruct it from Paul's criticisms, and that means that our picture is
almost certainly distorted. What is strange is that there seems to
be a blend of Jewish and pagan elements of a Gnostic type,
elements which are ordinarily considered incompatible. Paul
warns the Colossians, on the one hand, against making rules
about food and drink and the observance of festivals, new moons,
and Sabbaths. Except for the reference to drink, this sounds quite
Jewish. On the other hand, the warnings against speculations
about the nature of things, cultivation of visions, worship of a
whole system of supernatural powers, as well as the warnings
against both asceticism and immorality, call to mind religion akin
to Gnosticism.

Paul sees the key to the problem in the proper understanding
of the true position and role of Christ; and he is led by this to
develop his thought on the point well beyond what he expresses
in any of his other letters, so much so that, as has been seen,
some scholars question the Pauline authorship of the letter. But
this is hardly justified.

Christ, Paul says, is our sole deliverer, the image of the invisible God, existing before anything else, the one for whom and
through whom creation took place. Any other spiritual powers
which may exist are completely subordinate to him.

By him Christians have been redeemed. Thereby they are set
free from all outward regulations, as well as from all supposed
subjection to spiritual powers of any kind whatsoever. But, as
Paul always has to insist, this does not mean that moral conduct,
according to the highest standards, is not required. Having died
to earthly things, and having been raised with Christ, they will
seek the things above.

The latter part of the letter discusses in some detail what these

Excavation of the Roman Forum, the center of the life of the imperial city in Paul's time. (Brown Brothers)

things are. Special attention is given to domestic relationships: husband and wife, parent and child, master and slave. This last is elaborated with particular fullness, lending support to the idea that this letter was sent along with Philemon, and was intended to be read, along with Philemon, in Laodicea.

The letter addressed to Philemon and others shows Paul in his most winning, tactful mood. In his imprisonment he has met and converted Onesimus, a runaway slave. Paul sends him back to his master, with this appeal—though he really could make it a demand—that Onesimus be accepted as a Christian brother. As a runaway slave, the man was entitled to no protection from the law—his master could punish him as he saw fit; and it must have been no easy thing to send him back, and even harder for the slave to go. We have no direct evidence of the outcome, but it has been suggested that the letter would hardly have been preserved if its appeal had been rejected. It has also been argued, with much ingenuity, that this is the same Onesimus who appears somewhat later as the bishop addressed in the letter of Ignatius of Antioch to the Church in Ephesus.

PHILIPPIANS

When Paul wrote Philemon he was looking forward to being soon released. Philippians is less assured.

The immediate occasion seems to have been to thank the Philippians for a gift of money, and for sending Epaphroditus to look after Paul. He felt very close to the Philippians, for in general he was very careful not to accept any money from his churches lest he be accused of mercenary motives.

These thanks, however, come at the end of the letter. It begins with an account of how things are going with Paul, though there are allusions which we do not have the necessary background to follow. Something has happened, and Paul says that the unexpected result has been the further spread of the gospel. Some are acting from unworthy motives, but in any case the gospel is being proclaimed. He is not clear whether the immediate future holds death or life, and is not sure which he would choose if the choice were left to him. The Philippians are having their difficulties, too; and Paul encourages them to live worthily and stand fast in their faith, in humility and love, having the mind of Christ, who put aside his glory and took the form of a man, undergoing death on the cross, only to be highly exalted by God.

Paul expects to send Timothy as soon as he can be spared. Epaphroditus, whom they had sent, is returning, having been ill and at the point of death.

Abruptly the text as we have it shifts to a violent denunciation of Jewish (or Jewish-Christian) opponents who practice circumcision, only to return at the end to the mood and train of thought that Paul was previously pursuing, leading up to his farewell. If the letter was written from Rome, it would seem to be the last word we have from Paul.

EPHESIANS

Whether Ephesians is by Paul or not, it is a summary of Pauline thought. If it is by Paul, it seems to belong with the letters just discussed, especially Philemon and Colossians. If it is not by Paul, we are hardly certain as to its original occasion, in spite of Goodspeed's theory. It will be simplest, therefore, to discuss it at this point. In any case, it is probably not to be understood as a letter to a specific church.

Indeed, except for the unusually brief introduction and conclusion in letter form, we would naturally be inclined to classify Ephesians as a sermon or a tract. The composition is divided into two parts by a doxology in the middle (3:20–21). Preceding the doxology is a section in the form of a prayer, laying down basic principles; following it is a series of exhortations bringing out what these principles imply for conduct.

The formal address is followed by praise to God for his purpose of redeeming men through Christ. In accordance with this, God's chosen people have been destined from the beginning to live for the praise of his glory; and now the Gentiles have received the Holy Spirit, as the guarantee of their share of the inheritance.

An extended prayer follows, that those addressed may appreciate the greatness of what has been given them through Christ, who has been exalted by God above every other supernatural being and made head of the Church, his body. Thus they have been saved by grace, through faith, in spite of their former condition. Formerly the Gentiles had been strangers to God's promises. Now all have been brought together in Christ. To proclaim to the Gentiles this formerly hidden plan of God, now made plain, is Paul's mission. The prayer concludes with the petition that they may be strengthened by God's spirit, that Christ may dwell in them, that they may be able to comprehend what is "the breadth, length, height, and depth" and be filled with the fullness of God.

After the doxology, the author proceeds to develop the consequences that follow from this plan of God to unite all men and all things under Christ; and in Paul's role of prisoner, he begs them to be worthy of their calling. Especially does he stress unity, and the use of all spiritual gifts for the building of Christ's body, the Church.

In their personal conduct they must turn away from the lax standards they have had as Gentiles. Such faults as lust, anger, slander, and malice must be put away. They must be forgiving as they have been forgiven. They are to be imitators of Christ, turning away from darkness to the light.

In their relations with one another, proper subordination must be recognized, on the pattern of the subjection of the Church to Christ. This principle holds in the relation of wife and husband, children and parents, slaves and masters.

All this is part of a great struggle against evil, involving a host of supernatural powers. In defense, one must put on the whole armor of God, keeping alert and making supplication for all Christians everywhere, including the writer, that he may be able to proclaim the gospel boldly.

The close is in the usual form, though with less personal detail than Paul customarily gives.

CHAPTER 14

The Teaching of Paul

$\mathcal{P}$AUL was not a systematic theologian. He was a devoted and highly intelligent herald of a revolutionary conception of the nature of man's relation to God. His preaching was certainly not a crude appeal to emotion; but neither was it the exposition of a complex doctrinal system, adherence to which was somehow supposed to provide security for the future and an access of strength for meeting the problems of the present. His most comprehensive statement of his position, in the letter to the Romans —closely argued though it is—is an appeal, not a theological treatise. If Paul's thought is to be systematized, we shall have to do it ourselves, with the inevitable risk of addition, omission, and change of emphasis which that involves. Nevertheless, the attempt to make such a synthesis can be a help in the process of understanding Paul—if we do not make the mistake of substituting our construction for Paul himself.

MAN AND HIS SITUATION

Paul's teaching has two main aspects: a description of man and the unsatisfactory situation in which he finds himself, on the one hand; and a view of how that situation is to be met, on the other.

Paul's view of man is rooted in the Old Testament. This means—and it is a matter of fundamental importance—that man is the creature of God. God, having created the world, crowned his work by creating man in his own image and likeness. In this fact, man's possibilities of blessing originate; and from it, also, as will be seen, comes his problem.

This man is both body and spirit. In thoroughly Jewish fashion, Paul sees these as two aspects of the one man, equally real and equally essential. He believes in the existence of disembodied spirits; but such a spirit is not a man, and most certainly not the essential man, as if man were only able to realize his true nature when freed from a body. Such a notion would have been inconceivable to Paul.

Paul has a number of terms relating to man so conceived, which need to be understood if Paul's thought is to be understood. He uses these terms freely, with variations of meaning, so that their meaning and interrelations present a complex problem. Only a rough sketch can be given here.

First, there is the word *body*. Frequently, it simply means the living physical body (Paul would hardly have called a corpse a "body"). He bears on his own body the "marks of Jesus" (evidently scars acquired as a result of his missionary activity). But the body is also the instrument by which the person expresses itself, and is related to other persons and the world; so it frequently really means the person himself. "Present your bodies as a living sacrifice" (Rom. 12:1) means "present yourselves."

For the other side of this unity which is a man, Paul uses several terms. One is the Greek word *psyche,* which he uses for the "life" which seems to inhabit the body. It too can mean "self." This usage comes from the Old Testament. But Paul often uses an adjective derived from it with connotations of the merely natural life. Otherwise, he uses it in such expressions as "with one mind (*psyche*, "spirit") striving . . . for the faith of the Gospel."

Much more frequent is the term *pneuma*, "spirit" (originally "breath"). In many if not most cases, *pneuma* is practically synonymous with *psyche*. It is not itself a higher principle or an intellectual or spiritual faculty. However, Paul does recognize the activity of the divine (Holy) Spirit in man, as will appear later.

SIN

This man, a living unity of body and spirit, was created by God for fellowship with God, to be the recipient from him of all that is good forever. It is only too obvious that if this is so, something has gone seriously wrong. Not only does life have its share, or more than its share, of troubles; but it finally ends in death. Destined to receive the glory of God, man has fallen short; he has "missed the mark." That is to say, he has come under the dominion of sin.

By this basic term in Paul's vocabulary, he is not referring primarily to the fact that man transgresses God's will from time to time, each such transgression being *a* sin. Rather, as the etymology of the Greek word we translate "sin" suggests, he has "missed the mark," not just in some particular instance, but he has generally gone astray. Paul goes even further. Sin is practically personified, so that Paul can refer to "the sin which dwells within me" (Rom. 7:17, 20), and speak of it as if it had an independent activity of its own, contrary to the will of the man himself. Following Genesis, Paul attributes this to the disobedience of Adam, by which sin became a fact in the world, bringing punishment and death. Paul says nothing about inheritance of guilt. Man now comes into a world where sin is a present and persistent fact, and finds himself actually involved in it by the time he is old enough to know what he is doing.

But once again it must be stressed that, in Paul's view, there is something deeper here than a series of specific breaches of the rules God has laid down. The essence of sin is defiance, rebellion, self-assertion, against God. It is the attempt to act independently of God, or to use him. Even obedience to God can be sinful if its motive is to use God for one's own purposes, to obey him for what one can get out of him, so that if one did not happen to like what God had to offer he would have no reason to try to please him. What God demands is not conformity, but surrender of self.

Thus sin, for Paul, is primarily alienation from God; but the matter cannot stop there. Because man is out of proper relationship to God he is out of proper relationship to his fellow men, and indeed cannot be in right relation with himself; and by no effort that he can make can he get himself out of his predicament.

As has been said, man finds himself in this situation by the time he is able to act for himself. If this seems to be unjust, it is to be noted that, even though we prefer some other explanation of how things got the way they are to that given by Paul, we do not change the fact, nor does it become any more just. But in any case, such is the human predicament; and we need to look more closely at Paul's theory of how sin attacks us.

In some places, at least, Paul seems to be operating with a far-reaching theory, in which the physical world itself had become corrupted and had come under the dominion of spiritual powers in rebellion against God. These are the "principalities and powers" which God disarmed, "triumphing over them" in Christ (Col. 2:15). The triumph is a little ahead of our story; but Paul never mentions these powers without it, even though it is a triumph which had not yet become final. But the point is that he certainly believed that for ages man had been under attack by these powers hostile to God and to what is good.

Paul also assigns a particular role in man's predicament to the "flesh." This is another of his terms which is variously used, and it is not necessarily bad. Onesimus is described as a brother, both in the flesh and in the Lord. Christ "according to the flesh" was a descendant of David. In general, it is outward or external. It is what is "natural" in the sense that it includes all normal human desires, whether they are condemned by society or not. Thus it includes not only such things as lust, gluttony, avarice, disobedience to parents, strife, and deceit. Those who set their minds on the things of the flesh (Rom. 8:5) are not those dominated by sensual desires, but those who are seeking what is purely human, however fine that may otherwise be, and who do not recognize the prior claim of God to man's full allegiance. "Flesh" is human nature, good as well as bad, so far as "good" is only what is recognized as good by purely human standards no matter how exalted those standards may be. Even to serve God because this seems the best way to secure the maximum benefits from life, is for Paul "to live after the flesh."

THE REMEDY

Such is Paul's view of human nature as it naturally expresses itself. It inevitably misses the mark. Paul's message is that there is a remedy for this situation. He describes the remedy negatively as well as positively.

Negatively, the goal of man's life cannot be obtained as was (and is) commonly supposed: by obedience to God's commands. Paul was particularly interested in the Torah, because he had been brought up to see it as the embodiment of God's demands; but what he is criticizing is the whole idea that man can by obedience to God establish any claim on him, as he could if God had demanded obedience to certain rules and promised to reward the observance of them. When Paul criticizes the Law as unable to make a man righteous in the sight of God, he is not criticizing just the ritual aspects of the Law, claiming that they are of no importance for this purpose, while asserting that only the moral requirements are binding. Paul is criticizing the whole idea that man's relationship to God is determined by obedience to any rules whatever, and that the relationship is such that by obedience our own ends may be served.

This poses a problem for Paul with which he wrestles manfully, but hardly to anyone's complete satisfaction. After all, he still considers himself a Jew; and he finds in the Law (in the broad sense of "Scripture") an important source of argument, so he cannot simply say, "It is all a mistake: God is in no way responsible for the Law. Just forget the whole thing."[1] No, it does set forth God's standards of righteousness, even though man's whole attitude to them is warped by his intention of profiting by obedience. Moreover, it can make man aware of his shortcomings as he tries to live up to it. But Paul's main point is that whatever the function of the Law, it is not that of producing righteous men. Righteous men cannot be produced by conformity to law.

How, then, can they be produced? This is the crucial point in Paul's whole position. His answer is, briefly, that man cannot make himself righteous. He can only be made righteous (in some sense) by God. What man needs to realize is that God is ready to acquit him of the charges which can be brought against him when his conduct is measured by the Law. The traditional term for this in English is *justify,* but the central idea is that of acquittal. The judge says "Not guilty." This does not mean that God says, "We'll make believe it didn't happen," or "It doesn't really matter," or "Let's forget it." God is a righteous God who cannot abide iniquity, but he has shown himself ready to pass over former sins (Rom. 3:25) once man's basic relation to him is right.

Paul has several terms for this situation: *reconciliation, re-*

[1] He does say in one place (Gal. 3:19) that it was not given by God directly, but through angels.

demption, adoption. These are not to be understood as phases of a theological process, but as metaphors drawn from the legal and social institutions of the day, expressing in different ways the real fact that the Christian stands in a new relationship to God. The sinner can be thought of as being at enmity with God. In these terms, his new condition is that of having been reconciled. Again, the sinner can be thought of as being enslaved to his sin. In the Graeco-Roman world, where slaves were gained by capture in war, redemption was the process of securing the slave's release by paying his ransom. Man's new condition is like being redeemed from slavery. Once more, man's new condition is like that of a person—perhaps a former slave—who has been adopted into a family.

A comprehensive term for man's new situation is *salvation.* The root idea is "deliverance," "preservation." The related word *savior* (practically never used by Paul) was widely used as a title of honor for rulers and other important people. Asclepius, the god of healing, is so called, but so are philosophers. But *salvation* is used for security and preservation from threat of death—and then in religious writings for *salvation* in a religious sense. Paul uses it for the final attainment of the condition for which man was originally destined, and to express the fact that so a man would be preserved from the wrath of God.

But whatever term is used for the condition to which Paul looks forward, the important question is how it is attained. Not, as has been said, by keeping the rules, but by God's free act of acquittal. This rests on God's love of men and his benign purpose. He has no pleasure in the death of the wicked. Still, he cannot just ignore wickedness, not so much because this would encourage wickedness, or because it would not be right to ignore it, but because the basic trouble is not the specific transgressions, but that man has turned away from God in a radical way. What God really has to give is himself; and he cannot give himself to the man who has turned away from him, any more than you can give friendship to someone who sets up a barrier between you and him.

GOD'S GRACIOUS DEED

God's problem, if we may put it so, is to break through to the sinner. If God can reach the sinner, he will acquit him; but if the sinner stubbornly persists in his self-imposed alienation, he brings destruction on himself.

God's gracious deed, by which he tries to break through to men, according to Paul, was the sacrifice of his Son, who willingly divested himself of his high position and became a man, accepting a shameful and terrible death by crucifixion, that man might live. In Paul's thought, there is little suggestion that Christ became an example for us, or that he taught men "a better way of life." Indeed, Paul seems little concerned with Jesus' actual life. He rarely refers to what Jesus said, and never to any incident in his career. It is necessary, in Paul's thought, that Jesus should have had a real human existence; but if somehow that could have begun two minutes before the Crucifixion, Paul's ideas of the significance of Jesus would not have to be changed. What he is concerned with, however, is that Jesus in his human life should have plumbed the depths of humiliation and suffering, because in so doing Jesus could show that God was ready to go to the uttermost limit to make plain his concern for man.

To bring out the significance of this deed, Paul again resorts to a number of analogies. If we wish to think of man as a lawbreaker, then Christ can be thought of as one who paid the penalty which the law exacts for breaking it. If, in the framework of the Old Testament, we think of sacrifice as the appointed remedy for sin, then Christ can be thought of as the sacrifice for men's sins. Again, if we think of men as captured and enslaved by evil, Christ is the ransom for their redemption. And if men are seen battling against evil powers, then Christ has over-thrown the powers of evil so that we may be victorious.

How far Paul took these metaphors literally it is hard to say. Certainly he took them seriously. He had no doubt that Christ's work was God's deed, by which God revealed his nature as self-sacrificing love, the cost and meaning of forgiveness, and the awful nature of evil. "God was in Christ reconciling the world to himself" (II Cor. 5:19).

Inseparable from the Crucifixion in Paul's mind was the Resurrection. This was essential for Paul, because only so could it be known that the Crucifixion of Jesus was not an ordinary execution, but a divine act. Together the Crucifixion and Resurrection constitute an act of divine grace, intended to awaken men to their true condition and their real need.

FAITH

It is at this point that Paul's concept of faith becomes impor-tant. Certainly faith is not just the willingness to give assent with the mind that all this is true. If this were the case, there really would be no essential difference between the new way of sal-vation and the old. It is not that God in the first place said, "If you will obey the rules I will give you what you want," but now, finding that beyond men's power, he says, "All you have to do is to believe that Jesus was my son who died for you. If you do that, I will give you what you want." To Paul's way of thinking, the trouble with the Law was that it called forth a bargaining attitude. The attitude is what is wrong. That cannot be cured simply by offering an easier bargain.

So when Paul says that man is to be justified (acquitted) not by works of the Law but by faith, he means by faith more than belief, in the sense of assent by the mind to something as true. He also means more by it than simple trust, in the sense of relying on God to give you what you want. The crucial point is this "what *I* want." To ask, "How can I get what I want?" is, for Paul, to be without faith; and you can never have it as long as that is your question. Paul's great example of faith is Abraham; and Abraham's faith, according to Paul, consisted in trusting that God would carry out God's purposes through him. For Paul, the important thing was not the advantage that would accrue to Abraham from having numerous progeny, but the fact that God proposed to use Abraham to bring blessing to many nations (Gentiles). Abraham's faith consisted in his willingness to be used by God. This did involve belief and trust—the belief that God could do what he said, and the trust that he would do it— but Abraham's belief and trust were both meaningless apart from his willingness to put aside all claims and put himself in God's hands as an instrument of God's purpose.

This faith to which Paul summoned his hearers was basically of the same nature, but it had a new aspect. God, in the Crucifixion and Resurrection of his Son, had made a new approach to men. It was a challenge not just to one, as he had challenged Abraham, but a challenge to all. It was a challenge to appreciate the true significance of what had been done in Christ, to give up the effort to carve out one's own future, even with the help of God, and accept what God had done. Once more, belief and trust were involved. Unless Christ was believed to be God's Son, and unless it was believed that he had been raised from the dead, the events of Jesus' life and death would have had no more significance for Paul than any other miscarriage of justice in the execution of a righteous man. Trust in God was also involved. Unless this belief was a source of confidence and hope in actual living, it was not the kind of belief that was important. But the fundamental thing in faith, as Paul meant it, was the giving up of any attempt to win God's favor even by the effort to be righteous. To make an effort to win God's favor would be to set up a barrier to God's favor which God himself could not surmount. God had shown that his favor rested not on effort—legal, moral, or even religious—but on simple receptivity.

THE OUTCOME

Paul saw this as the looked-for fulfillment of God's promises of blessing which had always meant so much to him. Now, these promises had been promises to a people. Man was to be blessed with God's favor not as a separate individual but as a member of a group, the descendants of Abraham. In this he did not differ from other Jews. Where he differed was, first, in holding that membership in this group was not constituted by physical descent from Abraham and sealed by circumcision, but was constituted by faith. In the second place, he held that the events leading to the final fulfillment of God's promises had begun in the Crucifixion and Resurrection of Jesus. The end was at hand, and Paul expected to see the day. He shared the Pharisaic expectation (as Jesus had) that there would then be a resurrection of the dead and a judgment which would separate the good and the bad.

As has been seen, Paul believed that the physical universe itself had fallen under the dominion of supernatural but evil powers. In a way which he does not explain, Paul believed that the death and Resurrection of Jesus had brought about the overthrow of these evil powers. The victory had not yet been consolidated, so to speak, but that would be done when the final end came. Then "creation itself will be set free from its bondage to decay." (Rom. 8:21.) Along with this went Paul's belief that man's body would be changed to a "spiritual body." This did not mean a body which could exist in heaven. Paul did not expect to go to heaven when he died. He expected to live on earth—though it would be a renewed, purified earth, not subject to decay—and he expected to be given a real physical body appropriate for this new world and not subject to death.

THE COMMUNITY "IN CHRIST"

Meanwhile, the followers of Jesus were believed to be living in the (supposedly) short interval between the end of the old order and the beginning of the new. They were "in Christ" in the sense that they were a fellowship of those destined to have a place in the new order because they had been reconciled to God by their faith, called forth by the death and Resurrection of Christ.

Those who are thus "in Christ" have Christ in them, or have the Spirit of Christ, or the Spirit of God. Paul seems to use these expressions interchangeably without subtle distinctions. Through possession of the Spirit, believers have already by anticipation some of the blessings of the coming age. The experience of the Spirit was a very real element in the life of the early Christian communities. It bound the believers together into a functioning unity which could be described as "the body of Christ." They felt in themselves a newness of life which they attributed to the same Spirit. "The fruit of the Spirit is love, joy, peace, patience, kindness, goodness, faithfulness, gentleness, self-control." (Gal. 5:22–23.)

This doctrine of the Spirit provided Paul with a weapon against those who would take his teaching that man cannot be justified by the works of the Law to mean that it did not make any difference what a man did. The works of the flesh, he said, were plain: "immorality, impurity, licentiousness, idolatry, sorcery, enmity, strife, jealousy, anger, selfishness, dissension, party spirit, envy, drunkenness, carousing, and the like." (Gal. 5:19–21.) These things simply could not be the result of the presence of the Spirit of God. To act in such ways proved to Paul that the Spirit of God was not present, no matter what other "spiritual gifts" one might seem to possess. To claim that "faith" gave one the right to break the rules was the symptom of an attitude of self-seeking that was evidence that there was no real faith at all.

In the life of this community of those "in Christ," there were two ceremonies which Paul found already in use: baptism and the Lord's Supper. Baptism was the accepted procedure for entering the group; the Lord's Supper bound the members together in a common fellowship.

Paul indicates that he did not himself do much baptizing, but this was not because he held that it was unimportant. It was certainly baptism by immersion, and he interprets it as a participation in Christ's dying and rising again. But Paul surely had in view no magical conception of the efficacy of the ceremony. Only as the act was the expression of faith could it have any significance.

Basically, the situation is similar with regard to the Lord's Supper. It is a communion, in anticipation of the fuller communion which will be possible when the day of the Lord arrives. The bread and wine are not magic substances. Nothing is said of eating Christ. It is rather an experience of fellowship, of fellowship with one another and with Christ. If some seek that fellowship unworthily, their danger is not that the magic will go wrong and produce disastrous results; but that without faith (if they had it they would not be unworthy) they are of necessity exposed, as all unrighteous men are, to the wrath of God.

Actually, it would seem as if these ceremonies had no essential place in Paul's thought. They were already a part of Christianity when he was converted, and he simply fitted them into his central thought the best he could. But for Paul, the central thing was the recognition that man could not become righteous by trying. The essential was faith. If a man had faith, it was hard to see that anything else would be necessary.

JEW AND GREEK

Any presentation of the thought of Paul involves the consideration of a multitude of subordinate questions, often calling for expert knowledge of a highly technical sort. Such matters cannot be discussed here. There are two basic questions, however, which cannot be completely ignored.

The first is the question as to whether Paul's approach to religion was essentially Greek, and only superficially Jewish, or whether the reverse is true.

Part of the difficulty of this question lies in the difficulty of discovering just what is essentially Greek and what is really Jewish. Answers tend to be in terms of abstractions which represent what someone thinks real Judaism, say, ought to be, rather than in terms of what it ever actually was. This is a vice which seems to infect most comparisons of religions. Paul, of course, thought that his own position, whatever it was, represented real Judaism. Most Jewish scholars, if they study Paul at all, find much that is Jewish in him, but have also an impression of something quite alien to the Jewish ways of thought in which they have grown up.

Certainly Paul has much in common with Judaism. In the first place, there is his consistent and unquestioning monotheism. God was one—not just an abstract philosophical principle, but the living God who had appeared to Abraham, who guided the course of history, and who was accessible in prayer. Again, despite his contention that a man could not render himself acceptable to God by trying to keep the Law, Paul's moral standards were fundamentally those of Judaism. His reaction to the lax moral standards of Corinth or Ephesus was precisely that of any faithful Jew. His expectation of a Messiah, which he saw fulfilled in Jesus, was a uniquely Jewish hope. So was his belief in a coming judgment and a bodily resurrection. The existence and activities of angels and demons are conceived in quite Jewish fashion. His recognition of Scripture as God's revelation was Jewish, clearly, and so were his methods of using it, even though it be granted that this is far from proving that he had the technical training of a rabbi.

It is clear, however, that Paul's Judaism, whether essential or superficial, is not identical with the stream of Palestinian Judaism which eventually found expression in the Talmud and the Midrashim. It is generally agreed that Paul was familiar with the *Wisdom of Solomon,* a book found in the Greek Old Testament but not in the Hebrew, which represents a type of Judaism clearly influenced by Hellenistic thought. He also shows points of contact with another such book, *II Esdras,* especially in its pessimism about men's fate (Paul would add: "apart from hope in Christ"). There are a few details of Scripture interpretation similar to some points in Philo, but nothing to indicate that Paul had read the Alexandrian.

At two points especially there is dispute among the experts as to whether Paul's concepts can be adequately explained from purely Jewish suppositions. These are his conception of "the first Adam" and his idea of "flesh." In regard to the first, it has been alleged that Paul was making use of non-Jewish speculations about a primeval Man; but it does not really seem necessary to suppose that he goes beyond what he could get from Jewish sources. It is possible that Jewish thought about Adam was itself influenced by such speculations. As for what Paul has to say about "flesh," it seems more likely that he was influenced to some extent by the dualism that set flesh and spirit in opposition. But even here he does not adopt the essential point of such dualism—that flesh and spirit are inherently antagonistic, and that man's goal is to escape from the flesh entirely to dwell in a realm of pure spirit. The present world may have to be renewed, and a new body provided; but Paul certainly does not anticipate existence as disembodied spirit, beyond the world.

The crucial question, however, is as to Paul's conception of the true nature of the religious life. Is his goal a mystical vision, a union with the divine? Did he, as has been said of Philo, take "to his heart the pagan idea of salvation; that is, that the spirit be released from the flesh, in order to return to its spiritual source in God"?[2] However it may have been with Philo, it seems clear that Paul was not a mystic, in this sense at least. He speaks of having one vision which he valued highly; but there is no indication that he made the quest for such experiences the center of his spiritual life, or that the goal of his preaching was to show others how these were to be achieved. That his converts spoke ecstatically and manifested various spiritual gifts would hardly have been acceptable to his orthodox Jewish contemporaries; but to Paul, these things were simply the manifestation of the Spirit of God, not essentially different from the way the Spirit had seized Saul with similar results (I Sam. 10:6). The orthodox thought such manifestations had long ceased. Christians thought that with the coming of the last days they had begun again. There is nothing essentially un-Jewish about the idea, however unwelcome the practice may have been.

When the details of his thought and expression are explored, it may well be that at a number of points Paul used ideas which he either borrowed directly from Hellenism, or absorbed unconsciously from his environment; but Paul seems to be rooted in Judaism. Where he seems to deviate from that, it is mainly the result of his trying to apply concepts derived from Judaism to explain his experiences and those of his converts as Christians.

JESUS AND PAUL

It has been said that Christianity as we know it is the creation of Paul, not Jesus—that Paul transformed the religion of Jesus into a religion about Jesus. Is this so, and what is the relation between the two?

Certainly there is much in common between them. In the first place, Jesus proclaimed the imminent end of the present

[2] E. R. Goodenough, *An Introduction to Philo Judaeus,* Yale University Press, 1940, p. 16.

order; and this expectation of the end is a premise of Paul's message. For both, this involved, as it did for a large section of Judaism, the expectation of the resurrection of the body. Both called for a deeper righteousness than mere conformity to rule. Jesus never criticized the Law in the way Paul did; but when Jesus appealed beyond the letter to the ultimate purpose of God, he was in actuality undermining the whole conception that righteousness could be attained by conformity to a code. Paul's position is expressed in quite different terms, but at bottom there is more in common than appears on the surface. Both were concerned that man should live completely according to the will of God—not just on the surface, but from the inside.

On the other hand, there are obvious differences. As has been pointed out, Paul is to be understood in terms of Judaism; but it is in many respects a different kind of Judaism from what Jesus represents. Jesus' emphasis on repentance and forgiveness is not found in Paul. No doubt he has equivalent concepts, but different ways of expressing the same thing point to different routes for arriving at the same goal. In general, the Judaism of Jesus is closer to the form which eventually found expression in the Talmud and the Midrashim, while Paul's Judaism is a Hellenistic variety.

Another point of difference, at least in expression, is the use of the phrase *kingdom of God*. This, of course, was at the center of Jesus' teaching. Paul uses the phrase sparingly and rather incidentally. But this is again partly a matter of vocabulary, for Paul looks forward to the end of the present order and the establishment of a new order by God as surely as Jesus does. Nevertheless, the difference in vocabulary represents a difference in interests and emphasis. It is to be noted, also, that *Son of man*, which seems to have been Jesus' characteristic designation of the coming one, is completely absent from Paul's letters.

There is furthermore an important difference in the meaning attached by the two to the word *faith*. Here, part of the difference is accounted for by the fact that Jesus thought and spoke in Aramaic, while Paul thought and spoke in Greek. The Greek word used to translate Jesus' Aramaic did not have the same range of connotations. This is a common problem in going from one language to another, and it may be remarked that the English word *faith* has still a different set of connotations. But in any case, Jesus summoned men to a simple trust in the Heavenly Father, while Paul meant (as has been seen) something much more complicated.

Both speak of God as "Father"; but Jesus uses this expression to describe God's attitudes toward men, while Paul uses it chiefly to describe God's relation to Christ. When he uses it for God's relation to Christians, he generally does so in a much more formal way than Jesus. He never bases an argument on the implication of God's fatherhood, as Jesus does. There is nothing in Paul like the parable of the Prodigal Son.

The crucial question, however, is as to the position accorded Jesus. It has been pointed out above that it seems most likely that the conviction that Jesus was the Messiah represented a conclusion reached by his followers after the Resurrection rather than an attitude which he deliberately fostered, and that the interpretation of his death as a ransom for many probably was an application of Isaiah's Suffering Servant concept to the explanation of the otherwise difficult problem of the unexpected death of the Messiah. If this is correct, then the concepts certainly represent an important addition to what Jesus taught. If, on the other hand, as many would hold, these concepts go back at least in germ to Jesus himself, then nothing radically new was added. But in any case, the innovator, if there be one, was not Paul, who tells us, "I delivered to you as of first importance what I also received, that Christ died for our sins in accordance with the scriptures." (I Cor. 15:3.)

Even so, it is not correct to say that Paul's religion was primarily a religion about Jesus. It was primarily a religion about

God, his claim to man's allegiance, and how it was possible for man to satisfy that claim. Christ's work, according to Paul, was God's deed. In the end, Christ will deliver the kingdom to God the Father. "When all things are subjected to him, then the Son himself will also be subjected to him . . . that God may be everything to every one." (I Cor. 15:28.) Paul never speaks of worshiping Christ or praying to Christ, and he probably would have recoiled in horror from the thought. For him, Christ was God's Son; but this meant subordination, not "consubstantiality," as the bishops at Nicea called it. Christ was tremendously important to Paul; but he was important as the instrument of God's reconciliation, not as a member of a trinitarian Godhead. Both Paul and Jesus, however, were at one in holding that man's beatitude was dependent on God's totally undeserved action, though Paul's own concept of that action was completely transformed when he came to believe in the Resurrection of Jesus.

If, then, we want a short answer to the question, "Was Paul's teaching really different from that of Jesus?" it can only be "Yes and no."

PART IV

Christianity Faces a Larger World

INTRODUCTION

After the period of activity which centers about Paul, there is a gap in our knowledge of the history of Christianity. The letters of Paul, it must be emphasized, are the earliest writings of the New Testament; and the latest of these cannot be later than about A.D. 60. Perhaps the Gospel of Mark comes from about A.D. 70, but from then on there is a gap of about two decades. Some of the other books may have been written during these twenty years; but there is really nothing in them that demands a date much, if any, before the end of the first century.

The cause of this break in our tradition is uncertain; but one may suspect that it has something to do with the destruction of Jerusalem, the dispersal of the Church there, and the cutting loose of Christianity from its primitive foundations. Paul is generally depicted as the writer of the declaration of independence of Christianity from Jewish Christianity, and his story is told as if it were the story of Paul versus Jerusalem. But one of the points on which Paul's letters and Acts are in complete agreement is that Paul's work was fully recognized by the leaders in Jerusalem and that Paul was most eager to cement good relations between his Gentile churches and the mother church at Jerusalem. Moreover, despite his declaration that the effort to obey the Law will not make anybody righteous, some of his sharpest conflicts were with those who held that the new religion set them free from moral obligations. Whether this be due to "overconversion" or to the deliberate propaganda of an opposing point of view, Paul was convinced that any such view was utterly destructive of the essence of religion; and he must have found in Jerusalem an important ally in his struggle. With Paul gone, and the Church in Jerusalem scattered at the time of the Roman siege, a period of confusion must have ensued in which such tendencies as had shown themselves during Paul's lifetime in Corinth, Colossae, and probably even in Galatia, flourished without much effective opposition. Out of the conflict, whose details

This arch was erected to celebrate the victory of Titus over the Jews in A.D. 70. The panel inside shows Roman soldiers carrying off the sacred objects from the Temple. (Brown Brothers)

have been lost to us, there emerged by the end of the century a Church with an increasing homogeneity and a growing clarity in its point of view—a point of view which was heir both to Jerusalem and to Paul, even though it was not a Hegelian synthesis of two opposing views.

But whatever the cause, the fact is plain. The later books of the New Testament are to be understood in relation to a wider environment. The problems faced are those created by the fact that the new religion has now emerged on a world scene, with its characteristic complex situation—political, social, economic, cultural, and intellectual. Paul was, of course, in contact with such a world, and some of its features have already been sketched. But by the end of the century, the Church was not simply in this world; it stood self-consciously against it in many ways. In the first place, it found itself in increasing conflict with the Roman government, and faced the necessity of strengthening its members to withstand active persecution. The book of Revelation is directed explicitly to this situation. It is an important element in I Peter, and is in the background of Hebrews. Each deals with the problem in a different way.

By the end of the first century, the Church also found itself faced with the problem of developing an efficient organization in order to deal with dissension, to exercise discipline over its members, to regulate worship, and to administer charity. These problems are reflected in quite different ways in the Pastoral Epistles (I and II Timothy and Titus) and II and III John.

The remaining books have in common a set of problems which may be described as intellectual. Christians had to be instructed in the content and implications of their faith, it had to be defended from what the Church had come to see as dangerous perversions from within, and it had to be defended against the objections which would be brought against it from without. The intention, perhaps, was not so much that of winning over the objectors as it was to give the faithful an answer which would satisfy them when they encountered such objections. These motives tended to mingle in the mind of any writer, and no rigid division of the books is possible. To this general category belong James, the Synoptic Gospels, the Gospel of John, and the First Epistle of John, together with Jude and II Peter.

CHAPTER 15

Sources

THESE books themselves are the chief sources of information about this period and its problems. Before using them, we must ask the usual questions about date and authorship, even though these questions are here, if possible, even more difficult than usual, for the simple reason that we have so little to go on. In no case can we be sure of the traditional authorship, though in many cases we can be sure that the traditional author is not the true author. The traditional dates have usually little more to commend them. The best we can do is to try to see what sort of a situation the writings fit most nearly, and the notion that we can have anything more is, in most cases, a delusion.

A word should be said about the problem presented by the denial of the traditional authorship of so many books. In the first place, a distinction must be made between books which include within the body of the book (as distinguished from attached titles) a claim to authorship, and those which do not. In the first group are the Pastoral Epistles, which certainly claim to be by the apostle Paul; I and II Peter, which claim to be by Peter; and Jude, which claims to be by Jude, brother of James. In other cases, names are given which are very common; and if we inquire how we know which of the Jameses (the New Testament mentions three) wrote the Epistle, or that the writer of Revelation was John, the son of Zebedee, as is generally supposed, it is hard to get a satisfactory answer. Similarly with other books, such as the Gospels which have names attached to them. Once the question is raised as to when these names were attached, and how sound was the knowledge of those who attached them, we have nothing to go on which will bear much weight.

In the cases where it is a matter of identification of a name with a known figure who bore it, we need to remember the necessity the Church found itself under in the second century of appealing to apostolic standards. When valued books in common use bore names which had been borne by apostles, the conclusion that the apostles were the authors was natural and involved no intentional deceit. But unfortunately, good intentions are not a guarantee of accurate results.

As for the books which were deliberately issued under the names of people who were not their authors, we simply have to recognize a difference in point of view in ancient times. In the ancient world this seems to have been a fairly common practice, rather taken for granted. In any case, the real author doubtless believed that he was expressing the sentiments of the person to whom the book was ascribed. As he saw it, he was not trying to use the other man's name for his own profit, but on behalf of a cause that the other man had stood for. If in our eyes he was dishonest, in his own eyes and those of his contemporaries he was not.

HEBREWS

The one sure thing about Hebrews is that we do not know who wrote it. It was certainly not Paul. That it was originally an epistle is at best doubtful, and that it was originally addressed to "Hebrews" in any sense is also dubious. Apart from these three points, its designation in the King James Version as the "Epistle of Paul to the Hebrews" is entirely correct!

That the book was not by Paul is clear from a number of considerations. In the first place, the difference in style is clearly marked at just about every point where styles can be compared. Vocabulary, rhythm, and ways of putting words together are quite different; and although the difference can only be specified accurately in terms of Greek, the general difference is obvious enough even in English translation. What would not be obvious in English is that the writer of Hebrews shows himself much more aware of the rules of Greek rhetoric than Paul. All this was very plain to the early Christians who thought in Greek, and they did not hesitate to say so. Since it was necessary for a book to have apostolic sponsorship, the book was slow in gaining general acceptance. The problem was finally solved by the assertion that Paul had supplied the ideas and someone else the words. That this gained credence was not because there was any evidence whatever in favor of it. It was pure supposition whose only merit was that it allowed people to believe what they wanted to believe, in spite of the evidence against them.

Furthermore, the author's use of Scripture is not really like Paul's. The sustained allegory (or, more accurately, typology) involved in the comparison of Christ and the high priest goes far beyond Paul's reference to Hagar. Indeed, the ideas are different in many ways. The characteristic Pauline concern with justification is entirely absent (the word, either as a noun or the related verb, does not appear). Both emphasize "faith," but actually the word means different things to the two authors.

The general situation is not that of Paul's day. Hebrews presupposes a Church with some extended history, and a second generation which has lost the vigor and enthusiasm of their fathers. Finally, there is the decisive fact that the author clearly places himself in this second generation. "Salvation . . . was attested to us by those who heard" the Lord (2:3). Paul, with his insistence on his direct commission, could never have said this.

Unfortunately, when we come to recognize that Paul was not the author, we have no one to propose in his place. In the words of Origen, the greatest scholar of the ancient Church, "But who wrote the epistle, in truth God knows."

As to date, we do not have much more to go on. It is generally held that Clement of Rome has reminiscences of Hebrews in his letter to Corinth, and Clement's letter is usually dated just before A.D. 100. This would set an upper limit of, say, A.D. 95 for Hebrews, though the date of Clement is not free from doubt. If we could be sure that the sufferings of former days mentioned in 10:32–34 referred to the persecution of Christians by Nero in A.D. 64, that would give a lower limit. Attempts are sometimes made to date it relatively early, but they ignore the indications that the recipients were of the second generation, in an established Church with a considerable history behind it. These conditions would be best satisfied by a date toward the end of the century.

Who, then, were the intended readers of the book? At the close, those "of Italy" send greetings. Does this mean "we who are in Italy" are writing to those elsewhere, or does it mean "we from Italy" are writing home? In favor of the latter is the use of the letter by Clement of Rome. The references to persecution receive a natural interpretation on this hypothesis. On the other hand, the book has no obvious points of attachment to any other church.

It has often been inferred, from the fact that so much is made of the Jewish sacrificial system, that the book was intended for Jewish Christians; but against this are several points. In the first place, the author ignores the Temple entirely, in favor of the Tabernacle, its predecessor, as Jewish Christians would hardly have done. It uses the Scriptures in the Greek translation of the Septuagint. There is no indication that the author knew any

Hebrew or Aramaic. As for the emphasis on the Jewish sacrificial system, especially as connected with the Tabernacle, this after all is a feature of the Old Testament, which was also the Scripture of the Christian Church. That the writer was so familiar with it may indicate that his background was Jewish (though, if so, his familiarity with the Septuagint would indicate Hellenistic Judaism), but it affords no indication at all that his readers were Jewish Christians of any kind. In any case, emphasis on the Law, which was the characteristic feature of the Judaism of the time, is entirely foreign to this author.

As has been suggested, the book is not really a letter. The puzzling thing is that it closes like a letter although it does not begin like one. Perhaps the best suggestion is that it was originally a written sermon sent to Rome, to which the sender attached a brief note at the end.

THE PASTORAL EPISTLES

These letters, which were issued in the name of Paul, were certainly not written by him.

In the first place, the relationship implied in the letters "to Timothy" does not agree with the picture in Paul's other letters. They lack the intimate, affectionate tone of Paul's genuine letters (cf. Phil. 2:20–22, I Cor. 4:17); they suggest the affection of an older man for a promising young man (I Tim. 1:2, 18, II Tim. 1:2, 5), not the seasoned co-worker; the sufferings he is said in II Tim. 3:10–11 to have observed took place, according to Acts, before Timothy's association with Paul. Much of the advice is of such an elementary character that it is hardly appropriate for a trusted associate of long standing.

Another indication that the book does not really come from the time professed is found in II Tim. 3:1–9. This section starts out predicting abuses which will arise in the last days; but before the end of the section is reached, it is clear that the evildoers are not future but present. Moreover, as will appear when we consider the content of these Epistles, these abuses represent a development in the direction of Gnosticism well beyond anything in Paul's time.

Style, as usual, is another tell-tale. The vocabulary is different; the expression is much stiffer. Paul has so much to say that he can hardly get it out, with long, sustained arguments, not without digressions. The author of the Pastorals writes in neat little packages. Many of the characteristic Pauline ideas and emphases are absent. Examples are: the Spirit, and the idea of being "in Christ." The word *faith* is used, but in quite a different sense from Paul's usage, and different also from Hebrews. The author cannot be Paul.

Some of the more personal notes, especially in II Timothy, have seemed to various scholars to be different from the rest; and have led to the hypothesis that the author of the Pastorals had at hand some fragments of genuine Pauline letters which he incorporated in his own compositions. Just how and why these essentially unimportant personal details got detached and preserved, while the real substance of the letters was lost, is not explained. In any case, even if the hypothesis were true, such personal details without their original context would add nothing significant to our knowledge of Paul.

We have no closer knowledge of the date of these books than of other books of this period. They seem to be familiar to Church leaders like Ignatius and Polycarp in the first half of the second century; and the development in the direction of Gnosticism points to a time after the death of Paul. Sometime about the end of the first century is as good a guess as any.

JAMES

If we ask whether the Epistle of James was written by James, we shall have to decide first which James we are talking about:

James, the Lord's brother; James, the brother of John and son of Zebedee, or the shadowy James, the son of Alphaeus. It is also to be remembered that *Jacob,* which is the original from which the English *James* is derived, is one of the most common Jewish names. Actually, there is nothing in the letter to indicate which James was the author. He does not identify himself in any way.

Most often he has been identified with James, the Lord's brother; but the earliest trace of this identification comes only from the third century. The Church historian Eusebius indicates that even in the fourth century there was hesitation in some quarters about accepting the book as part of the New Testament. The obvious conclusion is that this was a book, valued in some quarters at least, whose position in the canon was secured finally as the opinion gained ground that its author was the James who had been head of the Church in Jerusalem. But a conclusion reached at such a late date, without additional evidence, has no value whatever.

There are numerous points which tell against this identification. It is true that the thought is in many respects quite Jewish, but the expression is Greek. The Greek is not elaborate, but it is good, obviously the product of a mind that habitually thought in Greek. In form, it shows more clearly than any other book in the New Testament the characteristics of the diatribe which the Stoics had popularized. Parallels to its phraseology and vocabulary can be found in Hellenistic Jewish books like the *Wisdom of Solomon, IV Maccabees,* and Philo. The author's Bible is the Greek translation of the Old Testament, not the original Hebrew. These facts point to a Hellenistic Jew as the author; and none of the three Jameses in the New Testament meets this specification. That his name was James we may perhaps believe; but if so, we learn more about this otherwise unknown James from his book than we can learn about his book from knowing his name.

One of the peculiar features of the book is that Christ is explicitly mentioned only twice, and both of these references could be cut out without any disturbance of the sense. This has led to the suggestion that the book was originally a Jewish writing which was adapted to Christian purposes by the insertion of the references to Jesus. As will appear when the contents are considered in more detail, this will not do; for the Christian element is much more pervasive than the two specific references to Christ. A recent modification of the hypothesis seems more probable, though it can hardly be said to be demonstrated. The suggestion is that the Christian author of unknown name used as the basis for his composition a "Letter of Jacob" (the Hebrew equivalent of James), addressed to Jews of the Dispersion and modeled after Genesis 49, where Jacob addresses each of his twelve sons, the "ancestors" of Israel, in turn. Moral exhortation addressed to each has left identifiable traces in the present form. This form of the hypothesis is certainly preferable to the original form, as it allows much more extensive additions and changes by the Christian who adapted it for those he believed to be God's true Israel.

We are hardly in a better position with regard to the date than with regard to the authorship. The discussions of faith have often been taken as an attack on Paul's teaching. If so, the author did not understand Paul; and it seems more likely that he was attacking Paulinism as misunderstood by others. In any case, he cannot be earlier than Paul. There is no reference to the conflict about whether the observance of the Law should be required of Gentiles, which suggests a period after this crisis had passed. The Church seems to include the rich and worldly, another indication of a relatively late date. All of these conditions would be satisfied by a date about A.D. 100, but there is nothing decisive for or against a date ten years or so earlier or later.

I PETER

The clue to the understanding of I Peter is to be found in its date. This question will therefore be considered first. Chapter 4,

326   *A Historical Approach to the New Testament*

verses 12 to 19, presupposes that those to whom the letter is addressed are being subjected to severe persecution. It is a "fiery ordeal." They are to share Christ's sufferings, which surely means that they are threatened with death. They suffer specifically as Christians and are urged "under that name" to glorify God. Since those addressed are Christians living in "Pontus, Galatia, Cappadocia, Asia, and Bithynia," the problem of dating would be solved if we could find when Christians in this area were being severely persecuted.

There are three known persecutions in this period: under Nero (A.D. 64), under Domitian (about A.D. 96), and under Trajan (about A.D. 115). The first is certainly to be excluded, since there is not the slightest indication in Roman or Christian sources that the Neronian persecution extended beyond Rome. Actually, we know very little about the persecution under Domitian, and some scholars have recently doubted whether there was any such. But if there was, the scene of it was Asia Minor; and it would thus be a distinct possibility. The persecution under Trajan seems even more likely. For this persecution we have correspondence between Pliny, who was then the Roman governor of Bithynia, and the Emperor, dealing with proceedings against Christians. Central is the question whether "the name itself, even if innocent of crime, should be punished, or only the crimes attaching to that name."[1] Now this seems to be just the situation in which the Christians addressed in I Peter find themselves, and various points in the letter are illuminated by accepting this date. But in any case, it cannot be earlier than A.D. 96.

The advantage of beginning with a discussion of the date is that the recognition that the book comes from the very end of the first century (and probably from the second decade of the second century) is that it disposes at once of the possibility that

[1] The issue may be easily understood today, if we think of "communism." Shall people be subject to legal penalties simply by virtue of party membership, or do they have to be convicted of some specific criminal act, such as conspiring to overthrow the government?

Peter, who probably died about A.D. 64, wrote it. Once this is accepted, facts which are very difficult to explain on the supposition of Peter's authorship easily fall into place. The Greek is far better than one would expect from a Galilean fisherman who learned it late in life and, according to the Papias tradition at least, was supposed to have needed an interpreter in his dealings with the Greek-speaking Church at Rome. Then, too, the author is thoroughly familiar with the Greek Old Testament. At points he seems to be influenced by some of Paul's writings. All this is natural enough if the book was written about A.D. 100 or shortly thereafter, but is hard to understand if Peter was the author. Actually, those who try to maintain the Petrine "authorship" are not only forced to explain away the clear indications of date but also to imagine that the actual writer was a man with just these non-Petrine characteristics, who expressed in his own way the ideas Peter is supposed to have given him. This is another of those hypotheses which clutter up Biblical study and rest on nothing more substantial than the fact that they make it possible to continue to hold a cherished idea in the face of apparently overwhelming objection. They have no positive support whatever.

JUDE

This little book offers few data for determining date and authorship. "Judas, brother of James" is presumably intended to identify the author with the brother of James of Jerusalem, the brother of Jesus, though both Judas (Jude) and Jacob (James) are among the most common of all Jewish names. It may be argued that if a later writer were borrowing a name under which to deliver what he believed was an apostolic message—as, for example, the author of the Pastorals did—he would surely have chosen a better-known figure. The author was certainly familiar with such Jewish apocalypses as Enoch and the Assumption of

Moses, and had the horror of sexual perversion which Christianity inherited from Judaism. If these points are compatible with authorship by Judas, the brother of James, we still do not know enough about this Judas to know where to fit the book into his career; but if it was this Judas, his book could not be later than the latter part of the first century.

However, taken by itself, the book gives a distinct impression of being quite late; and the fact that the ideas are not otherwise such as to preclude Jude's authorship ought not to override these indications of lateness. That part of the data allows a certain possibility does not overbalance positive indications that weigh against it.

The indications of lateness are that the views combatted are of the Gnostic variety, developed at least to the degree revealed in the Pastoral Epistles; the use of the term *faith* in the later, static sense, referring to assent to a body of teaching "delivered" to a former generation (verse 3). Verse 17 looks back to the days of Jesus and the apostles as lying well in the past. Once more, a date about the end of the first century would seem to be as close as we can come.

II PETER

When II Peter is compared with I Peter it is immediately clear that they cannot possibly be by the same author, since the style is entirely different, being obscure and awkward, with striking differences in vocabulary. Jerome tells us that even in his day many denied that Peter wrote II Peter because of its stylistic differences from I Peter.

We have concluded that I Peter was not written by the apostle; but this does not make it possible to take the second Epistle as having been written by him, for the marks of lateness are more apparent here than in any other book in the New Testament. References to "this second letter" and to being present at the

Transfiguration of Jesus are simply part of the fiction of Petrine authorship. In 3:16 we have a direct reference to Paul's writings as recognized Scripture, an indication of a date well on in the second century. It is also clear that the author borrowed largely from Jude, especially in Chapter 2 (cf. Jude, verse 4 ff.).

All these facts point to the conclusion that II Peter is the latest book in the New Testament, written not long before A.D. 150.

THE SYNOPTIC GOSPELS

Questions as to the date and authorship of these books have already been discussed in connection with the use of them as sources for a knowledge of the life and teachings of Jesus. But it must be remembered that these books find their place in the life of the Church in this later period. They were not composed to serve as a collection of sources to be used by scholars engaged in the study of the life of Jesus, and they will need to be studied in relation to the problems and needs of this period in which they were produced.

THE WRITINGS ASCRIBED TO JOHN

The New Testament contains five books ascribed to John, who is traditionally identified with John, the son of Zebedee, one of the original twelve apostles. These books include a Gospel, three letters, and an Apocalypse.

In discussing the date and authorship of these books, the first step is the recognition that on the basis of the character of the Greek in which they are written, they fall into two clearly marked groups, the first consisting of the book of Revelation, and the second consisting of the rest of the books. The Gospel and Epistles are written in simple but correct Greek; Revelation is written in a Greek which had indeed its own rules, but they are not the rules to which any other Greek anywhere conforms. *"The lin-guistic character of the Apocalypse is absolutely unique."*[2] It is the Greek of a man who thought in a Semitic language, to whom Greek always remained a foreign tongue. This clearly indicates that Revelation could not possibly have the same author as the rest of the books. It is sometimes suggested that the same author wrote the books, with some considerable interval of time between them; that in the meanwhile he had taken pains to improve his Greek. Those who make this suggestion are concerned to defend the authorship of all five books by John the Apostle. But even if we could accept a date in the decade between A.D. 50 and A.D. 60 (actually quite impossible, as will appear) that would make the author well along in middle life. No one who has tried himself to learn a foreign language in middle life, or who has observed, say, the refugees who have come to this country either before or since the war (some of them men of outstanding intellectual ability) will consider this sort of radical improvement even a remote possibility.

If the two groups are not by the same author, is it possible that either of them was by John the Apostle? Reasons have already been given for thinking that John the Apostle was not the author of the Gospel. Can this John be identified with the author of Revelation?

It would seem that the answer is no. The author calls himself John; and in spite of the fact that it was the custom of writers of apocalypses to issue them under the names of prominent figures of the past, in this case *John* may well have been his real name, just because the book does not identify its author explicitly or by implication with an apostle. Chapter 21:14 would imply that the author was not an apostle. In 22:9 he is called a prophet; and he is frequently referred to as a servant of God, an expression which in this book is generally associated with prophecy. The

---

[2] R. H. Charles, *The Revelation of St. John,* International Critical Commentary, Scribner's, 1910, vol. I, p. cxliii. Charles italicizes the statement.

first known statement that the author was John the Apostle is by Justin Martyr, about A.D. 150. Of course, if the tradition of John's martyrdom before A.D. 50 is correct, as it may well be, then, as will appear when we come to examine the date of the book, he could not possibly have written it.

THE DATE OF REVELATION

The oldest traditions as to the date of Revelation place it in the reign of the Emperor Domitian (A.D. 81–96), although some later writers give earlier dates. But the earliest tradition comes only from the end of the second century, in the writings of Irenaeus. It may well be that traditions about dates are often more trustworthy than those about authorship (where there was pressure to find an apostolic author for a valued book), especially when the dates given are so late as really to make apostolic authorship unlikely. Still, we would like confirmation.

If we turn to the internal evidence of the book itself, we find it very confusing. Chapter 11 implies that the Temple in Jerusalem, which was destroyed in A.D. 70, was still standing. Chapter 17:10 implies that the reigning emperor was the sixth, who would naturally be Vespasian.[3] But the book also presupposes persecution for refusing to take part in the worship of the emperor. There is no ground for seeing such persecution before the reign of Domitian. Chapter 6:6 may refer to a price-fixing regulation from Domitian's reign. The letter to the Church at Smyrna (2:8–11) implies a fairly long and honorable history, although an early bishop tells us that it was founded subsequent to Paul's time. Finally, the book presupposes the legend that the emperor Nero was to return as the anti-Christ, a legend which in this form is dated by students of the subject toward the end of the century.

[3] Augustus 27 B.C.–A.D. 14
  Tiberius A.D. 14–37
  Gaius (Caligula) 37–41
  Claudius 41–54

Nero 54–68
Vespasian 69–79
Titus 79–81
Domitian 81–96

USE OF SOURCES

It seems plain that these contradictory indications arise because the author, after the manner of the writers of such books, has, with a minimum of editing, borrowed and incorporated earlier materials. Some of these sources bear internal evidence of earlier date, but the date of the book as a whole must be that of the latest elements. The earliest date that meets this requirement is thus one during the reign of Domitian. If those are right who doubt that there was a persecution under Domitian, then the persecution under Trajan, reflected in I Peter, would be the most likely occasion.

This recognition of the use of sources not completely assimilated calls attention to one of the difficult problems in the book of Revelation, the apparently contradictory character of different parts. Chapter 14:8 indicates that the fall of Rome has already taken place; 17:16 predicts it; 18:2 proclaims again that it has happened; 18:21 and 19:2 predict it once more. Finally, in 19:11–21 it is described for the last time as having taken place. There are other instances of similar phenomena. The result has been a wide variety of hypotheses of use of sources, accidental displacement of leaves, and interpolation. Charles, the commentator already referred to, supposed that the author died before he got his manuscript in final shape, leaving it to be issued by a faithful but not very bright disciple. It is clear that whoever issued it was not concerned primarily for logical consistency; but that is a characteristic of the authors of apocalypses in general, rather than a peculiarity of this one.

THE GOSPEL AND EPISTLES OF JOHN

The question of the authorship and date of the Gospel of John has already been discussed in Chapter 5, with the conclusion that the book was written at the end of the first century, and not by John the son of Zebedee. The considerations leading to these conclusions for the Gospel are equally applicable to the three

Epistles, whoever wrote them. The question still remains as to whether Gospel and Epistles were all written by the same author.

Certainly all four show a general similarity of style and ideas. Whether, within this general similarity, individual differences can be detected which warrant the conclusion of different authors for some of them, is a matter about which there is much difference of opinion. The differences in style are by no means of the obvious character which distinguish, say, Hebrews from Paul, and can only be presented in terms of Greek vocabulary and usage. As to whether the differences are so sharp as to demand difference of authorship the experts do not agree.

In the realm of ideas there are differences between the Gospel and first Epistle which can be seen without a knowledge of Greek. In the first place, the Epistle looks forward to an imminent advent of Christ, in agreement with many of the books of the New Testament. This is an emphasis which is quite lacking in the Gospel. Again, the Epistle presents Christ's work as one of "expiation," while the Gospel lacks this idea but emphasizes Christ's drawing all men into the unity of the divine love. Finally, the conception of the Spirit in the Epistle is much more primitive than that in the Gospel. The Epistle does not indicate any role for the Spirit in regeneration, as does the Gospel in 3:5–8. It is possible to imagine explanations of these differences, and such explanations may be valid; but the simplest conclusion would be that the Gospel and first Epistle are by different authors.

The second and third Epistles are short and quite different in subject matter from either the first Epistle or the Gospel, so that the argument from style is harder to apply, while the difference in subject matter makes comparison of concepts almost impossible. Some scholars have believed they could find indications of a closer tie between Gospel and second and third Epistles than between Gospel and first Epistle. If in this way or some other, the Gospel and second and third Epistles can be shown to have a common author, then there is added evidence that the author of the Gospel was not John the Apostle, one of Jesus' close companions. In the two Epistles the author refers to himself as "the Elder." Since in both cases he is making demands by virtue of his authority, he would surely not have claimed anything less than his highest title. But once again, the importance of authorship can be exaggerated, since our knowledge of most people of this age is so shadowy that we would learn next to nothing about the book even if we could definitely identify the author.

One further question about the Fourth Gospel needs discussion. Is the book in substantially the form in which it left its author's hand, or has it been added to or disarranged?

It seems quite clear that the twenty-first chapter is a later addition. Chapter 20 tells of a series of appearances of the risen Christ in Jerusalem, concluding with the statement that those who believe without the physical evidence which Thomas demanded would be blessed. The purpose of the book is then stated as being to recount the signs which would lead to belief, and the resulting life in Christ's name. The book has come to a climax and a clearly marked conclusion. Chapter 21 starts all over again, with the disciples after the Crucifixion back in Galilee fishing. When Jesus appears on the shore they do not recognize him at first, and so on. The chapter seems clearly a later addition.

The recognition does not increase our confidence that the concluding verse, which explicitly asserts that the book was written by the "beloved disciple," was really based on sound knowledge as to the authorship. Actually, the identification of the "beloved disciple" with John the Apostle rests on very weak ground; and, apart from this appendix, it cannot be arrived at from the data furnished by this Gospel. There is, of course, no reference at all to such a figure in the other Gospels.

Within the body of the Gospel, the story in Chapter 8 of the woman taken in adultery is not found in the oldest manuscripts, and is not included in modern editions.

There are a number of rough places in the Gospel as we have it which are widely believed to indicate some disarrangement of the original text. The most obvious of these is at 14:31 where Jesus says, "Rise, let us go hence." He continues speaking, for three more chapters, without any indication of change of scene, with a concluding prayer which one can hardly imagine as spoken en route. Again, the sequence of movements in Chapters 4, 6, and 7 is quite awkward. It would seem plain that there is some disturbance of the original order; but as soon as the attempt is made to propose a specific rearrangement, difficulties appear, and no one has been able to propose a generally acceptable solution. Some have suggested that the awkward passages are later insertions by someone who did not notice the difficulties he was creating. Others try to make something of the passages as they stand, with results which are perhaps as plausible as the alternatives.

CHAPTER 16

❦❦❦❦❦❦❦❦❦❦❦❦❦❦❦❦❦❦❦❦❦❦❦❦❦❦❦❦

Christianity and the State

$\mathcal{B}$ Y THE END of the first century, Christians were unpopular; and from time to time and from place to place were subject to persecution, though it was not till the middle of the third century that there was any organized effort to stamp Christianity out. The factors involved are complex and, in some respects, are still not completely understood.

In the first place, the hostility of the government was never directed against the Christian beliefs as such. The Roman attitude was not, "We just can't have people believing that Jesus of Nazareth was the Son of God." To the sophisticated Roman official such a belief was a crude and worthless superstition; but the government did not undertake to deal with that sort of thing so long as it did not lead to criminal or subversive acts.

The Roman empire had come to include a wide variety of peoples and religions, and in general the Roman policy was one of toleration of local customs and religions. Thus, the Jews had full right to practice their religion and even were entitled to legal protection of that right. A Roman official who violated it could be compelled by imperial order to desist, as when Pilate set up certain shields offensive to Jewish religious sensibilities and was ordered by Tiberius to take them down.

At first, Christians were looked on by the Roman authorities as simply a branch of Judaism, and as such entitled to the same rights and immunities. As Christianity became prevailingly a Gentile religion, and friction between Jews and Christians in-

Nero accused the Christians of arson in A.D. 64. This was the first imperial persecution of Christians. (Brown Brothers)

Trajan. His correspondence with Pliny dealt with the treatment of Christians in Asia Minor. (Brown Brothers)

creased, frequently leading to civil disturbance, it was doubtless the Jews who insisted to the Roman authorities that this was not Judaism and not entitled to share in the legal privileges of Judaism. When it became clear that Christianity was not the native religion of a conquered people, it ceased to have any legal status. This did not mean that it became thereby illegal, so that it constituted a crime simply to profess it, but that it could not now claim the protection of the law.

The first imperial persecution of Christians seems to have

taken place under the emperor Nero in A.D. 64. Prior to that, under Claudius, about A.D. 50, Jews in Rome had been expelled for rioting; and there are reasons for thinking this may have been the result of Christian preaching. If so, from the Roman viewpoint, Christians were still not distinguished from Jews at this time. But in any case, the distinction was clear by the time of Nero. In A.D. 64 a bad fire broke out in Rome, in an area where Nero had vainly proposed a slum-clearance project. Not only so; but several times when the fire seemed under control, it got away again. Ancient Rome, of course, with its many "apartment houses" three or four stories high, of wood construction, with only the crudest fire-fighting equipment, was the scene of many disastrous fires; and even modern fire departments have thought they had a fire under control, only to have it break out again. So nothing could be proved. But the historian Tacitus tells us that there was a persistent rumor that Nero himself had been responsible for having the fire set. As a countermeasure he accused the universally despised Christians of incendiarism, and many were executed on this charge. Certain points are to be noted. The existence of Christians in Rome prior to this time was a matter of common knowledge. They were generally unpopular, which made them natural scapegoats. They were not, however, accused of Christianity but of arson, which is always a serious crime. The inflamed state of public feeling may have prevented their getting a fair trial; but the point is that they were proceeded against as criminals, not as practicing an unlawful religion. It is also to be noted that after the alleged incendiaries were executed that was an end to the matter in Rome, and that Christians elsewhere were never involved in any way.

The second imperial action against Christians seems to come from the reign of Domitian. The Roman historian Suetonius tells us that Domitian was inclined to take the ascription to him of divinity very seriously, even issuing a circular letter in the name of his procurators beginning, "Our Master and our God bids this," referring, of course, to himself. Cassius Dio, a later Roman historian, tells us that in A.D. 95 "Domitian caused Flavius Clemens along with many others to be put to death, although he was his cousin and had for his wife Flavia Domitilla, who was also related to him. The charge of atheism was made against them both, in consequence of which many others also who had adopted the customs of the Jews were condemned. Some were put to death, others lost their property. Domitilla, however, was only banished to Pandataria."[1] Many scholars are of the opinion that Clemens and Domitilla were Christians. If atheism seems a strange charge, it was nevertheless one often made against Christians. It is generally assumed, though without explicit confirmation, that during Domitian's reign worship of the emperor was particularly promoted in Asia Minor. It is true that the Roman province of Asia in general was especially active in promoting this worship.

The attempt to encourage emperor worship was not, however, enforced by a specific law. There was no statute directing people to worship the emperor and prescribing penalties for failure to do so. But when Christians refused to take part, and spoke of their expectation of the coming of a king from heaven who would destroy all earthly kingdoms, this brought them under suspicion of disloyalty. Doubtless, too, the general unpopularity of Jews which was directed against them before the distinction was clear (even to the Jews and Christians) still continued after the distinction was recognized. Those who can remember the attitude of Americans to other Americans of German descent during World War I can get some idea of the social and economic pressure, and even the abandonment of the principle that a man is innocent until proved guilty, which operated against a group suspected of disloyalty even though there was neither overt action nor legal basis for prosecution.

[1] Cassius Dio (excerpts by Xiphilinus) Hist. Rom. LXVII, 14–15, quoted in Ayer, *Source Book for Ancient Church History*, Scribner's, 1913, p. 11. *Pandataria* seems to be more frequently, and better, spelled "Pandateria" in English works.

In addition, the Roman administrator had the power, based on the principle, "The safety of the people shall be their supreme law,"[2] to proceed against individuals when it was judged to be in the public interest, even though there was no specific statute which they could be accused of violating.

This seems to have been the basis underlying the action of Pliny, Roman governor of Bithynia about A.D. 113. We are fortunate in having the correspondence between Pliny and the emperor Trajan in which Pliny states what he has done and inquires as to proper procedure. On assuming office he found himself confronted with the problem of how to deal with Christians. Temples were deserted, and those who provided fodder for sacrificial animals were feeling the pinch. He knows that Christians have been proceeded against, but does not know what crime is to be punished, or whether distinctions of age and strength are to be made; whether on repudiation of Christianity a previous offender should be set free; whether the name *Christian* is sufficient ground for condemnation, or whether specific crimes must be proved. Meanwhile, he has questioned those accused, freed those who were willing to sacrifice to the gods and the emperor, and executed those whose "obstinancy and unbending perversity" deserved in any case to be punished.

Trajan replies that Pliny has done well. There is no general rule of universal application. Christians are not to be sought out, but if accused and convicted they are to be punished. If they make it evident by an act of worship that they are no longer Christians, they should be released.

This correspondence makes it clear that there was no statute against Christianity as such, and that the imperial policy was to ignore it unless it was specifically brought to attention. But where it led to economic or civil disturbance, it could be proceeded against with the harshest measures.

---

[2] Cicero, *Laws*, III, iii, 8, C. W. Keyes (trans.), Loeb Classical Library, Putnam's, 1928, p. 467. *Their* refers, of course, to the administrators.

HEBREWS

The Epistle to the Hebrews is one of three books in the New Testament which reflect the hostility of the Roman state to Christianity. In former days, those to whom it was addressed had "endured a hard struggle with sufferings, sometimes being publicly exposed to abuse and affliction, and sometimes being partners with those so treated" (10:32–33). They had had compassion on prisoners and accepted the plundering of their property.

The author sees further trouble ahead. The final end, he thinks, is now approaching, and with it will come woes (including further persecution?) which they are not prepared to meet. They are of the second and third generation, and the glowing faith of their fathers has cooled. They are still immature, not yet ready for solid food. The author tries to rekindle their earlier zeal by a presentation of Christianity as the final religion, inherently superior to all others. They must not neglect such a great salvation.

The author begins by contrasting previous forms of worship and revelations with what is available through God's Son, far higher than the angels through whom the old covenant was given.[3] Even the faithfulness of Moses was that of a servant, not that of a son. As for the people whom Moses led, it is clear that they have been rejected by God. It is not they but the Christians who are to enter into the promised rest.

The purpose of religion is to maintain the proper relation between man and God. This relationship is continually marred by man's transgressions of God's will. For the writer of Hebrews, this is the essence of sin. (In this he differs from Paul, for whom sin was a basic alienation of man from God, consequent on man's failure to recognize his utter dependence on God, even in the

---

[3] The idea that the Law was given not directly by God but through angels is alluded to by Paul, and there are traces of it in Jewish sources. See Pesikta Rabbati 21 (103b) cited in Strack-Billerbeck, *Kommentar,* iii, 556 (on Gal. 3:19).

quest for righteousness.) Now God had entered into a covenant with his people, promising rest and blessing if they would obey his will, and had provided a sacrificial system by which transgressions of his will could be atoned for. The system culminated in the rites of the Day of Atonement, when the high priest went into the sanctuary and sprinkled blood as a means of purification of himself and of his people. The author of Hebrews asserts that this had now been done away with—not because it was wrong in principle, but because the sacrifice of God's own Son, once and for all had rendered the old system of repeated sacrifices useless.

This, however, was something more fundamental than just the replacement of the old system by a revised form. The author operates with a dualism, doubtless related ultimately to Platonism, though there is no reason to suppose that the author was himself a reader of Plato. His dualism is not so radical as to set the world we know in sharp opposition to the heavenly world. Rather, the relation between the two systems is that between the perfect pattern and the imperfect copy. The earthly tabernacle, the high priest, and the sacrifices of the old covenant were imperfect copies of the heavenly tabernacle, the true high priest, Jesus, and the one perfect, completely efficacious sacrifice.

Not only is the new covenant superior in its effectiveness, it is superior in its promises.

A roll is called of those who under the old covenant showed outstanding faith. Here, faith is confidence in the hoped-for outcome, the conviction that the fulfillment which is still unseen is nevertheless real. Now, the heroes of the old covenant never received what they looked forward to; but their failure to do so was not because of the failure of God's promises, but because God had always intended to bestow the heavenly reality, not the earthly copy. Now the time has come for them and those of the new covenant to share together in the heavenly Jerusalem, the city of the living God.

Christians are exhorted, then, to renew their faith in God's offer of the perfect salvation, even though they have to suffer for it. For those who have received the truth and turn away from it, there will be no second chance.

REVELATION

The book of Revelation can be understood only if it is seen in its immediate relevance to a situation somewhere about the end of the first century. The matters the seer was talking about he believed would "soon take place." (1:1.) The time was near. (22:10.) "He who testifies to these things says, 'Surely I am coming soon.' " (22:20.)[4]

Revelation belongs to a class of books known as *apocalypses*,[5] to which also belong the book of Daniel and parts of a number of other Old Testament books, as well as a series of Jewish books dating from the second century b.c. down into the first century of the Christian era. All of these arose when oppressors, usually foreign, were threatening God's people. Their purpose was to encourage God's people to be faithful in the face of persecution. In each case, the seer believed that he had been given a message that God was soon to take action to relieve his people's distress.

Such books are often supposed to present the essence of prophecy; but they have important differences from, as well as certain things in common with, such books as Amos, Hosea, Isaiah, and Jeremiah. In common, there is a faith in God's control of history and the ultimate victory of righteousness in a coming "day of the Lord." On the other hand, where the great prophets stressed the need of national repentance, and could only see doom if repentance was not forthcoming, the apocalyptists denounced the wickedness not of God's people but of their enemies, and threatened

---

[4] The theological problem presented by the obvious fact that what was predicted did not come to pass must be solved by an adequate conception of revelation, not by the violent warping of such plain words as *near* and *soon*.

[5] Actually, *revelation* is the Latin equivalent of the Greek word apocalypse.

doom for them. All this was expressed in the apocalypses in highly conventional language[6] and elaborate symbolism. It is this symbolism which makes these books seem so mysterious, and offers an opportunity for the fertile imagination to read all sorts of supposed meanings into the text. The requirement for sound interpretation is a wide and detailed knowledge of the history and literature of

Reconstruction of the temple and great altar of Pergamum. Pergamum was the center of emperor worship in Asia Minor. (The Bettmann Archive)

the time when the book was written. The notion that such books were deliberately written for the mystification of those who first read them is in itself a most improbable hypothesis, and one which gains currency only because few people have the necessary knowledge to put themselves in the place of the first readers. But it ought not to be surprising that, when this knowl-

_____

[6] Thus, Charles' commentary on Revelation has some sixteen pages listing in parallel columns phrases in Revelation and passages in other books, chiefly apocalypses, of which they are more or less directly reminiscent.

edge is neglected and so-called interpretation is really the reading into the text of the products of one's own imagination, there is no way of arriving at common agreement.

In the book of Revelation, however, some of the symbolism is fairly transparent. In the first place, the enemy is clearly identified as Rome, by the reference to the "seven hills on which the woman is seated" (17:9) and the statement "the woman that you saw is the great city which has dominion over the kings of the earth" (17:18). Rome is also depicted under another symbol, that of the beast rising out of the sea, which was allowed to have "authority over every tribe and people and tongue and nation" (13:1–8). The second beast is the worship of the emperor (13:11–12) that "makes the earth and all its inhabitants worship the first beast," and by various signs—pretended miracles of the kind frequently practiced at the pagan shrines of the period—convinces the ignorant of supernatural powers.

Though many details are still obscure, because even at best our knowledge of any part of the ancient past is limited, the main purpose and movement of thought in the book are also clear. The purpose is to encourage Christians, threatened by persecution because they refused to participate in the worship of the emperor, to remain faithful to their religion. The ground for encouragement is found in a vision which gives assurance that the end is at hand and that God's enemies will finally be overthrown with terrible slaughter.

The book opens with a series of short letters: a general letter recounting a vision of the risen Christ in the midst of his churches; then letters to seven (a symbolic number) churches in Asia Minor, assessing their strengths and weaknesses, with many allusions to specific local conditions. Thus, the lukewarm Church in Laodicea, a banking center, famous for white cloth and for a salve for sore eyes, is enjoined: "Therefore I counsel you to buy from me gold refined by fire, that you may be rich, and white garments to clothe you and keep the shame of your nakedness from being seen, and salve to anoint your eyes, that you may see." (3:18.)

The scene shifts to heaven, with a vision of the Almighty on his throne, with a scroll in his hand which can only be opened by Christ, the Lamb. As the seven seals are broken, one by one, various woes, to be inflicted on the inhabitants of the earth as the end approaches, are revealed. The seventh seal introduces a new series of woes proclaimed by seven trumpets. The two series of woes include, among other things: war, famine, pestilence, drought, earthquakes, cosmic disturbances, a supernatural plague of locusts. The trumpets, in turn, lead to the pouring out of seven bowls, culminating in the destruction of Rome, the harlot city. Christ, the Word of God, goes forth, with his heavenly hosts, to overthrow his enemies, treading "the wine press of the furious wrath of God the Almighty." Satan is bound; and Christ reigns for a thousand years over those who had been faithful during the persecution, those who had suffered martyrdom being raised from the dead for this purpose.

At the end of the thousand years, Satan is loosed, and there is a great battle in which he is finally overthrown. The rest of the dead are raised and judged; those whose names are not written in the book of life are thrown into the lake of fire. A new heaven and a new earth replace the old ones, with a new Jerusalem, where God himself will dwell in the midst of his people, without need of a temple. The book closes with an appeal: "The Spirit and the Bride say: 'Come'. . . . And let him who is thirsty come, let him who desires take the water of life without price. . . . He who testifies to these things says, 'Surely I am coming soon.' " (22:17, 20.)

In sum, though troublous times are just beginning, they are part of God's plan. His eventual victory is sure; and those who are faithful will receive their just reward while they enjoy the sight of the blood of their enemies being poured out like water.

I PETER

This book, which may even come from the same time and place as Revelation, is a very different sort of book. The meaning is clearly expressed rather than hidden under an obscure symbolism. The message, of course, is based on an assurance of God's coming triumph over the forces of evil; but it calls on Christians to be faithful in persecution, rejoicing insofar as they share in Christ's sufferings. There is no trace of the easy doctrine that Christ's followers may be expected to escape unjust suffering, any more than there is any trace of the doctrine that the time will come when they can gloat over their fallen enemies.

Actually, the specific references to persecution are confined to 4:12–5:11. Chapters 1:3 to 4:11 are more general. The references to being born anew (1:3, 23), to newborn babes (2:2), and to baptism which "*now* saves you" (3:21, italics added), have led many scholars to the conclusion that this part of the Epistle, at least, was originally a sermon (no doubt repeated on various occasions) to a group of newly baptized converts. Read with this in mind, these chapters seem very appropriate for this use; and the tone of them is more that of an address than of a letter. If this is so, however, it is hard to see why the author of the letter calling for faithfulness in persecution should have prefixed an old sermon, which presumably his readers had heard at their baptism. The suggestion that he wanted to recall them to that high moment is well enough; but this would hardly be the way to go about it. It would seem more plausible to think that two compositions by the same author were joined later, and provided with an address and close, claiming for the result the name of Peter.

Whatever the solution of this problem, the book as we have it, after the formal address, sets forth the greatness of the salvation which is the privilege of Christians. Now they must live in a way worthy of their redemption by the blood of Christ. They must live in love to one another, first of all.

But they must also conduct themselves among the Gentiles in such a way as to reflect credit on their religion. They must be subject to the emperor and the governors he sends out. Similarly, slaves are to submit to their masters, even if these are tyrannical and unjust. Christ's acceptance of unjust suffering is an example to be followed in such situations. The same principle is to govern the relations of husbands and wives. Finally, all are to live in unity of spirit.

Once more, Christ is set forth as an example to those who are reviled and abused for their devotion to righteousness. Christ's faithfulness to death has made possible their baptism. They must be ready to give an account of themselves to him who is to judge the living and the dead, for the end of all things is at hand. This part of the Epistle closes with a benediction (4:11).

In the remainder of the book, the threat of persecution is more vivid; but the principle of bearing it with patient suffering, after the example of Christ, is the same. The leaders, the elders, are especially exhorted to tend faithfully the flock of God in their charge, and the others to be subject to them. Those who humble themselves under God's hand will be exalted. "After you have suffered a little while, the God of all grace, who has called you to his eternal glory in Christ, will himself restore, establish, and strengthen you." (5:10.)

CHAPTER 17

Development of Organization

WHENEVER a number of people undertake to work together for a common goal, there must be some type of organization, some division of responsibility and function, and coordination of effort. This was as true of early Christianity as of anything else.

However, the system of Church government which was in existence by the latter half of the second century, and which endured without a rival until the Reformation, was of gradual growth and had no common origin. Much of the process by which it came into being is obscure. The one sure thing is that the later-developed form was not primitive, and was not propagated and imposed from Jerusalem, the original center, along with the gospel. In saying that the later form was not primitive, there is no intention of implying that there was another primitive form which was corrupted or displaced. The truth seems to be that different forms and practices arose at different times and places, and the types of Church order known as *episcopal,* from the key role played by bishops; *presbyterian,* where the chief role is played by a relatively democratic assembly of "presbyters" or "elders"; and *congregational,* where the local unit is self-governing and largely independent of other congregations—all seem to have been primitive in some place or other.

An understanding of this complex and disputed subject is perhaps best approached by a consideration of the functions which had to be performed.

First of all would be preaching, the proclamation of the good news of salvation, and the exposition of what this meant in terms of conduct. This was originally the function of apostles and prophets. These were never officials holding office in a settled congregation. The word *apostle* is used in a number of senses in the New Testament, but particularly of the twelve associated with Jesus. By Paul it is used for those who were witnesses of the Resurrection of Jesus. Prophets were men with a special gift of inspiration. To themselves and to their hearers, their messages seemed to be given to them by the Spirit, when and as the Spirit chose. These prophets formed a traveling ministry, moving from place to place, again under the direction of the Spirit. Several might be present at a given assembly for worship. Later, with the disappearance of the apostles and the appearance of "prophets" whose messages were judged to be in conflict with the true gospel, this condition was replaced by a different one, with the preaching done by a settled local official. The process by which this came about cannot be traced in any detail.

That the "ministry of the word" was carried on by traveling apostles and prophets did not mean that there was no local organization. "In the least organized communities decisions had to be made as to where meetings were to be held and when, who could conduct [or contribute to] services, who should visit certain sick persons, etc., etc.; there were accounts to be kept, records to be made out, bills to be paid—and so on indefinitely."[1]

For the performance of such functions, both Jewish and Greek practice offered forms and terminology. In Jewish practice,

[1] B. S. Easton, *The Pastoral Epistles*, Scribner's, 1947, pp. 223–224.

the "elders" played a leading role. Originally these were just what the name implies—the older members of the community —it being supposed then that age and experience gave a basis for sound judgment. The prime duty of elders was to administer the Law which had been given by God. In each city and village they constituted a *sanhedrin* ("session"). They sat as a civil and religious court, managed community property, and levied taxes. "In each community, no doubt, the elders were responsible for the upkeep and repairs of the synagogue, provided the rolls of the Law and other necessities for the services, and appointed the sexton [*hazzan*] (usually the schoolmaster as well) and the 'ruler' whose task was to see that the services were properly conducted."[2]

As officials charged with administration of the Law, the elders were responsible for the good discipline of the community; and, as necessarily students of the Law given by God in times past, they were guardians of tradition. It is important to notice that these elders had as such no function in the actual conduct of the synagogue worship.

In addition to the local sanhedrin, there were seventy-one "elders of Israel," presided over by the high priest, who constituted what is often called "the Sanhedrin," meeting in Jerusalem. It had various functions, most of which are irrelevant to the present discussion; but it also functioned as a supreme court.

It is easy to see how these functions of the Jewish elders covered a great many of the needs which had to be met in the growing Christian movement, and how, with its Jewish roots, it was natural that this institution was taken over. What is not so obvious is how "elders" or "presbyters"[3] came eventually to be those who conducted the services and did the preaching. It would seem most likely that this took place in connection with the conflict with false teaching, to which reference has fre-

[2] Easton, *op. cit.*, pp. 191 f.
[3] *Presbyteros* is Greek for "elder." It is the source of the English word *priest*.

quently been made. As Christianity developed and became conscious of its possession of a tradition of its own, the effort to exclude false teaching, which would be the duty of the elders, could easily lead to their undertaking to set forth the true teaching themselves. Still, modern Protestant emphasis on the sermon should not blind us to the fact that other functions of the later priest are not thus accounted for.

Meanwhile, we need to give attention to the Greek word *episkopos*. By derivation, this means "overseer" or "inspector"; but, as usual (contrary to popular opinion), etymology throws little light on the actual meaning of words. This one has a wide variety of meanings—indeed, it has been said "almost anyone who exercises almost any kind of authority over almost anything can be called an *episkopos*."[4] It is worth noting, however, that among the many uses of the word, there is its use for officers of administration and finance. This use would cover part of the functions of the elders in a Jewish Community. In addition, the Christian congregation placed special emphasis on giving to the poor, in a day when there was in most places no such organized governmental program of public welfare as there is today. The gifts were not, however, made directly by individuals to the needy, but brought as an "offering" to be distributed by members of the group. Soon, at any rate, this distribution would be the duty of regularly appointed officials, under the general supervision of the governing body. It would seem likely that it was in this connection that *diakonoi* were first employed. This word, which in the singular we write *deacon*, means primarily "servants" or "helpers." Their functions in the Christian communities seem to have been in many ways analogous to those of the modern social case worker.

If we turn now to the New Testament, we naturally go first to the oldest part of it, the writings of Paul. As is likely to be the case in the first enthusiasm of a new movement, we find there

[4] Easton, *op. cit.,* p. 222.

relatively little concern with the machinery of organization. (That is likely to come later, in the attempt to compensate for the lost enthusiasm of later generations.) In one important passage, Paul says, "God has appointed in the church first apostles, second prophets, third teachers, then workers of miracles, then healers, helpers, administrators, speakers in various kinds of tongues." (I Cor. 12:28.) His concern is not to define or regulate these functions, but to urge each to see his own God-given task as part of a larger whole. With regard to elders, bishops, and deacons the passage is notable chiefly because it fails to mention any of them. The whole context gives the impression that the functions of the Corinthian Church were carried on by persons "inspired" for them, rather than by duly appointed and ordained officials.

Perhaps in this light we should understand Paul's reference to the saints with *episkopoi* and *diakonoi* in the address at the beginning of the Epistle to Philippi (1:1). Two points may be noted. In the first place, both words are plural and neither has the definite article. He does not address "the bishops (and certainly not *the* bishop) and the deacons," as would be expected if these were the regular titles of duly appointed officials. Also noteworthy, in connection with the fact that *episkopoi* and *diakonoi* were associated with the raising and distribution of financial assistance, is the fact that in this letter (and this letter only) Paul is thanking a church for a gift of money.

It is true that Acts says that Paul and Barnabas "appointed elders for them in every church" (14:23), and that on his last visit to Ephesus he summoned the "elders of the church" (20:17) and later addresses these as *episkopoi;* but the difficulty is in knowing how far we can press such details in Acts, written as it was toward the end of the century. Nothing would have been easier than for the author to have read back the later situation into the earlier. If he had a source which said, for example, that Paul summoned the leaders (meaning really those who had a recognized gift of leadership) it would have been easy to supply *elders,* supposing that of course this was their proper title. In any case, the word cannot have its later technical meaning, since *elders* and *bishops* are here interchangeable.

The later situation is clearly pictured for us in the pastoral Epistles (I and II Timothy and Titus). Here we have mention of bishops, elders, and deacons, but the still later concept of these as constituting a graded system has not been reached. In these letters, as elsewhere in early Christian literature,[5] bishops and elders ("presbyters") are not sharply differentiated; but the two names can be used interchangeably, as is shown most plainly in Titus 1:5–7, which begins by speaking of elders and their qualifications, and continues "for a bishop, as God's steward, must be blameless." The "for" makes it clear that the author is continuing to talk about the same people, not shifting to another group. But despite this lack of sharp differentiation between elders and bishops, it is clear that these are now duly chosen and ordained officials.

THE PASTORAL EPISTLES

We turn now to the contents of these Epistles, written in the name of Paul to deal with a crucial situation in the way the author believed Paul would have done. The situation they face is clear enough in the letters themselves. The threat is from the sort of teaching which we have called *Gnostic.* Timothy is explicitly warned against "what is falsely called knowledge [*gnosis*]" (I Tim. 6:20). The nature of the threat is shown plainly in 4:1–5, which implies that the opponents deny that God is the creator, and hold an ascetic attitude to marriage and food. The defense of the Scriptures (that still meant only the Old Testament) in II Timothy 3:15–17 implies the typical Gnostic attack on the Old Testament, which, with the creation of the world of which it tells, they regarded as the work of an in-

[5] E.g., Acts 20; I Clem. 44.

ferior deity, not the true God. Their doctrine, called *Docetism,* that Christ had no true human body but only the appearance of one, is attacked in I Timothy 3:16: "he was manifested in the flesh." II Timothy 4:4 refers to the elaborate Gnostic mythology which attempted to explain man's present predicament and how he could be delivered from it.

The letters attack all this in various ways. There is, first, direct exhortation, ostensibly for Timothy and Titus, but intended for every hearer, to avoid such things. However, such Gnosticism is especially to be combatted by the appointment of suitable church officials—*episkopoi* or *presbyteroi,* and *diakonoi.* Their qualifications are carefully described: "Now a bishop must be above reproach, married only once, temperate, sensible, dignified, hospitable, an apt teacher, no drunkard, not violent but gentle, not quarrelsome, and no lover of money. He must manage his own household well, keeping his children submissive and respectful in every way; for if a man does not know how to manage his own household, how can he care for God's church? He must not be a recent convert, or he may be puffed up with conceit and fall into the condemnation of the devil; moreover he must be well thought of by outsiders, or he may fall into reproach and the snare of the devil." (I Tim. 3:2–7.)

Similar qualifications are prescribed for deacons.

Especially are the leaders urged to be careful to preserve "the faith," "sound doctrine" (I Tim. 1:10; 4:6; 6:3, etc.); to guard what has been entrusted to them (I Tim. 6:20); to "follow the pattern of the sound words which you have heard" (II Tim. 1:13).

This faith which is to be so carefully guarded is something quite different from the abandonment of self to God which Paul meant by the term, as it is also different from the assurance of what is not now present, which was its meaning for the author of Hebrews. For the author of the Pastorals, it is something which can be expressed in words, and taught, which can be mistakenly identified with false knowledge (*gnosis*). He is sure that Christ died for our salvation, but he says nothing of faith as the means by which a man appropriates this salvation. Faith and "sound teaching (doctrine)" are here closely akin.

One may even say that, for the writer of the Pastorals, "sound teaching" is practically Christian teaching uncorrupted by Gnosticism. As far as the emphasis is not on some of the Gnostic corruptions, the really meaningful part of Christian teaching seems primarily ethical.

> But as for you, teach what befits sound doctrine. Bid the older men be temperate, serious, sensible, sound in faith, in love, and in steadfastness. Bid the older women likewise to be reverent in behavior, not to be slanderers or slaves to drink; they are to teach what is good, and so train the young women to love their husbands and children, to be sensible, chaste, domestic, kind, and submissive to their husbands, that the word of God may not be discredited. Likewise urge the younger men to control themselves. Show yourself in all respects a model of good deeds, and in your teaching show integrity, gravity, and sound speech that cannot be censured, so that an opponent may be put to shame, having nothing evil to say of us. Bid slaves to be submissive to their masters and to give satisfaction in every respect; they are not to be refractory, nor to pilfer, but to show entire and true fidelity, so that in everything they may adorn the doctrine of God our Savior. (Titus 2:1–10.)

Christ "gave himself for us to redeem us from all iniquity and to purify for himself a people of his own who are *zealous for good deeds.*" (Titus 2:13, italics added.) In Paul's mind, being zealous for good deeds was the antithesis of faith.

II AND III JOHN

These two brief letters represent another phase of the struggle against Gnostic tendencies. They belong here because they also reflect the effort to deal with the problem in terms of disciplinary action rather than by argument against opposing positions.

II John is addressed to a Church and its members ("the elect lady and her children"). III John is addressed to an individual member of the same Church. The letters show the operation of the power of the leaders to exclude persons of wrong views from a hearing in the local Church. II John warns the Church not to receive those who do not acknowledge the coming of Jesus Christ *in the flesh* (as opposed, not to those who deny that Jesus was the Christ, but to those who assert that he had no real fleshly body). Anyone coming with this latter message is not even to be greeted politely. III John, written to a friend, reveals the situation more fully. Actually, a certain Diotrephes seems to be in control in this Church and is using his power on the other side! The recipient of the letter is commended for receiving the right people in spite of Diotrephes; and the writer, who is evidently a man of considerable authority himself, threatens to come and deal with Diotrephes in person. One wonders what the final outcome was. Perhaps the preservation of the letters indicates that Diotrephes was overthrown.

~~~~~~

CHAPTER 18

Books Presenting Christian Teaching

T HE BOOKS of the New Testament may be classified for convenience into Pauline writings, books reflecting a background of
persecution, books reflecting the developing organization, and
books presenting Christian teaching. These categories will be
helpful only if they are not taken too seriously, for actually they
are not really sharply defined; and they represent our point of
view, not that of the original authors. Whoever wrote Hebrews,
for example, did not undertake his task thinking, "Now I am
going to write a book with a background of persecution."

These cautions need stating particularly in connection with
the present group of books; for, in a sense, all the books in the
New Testament are presentations of Christian teaching. However, in the Epistle of James, the Epistles of Jude and II Peter,
the Synoptic Gospels, and John's Gospel and first Epistle, the
primary intent is to instruct, to answer questions in the minds
of believers, to deal with arguments advanced against Christian
claims, and to combat what are believed to be misunderstandings
or perversions of Christian teaching. In the books just mentioned, there is not always a sharp division between these various
approaches; but, in general, the emphasis is rather on teaching

than on appeal or on special problems like the organizational machinery of the Church.

JAMES

This book represents a very practical outlook, in many ways similar to that of the Synoptic Gospels. This is seen in its recurring insistence on *doing;* the value it sets on poverty, with warnings to the rich; the injunctions to prayer; the warning against oaths (practically a quotation from Matthew); injunctions for restraint in judging others and against unkind speech; and for complete devotion to God.

On the other hand, there are significant omissions. Nothing is said about the incidents of Jesus' life; the term "Son of man," by which Jesus refers to himself according to the Synoptics, is missing; the kingdom of Heaven (or God) is never mentioned. There is nothing to indicate that the author attached any special significance to the death of Christ.

The latter part of the second chapter seems clearly directed against a misunderstood Paulinism, though whether the misunderstanding is that of James or of his readers is not altogether clear. Certainly Paul would not have recognized faith as genuine which did not find expression in concrete deeds; but it is equally clear that he would never have put this in the form, "faith without works is dead." The reference to Abraham as having proved his faith by his deed in preparing to sacrifice Isaac recalls Paul's use of the story of Abraham to establish the fact that men became acceptable to God through faith, not by obedience to requirements which had not yet been put before Abraham. The illustration was a striking one and must have been often repeated, so that James might have encountered it without reading Paul. However, there are a number of phrases in James strongly reminiscent of Romans. If James knew Romans, he evidently found much in it which appealed to him.

It is hard to make a clear-cut outline of the book. In addition to topics which have already been mentioned, it calls for endurance under trial, warns against the power and danger of the tongue, and speaks of the imminent coming of the Lord. Moffatt gives the following outline; and it will be a useful exercise to compare it with the Epistle itself to see how adequately it succeeds in gathering together the various threads:

> The homily begins with five paragraphs loosely strung upon the thread of trial or temptation (i:1–16), followed by reflections on the true word and worship (i. 17–27), which open up into a denunciation of some abuses in contemporary worship (ii. 1–13, iv. 11–12). Then comes an indignant refutation of a merely formal faith (ii. 14–26, iv. 17). But excess of words is as fatal as lack of deeds in religion, and James now proceeds to expose the vices of the tongue (iii. 1–12), closing with a passage on the true wisdom of life (iii. 13–18), as opposed to the factiousness and worldliness which are rampant in the church (iv. 1–10). He then censures scheming traders (iv. 13–16) and oppressive landlords (v. 1–6), and exhorts the poor, patient Christians to be of good cheer (v. 7–11). Some scattered counsels (v. 12, 13, 14–18, 19–20) conclude the homily.[1]

JUDE AND II PETER

These two late letters, the second dependent on the first, are specifically directed against false teaching of the Gnostic variety.

Jude is a brief, straightforward denunciation of the "ungodly persons who pervert the grace of our God into licentiousness and deny our only Master and Lord, Jesus Christ." This opposes the tendency of Gnostics to infer from their basic dualism that what the body did made no difference to the soul, and that Jesus Christ was not a real flesh and blood man. In his denuncia-

[1] J. Moffatt, "The Epistle of James," in *The General Epistles,* Moffatt New Testament Commentary, Harper, n.d., pp. 3–4.

tions, the writer reminds his hearers of the fate of Sodom and
Gomorrah, Cain, Balaam, and Korah, and refers to a legend
found in a Jewish apocalypse known as the Assumption of
Moses, and to a passage in Enoch, another Jewish apocalypse,
prophesying judgment on the ungodly. With this is put a prophecy ascribed to the apostles that such perversions are to be expected in the last time. The hearers are exhorted to build themselves up in the holy faith, keep themselves in the love of God,
and wait for the mercy of Jesus Christ.

II Peter has essentially the same message and even borrows
the identical language in spots. The denunciations and descriptions of the opponents are more extensive, though no more
explicit as to the details of the false teaching—except that those
opposed in this book make a point of denying the reality of a
second coming by Christ, saying that time has passed, the original
apostles have all died, and nothing has happened. To this the
author replies that God's time scale is different from ours, but
the day of the Lord is sure to come.

One thing which adds to the length of the book is the labored
effort to bolster the fiction that the book is by Peter. He states his
purpose to leave a reminder of what he always has told them, and
refers to his position as an eyewitness to the Transfiguration of
Jesus. He evidently knows of the existence of I Peter and refers
to "this second letter" he now writes, though one of the certainties in a sometimes uncertain field is that these two letters
cannot possibly be by the same author.

Interesting is the reference toward the end to the letters "of
our beloved brother Paul" (3:15–16). He is eager to claim Paul's
support, but it is clear that his opponents are using Paul's letters,
too. Paul's criticisms of the effort to obtain righteousness in God's
sight by trying to observe the Law were obviously being distorted
—as they were in Paul's own day—into a justification for
scandalous conduct. So II Peter says of Paul's letters, "There are
some things in them hard to understand, which the ignorant and

unstable twist to their own destruction, as they do the other scriptures" (3:16). But forewarned, his readers should be fore-armed.

THE SYNOPTIC GOSPELS

MARK

The Synoptic Gospels have already been considered as sources for a knowledge of Jesus. They now need to be considered in their own right. They were not written with the conscious inten-tion of preserving for all time the knowledge about Jesus avail-able to their authors, but to meet certain definite needs of Christians at the time of their composition. It is a mistake to call them biographies.

For this problem, the questions of date and place of composi-tion assume much less importance than might be supposed. One might naturally expect that, if we knew when and where Mark was written, we would then be able to place it in its setting and see more clearly its purpose. But this is not actually the case. Suppose we could be absolutely certain that, as is often held, Mark was written in Rome about A.D. 70; this would really throw little light on Mark, for the fact is that we know next to nothing about the Church in Rome at that time. If these facts could be established, they would throw much more light on the Church at Rome than they would on the meaning of Mark. We shall have to take Mark (and the other Synoptics) as they stand, with-out knowing, to start with, the situation in which they arose.

Even a superficial reading of Mark makes it plain that its author was concerned to present Jesus as the Messiah. But we cannot stop here. All of the books in the New Testament are concerned, in some way or another, with presenting Jesus as the Messiah. Our problem is to discover the specific features of Mark's presentation, and what determined them.

It is sometimes supposed that Mark and various other books in the New Testament were written with the purpose of demonstrating the fundamentals of Christian belief to unbelievers. The truth is that no book in the New Testament was written chiefly for unbelievers. All the books presuppose that their readers will be chiefly people who already consider themselves, in some sense, Christians. Why, then, for example, write a book to present Jesus as the Messiah? Surely all Christians acknowledged him as that to start with. Nor can it be said that the book attempts to correct a false notion of the nature of Jesus' Messiahship.

What the book really does is to answer two objections to the proposition that Jesus was the Messiah. They are objections which would be raised by opponents, Jewish and pagan; but they are really answers for the faithful, not for the opponents. The objections were two. Why, if Jesus was the Messiah, was he not recognized by those who were expecting the Messiah; and, second, how could a man who had been executed by the Roman provincial government as a disturber of the peace be the Messiah? It is not likely that Mark's answers would have satisfied the objectors, but they satisfied the believers and put to rest the disturbing doubts raised by the questions.

In essence, Mark's answer was that Jesus *was* significantly recognized, that his execution by the Roman governor was actually carried out unwillingly, and that the whole process of rejection and execution was part of a divine plan which Jesus knew and made known to his disciples before it happened, though they—like later objectors—found this difficult to comprehend. Only after the Resurrection did they understand it. Finally, it is asserted that the future will shortly vindicate all this, when Jesus returns as he promised.

The book opens with the preaching of John the Baptist, thus from the beginning relating the mission of Jesus to the divine plan and telling of Jesus' recognition by God himself. A few begin to follow him; and when he heals, supernatural beings are ready to testify to his true status, though he forbids them to do so. Meanwhile, in a series of controversies, the opposition of the Jewish leaders is aroused. Jesus chooses a group of twelve to accompany him and share his work of healing and teaching. He performs many wonderful deeds, and finally is recognized as Messiah by those closest to him—though they did not then understand that his Messiahship implied suffering and death. He tells them this, but they remain uncomprehending. He goes up to Jerusalem and is hailed by the crowd; but due to the opposition of the leaders, the crowd turns away and the Roman governor is forced to accede to their demand that he be crucified, and he is executed. At the execution a Roman soldier acknowledges that he is a divine being ("a son of God"). Before his execution he had predicted his escape from the grave and his return to gather his elect throughout the world. The book closes with the visit of women to the grave, where they meet supernatural beings who assure them that Jesus has risen and will return as he said.[2]

MATTHEW

Neither Mark nor Matthew is a biography of Jesus. But while Mark is really an answer to what are basically theological questions, Matthew is a handbook of God's new revelation, the new "Law" for his new people. It is "the book of the generations of Jesus Christ, the son of David, the son of Abraham." That is to say, it is the book of the spiritual descendants[3] of Jesus, the Messiah's people, the true heirs of Abraham.

---

[2] Mark 16:9–20 is not in the oldest and best manuscripts and is generally acknowledged by scholars to be a later addition to the text. It is then often supposed that the book originally had a different ending which was lost. Of this there is no evidence, and the belief rests on our assumption that an early Gospel would necessarily have included accounts of the actual appearance of the risen Jesus. But though from the literary point of view the ending is rather awkward, the book really comes to a perfectly good climax in thought; and no hypothetical "lost ending" needs to be looked for.

[3] This seems more likely than the interpretation of what the King James Version called *generations,* as "ancestors." The Greek word is the same word which appears in the Septuagint of Genesis 5:1, etc., and 2:4, where it clearly means, as the Hebrew lexicon says of the original word, "an account of men and their descendants" and "an account of heaven and earth and what proceeded from them." (Brown-Driver-Briggs, *Hebrew Lexicon,* Houghton Mifflin, 1907, p. 410.)

The book is carefully and systematically arranged. The core of it is found in five large sections of teaching, each of which is preceded by a block of narrative material related to the theme of the teaching, and concluding with the regular formula "after Jesus had finished these sayings (words, parables)," he proceeded to something else (Matt. 7:28, 11:1, 13:53, 19:1, 26:1— the last has, significantly, "when he had finished *all* these sayings"). Concerned as Matthew is with the relation of the teachings of Jesus to the Law, it is hardly farfetched to see a deliberate analogy of these five central sections to the five books of the Mosaic Law, or to attach significance to the fact that Jesus gave the great Sermon which introduces these from a mountain, as God gave the bulk of the Law from Sinai.

The book opens with a prologue which tells the story of the divine origin of Jesus, with stress on the fulfillment of the prophecies that show him to be the true founder of a new spiritual race.

The first of the main divisions deals with the *foundation of the new community*. After a period of preparation, Jesus comes forward in Galilee of the Gentiles to proclaim the kingdom and summon men to enter it. In the discourse section, the Sermon on the Mount, he then lays down the conditions for entering it, contrasting old and new righteousness and old and new piety.

The new division which begins at Chapter 8 and extends through 10 has as its subject the *promulgation of the new community*. The narrative gives typical incidents in the career of Jesus which foreshadow the experiences of those who were later to undertake to spread the gospel. The division closes with specific injunctions to those who would be the missionaries to gather the new community.

Division three deals with the *present apparent insignificance of the new community* of Jesus' spiritual descendants. The incidents show how Jesus was faced with bewilderment, indifference, and violent opposition, and the hostility of the divinely blinded leaders of the old community of heirs of the promises. The chapter of parables (Chapter 13), which is the discourse section of this division, explains how this hidden community must eventually be revealed in triumph, and the consequent importance of loyalty to it.

The subject of the fourth division is the *faith of the community* and how the community must act to preserve it. The narrative depicts first the lack of faith, even among Jesus' followers; then, in Peter's confession, the dawning of faith; and the confirmation of it in the Transfiguration and the following healing. The discourse deals with the problem of the community's exercise of its disciplinary powers, especially with the problem of those who scorn the simple faith in the Messiah.

The fifth book or division deals with the *final rejection of the old community*. In the narrative portion, the standards are announced, while the leaders of the old Israel seal their fate in their controversies with Jesus during the last week. In a discourse which matches in length the opening discourse, Jesus proclaims the fate of the religious leaders and goes on to describe the course of the judgment soon to take place, and gives injunctions to his followers so that they may be prepared when the judgment comes.

The conclusion relates the temporary victory of the powers of evil, which, however, quickly issues in the triumph of the Resurrection, by which the hopes of the community of Jesus' followers are assured. The book closes with the injunction to go throughout the world accepting men into the new fellowship of those who obey Jesus' injunctions, to whom he promises his continued presence.

Such is the "book of the origin of Jesus and of the community which he brought into being."

LUKE–ACTS

As has been pointed out, these two books were planned as the two "volumes" of a single work. The suggestion has sometimes been made that the author planned a sequel which would tell what happened to Paul when his case came to trial. Others have suggested that Acts was written before the trial was over. Both of these suggestions grow out of the fact that Acts does not end the way we assume it should. They presuppose that the purpose of the book is to give information for its own sake; and because it does not give interesting and important information we would like to have, we infer that something is lacking.

No doubt Luke undertook to give detailed and accurate information; but he was hardly interested in providing the necessary facts for candidates proposing to take a true-false, multiple-choice achievement test for admission to the kingdom of God. In considering Luke's purpose it would seem natural, perhaps, to begin with the preface, intended of course as the preface to both volumes. But prefaces, then as now, were highly conventional; and what Luke says is just the sort of thing generally said in contemporaneous prefaces. This does not imply that Luke does not really mean what he says there, but it may well be that he has not said all he might have said. Did he have any deeper purpose than a Hellenistic historian who undertook to entertain and instruct his readers?

The situation becomes plainer if, instead of looking at the beginning of his work, we look at the end. Paul has arrived in Rome, capital of the great empire which seems to be the final achievement of the human race. For the last time he presents the gospel of the Messiahship of Jesus to the Jewish community. He gets a prevailingly negative response. So, after a reference to Isaiah's statement that "this people" would never understand (Is. 6:9–10), Paul concludes: "Let it be known to you then that this salvation of God has been sent to the Gentiles; they will listen." He then preaches the gospel openly and unhindered to those who will receive it.

These two volumes, then, are the story of how the promises which God had originally made to Abraham and his descendants in the literal sense had become the possession not of the Jews but of the Gentiles. When Luke wrote, Christianity had become for all practical purposes a completely Gentile religion—a fact which certainly needed explanation, since Christianity based its claims on the events and prophecies of the Old Testament, which are presented there as made to Jews.

The closing scene in Acts is simply the climax of a long series of rejections. Book I, which we call Luke, is the story of how the divine Savior was rejected by the Jews and put to death at their instigation. The theme is announced in the carefully constructed scene of the rejection at Nazareth at the very beginning of Jesus' ministry. Jesus is cast out of the city and almost killed then and there because he quoted the Old Testament to show that, even in the days of Elijah and Elisha, God was concerned with the welfare of Gentiles like the widow of Zarephath near Sidon, and Naaman the Syrian. Actually, there seems to be little in the teaching of Jesus to support this interpretation of Luke; and in telling the story of Jesus' career, he uses the materials provided by Mark and what we have called Q, plus a series of valuable parables, including the Good Samaritan and the Prodigal Son. In his material he can evidently find no particular evidence of Jesus' interest in Gentiles; but he does give two favorable comments on Samaritans, and omits the story of Jesus' apparently reluctant healing of the Syro-Phoenician woman's daughter, given in Mark and Matthew. The role of the Jewish leaders in the execution of Jesus is stressed.

The theme of the second volume is also announced in a carefully constructed scene, the coming of the Holy Spirit at Pentecost, when the gospel was proclaimed to representatives of peoples throughout the world. Since Jesus' death was after all "according to the definite plan and foreknowledge of God" (Acts 2:23), the Jews are now offered another chance, and many respond. The leaders are still opposed, however; and when men of Gentile antecedents (the Hellenists) become active, there is severe persecution, which nevertheless leads to the spread of the Church to Samaria and then, under Peter's auspices, to the Gentiles. According to Acts, the decision to accept Gentiles had already been reached before Paul's conversion. The last sixteen chapters are the story of Paul, the great missionary, who carried the gospel first to Asia Minor and then, in response to a heavenly vision, across to Europe. Throughout this story Paul continues to offer the gospel to the Jews but is regularly rejected. Finally, on a visit to Jerusalem, he is beset in the Temple by hostile Jews who are determined to kill him. He is arrested there and, on appeal, taken to Rome, where the story of the Jewish rejection of the salvation which God offered through Jesus reaches its climax. The Jews have rejected God and God rejects them. It has become clear, once and for all, that the good news has become the heritage of the Gentiles.

If this is the main theme of Luke's work, it does not always lie on the surface and does not exclude other interests. Luke's presentation of his material in the Gospel is determined in general by what has come to him in his sources. He does not warp it violently to make it illustrate his theme in detail. Moreover, he has two secondary themes. The first is that Jesus, in all respects, represents true Judaism. So if Jesus pointed out God's concern for the Gentiles, he quoted Old Testament precedent. It is the Jews who, as always in the past, are false to God's real requirements. Again, Luke is careful to point out that whenever Christianity had come to the attention of Roman authorities, whether in the person of Jesus or of Paul, the authorities, when they had understood the situation, had found no fault with Christianity. Pilate, the Philippian magistrates, Gallio the proconsul, the Asiarchs at Ephesus, the procurator Felix (though his hope of a bribe prevented him from releasing Paul), the procurator Festus —none found anything to condemn. Even the puppet-king Herod Agrippa (Jewish at least nominally) is reported as saying to the Roman procurator after hearing Paul, "This man could have been set free if he had not appealed to Caesar." (Acts

26:32.) In view of the growing hostility of Rome to the new religion toward the end of the century, this stress on the precedents set by former Roman officials is hardly coincidence.

THE GOSPEL OF JOHN

The author of the Fourth Gospel states his purpose thus: "These [things] are written that you may believe that Jesus is the Christ, the Son of God, and that believing you may have life in his name." (Jn. 20:31.) To characterize Jesus as the Christ (that is, the Messiah) is to set him in the framework of Jewish thought; to call him son of God is to relate him to the quite different concepts of the Gentile world.

The deliberate choice of these two characterizations indicates the author's familiarity with both worlds of thought and his conviction that Jesus was the fulfillment of the hopes of both. Probably his own world was one in which a fusion of the two cultures was already well advanced. We cannot understand the book without taking these two aspects of his viewpoint into account.

This observation is necessary because the very obvious differences in point of view between this Gospel and the Synoptic Gospels have often led to the attempt to account for the differences by the supposition that they are due simply to the fact that John's Gospel is wholly Greek in outlook while the other three are Jewish. Because there are, after all, elements in the Fourth Gospel which are unmistakably Jewish, this has led to a reaction which is just as blind to the presence of Hellenistic elements. The truth, this time at least, lies somewhere in between these extremes.

SOURCES

It is natural to suppose that part, at least, of the difference between this Gospel and the other three is due to a difference in sources, though the general opinion is that the author of the Fourth Gospel was acquainted with one or more of the Synoptics, and he has often been credited with the deliberate attempt to correct or supplement them. But when the evidence for these assertions is sought, it is hard to find; and what is offered only seems relevant because of prior question-begging assumptions. Thus, John's knowledge of Mark is asserted on the basis of such details as the common use of a rare word (translated "pure" by RSV) in the story of the anointing of Jesus (John 12:1–8, Mark 14:3–9), and resemblances in the stories of the Feeding of the Five Thousand (John 6:5–14; Mark 6:35–44). There is nothing here that cannot be accounted for in terms of common unwritten tradition; and the fact is that the differences are more striking than the resemblances. Even more flimsy is the "evidence" supposedly supporting John's acquaintance with Luke, which is hardly more substantial than the fact that they both know of Mary and Martha, though what they specifically say about them does not overlap at all.

Other attempts have been made to distinguish sources within the Gospel by means of internal evidence, but none of them has ever succeeded in gaining very wide acceptance. No doubt the author had sources, and sources which were independent of the Synoptic Gospels; but just what they were we simply do not know.

BACKGROUND

That the background of this Gospel included both Jewish and Hellenistic elements has already been stated. This assertion must now be made more specific.

The presence of Hellenistic elements is unmistakable. Augustine, in a famous statement, says:

> . . . thou procuredst for me, by means of a certain man, puffed up with a most unreasonable pride, to see certain books

of the Platonists, translated out of Greek into Latin. And therein I read, not indeed in the self-same words, but to the very same purpose, persuaded by many reasons, and of several kinds, that In the beginning was the Word, and the Word was with God, and that Word was God: the same was in the beginning with God. All things were made by him, and without him was nothing made. In that which was made, was life, and the life was the light of men. And the light shined in the darkness, and the darkness comprehended it not. And for that the soul of man, though it gives testimony of the light, yet itself is not that light, but the Word, God himself, is that true light that lighteth every man that cometh into the world; and that he was in the world, and the world was made by him, and the world knew him not. But that he came unto his own, and his own received him not, but as many as received him, to them gave he power to become the sons of God, as many as believed in his name: all this did I not read there.

There also did I read that God the Word was not born of flesh nor of blood, nor of the will of man, nor of the will of the flesh, but of God. But that the Word was made flesh and dwelt among us, did I not read there.[4]

This is striking testimony to the fact that when Augustine wrote, such cardinal Johannine ideas as the creative activity of the divine Word (Logos), the spiritual nature of the Word, and the Word as the source of life and light, unrecognized in the world, were current ideas outside Christianity. There is no reason for supposing that these ideas were derived from Christian sources, and in the Hermetic literature they can be traced to a considerably earlier date. In this literature we find a number of points which indicate a background of thought shared with the Fourth Gospel. In addition to the assertion of the existence of spiritual reality, the Logos doctrine, the stress on life and light, the contrast between light and darkness already mentioned, we

[4] Augustine, *Confessions,* vii, 9, William Watts (trans.), Loeb Classical Library, Putnam's, 1919, vol. I, pp. 365, 367.

find many other similarities, extending to details of expression. For both, "rebirth" and "knowledge" are fundamental, though the Johannine concepts have their unique features. The expression *the Son of man* is an interesting example. In the Synoptic Gospels this phrase has its normal Jewish connotation of the supernatural judge at the end of the age. In John's Gospel the phrase appears, indeed, but its connotations are much more nearly those of the "archetypal man" to which Paul's doctrine of the first Adam is related, and which is also found in the Hermetic literature. There is no doubt that in all these cases the Johannine concepts have their own individual character and are by no means simply taken over unchanged by John. But that the author was unacquainted with this general type of thought is incredible. Indeed, it is hardly possible to doubt that one of the purposes of the author was to speak to just such people, leading them to what he believed was the true meaning of what they had partially grasped.

If we use the word *Gnostic* in the broad sense, as referring to a type of religion which emphasizes salvation by knowledge, then this Hermetic literature represents one of the higher phases of Gnosticism. At the other extreme is the religion known as *Mandaism*. The Mandeans, found in lower Mesopotamia, are the only Gnostic group to survive to modern times. The central figure of this system is known as *Manda d'Hayye,* and this expression is simply Aramaic for "knowledge of life." The sect is anti-Christian and gives an important place to John the Baptist. Some scholars hold that this sect stems from a group of followers of John the Baptist, but it seems significant that the references to him are found in obviously late strata of their literature. In expression, there are certainly some striking parallels to the Fourth Gospel: "the true envoy am I, in whom is no lie"; "a vine are we, a tree of life, a tree which cannot lie"; "a Shepherd am I who loves his sheep, I keep watch over my sheep and my lambs . . . I bring them into the fold, the good fold, and then with me they find pasture."[5] A few scholars believe that this literature is dependent on the Fourth Gospel, as is chronologically quite possible; but it seems more probable that the two have some common roots rather than that either influenced the other directly.

That there is some relationship between the Gospel of John and Gnosticism is plain. On its face, nothing could be more Gnostic than the saying, "This is eternal life, that they know thee the only true God, and Jesus Christ whom thou hast sent." (John 17:3.) On the other hand, John seems to take great pains to avoid or combat Gnostic tendencies, even in the narrower sense. The assertion that the physical world is (through the Logos) God's creation, and that Jesus had a real physical body as shown by his thirst, his weariness, the nail prints, and the spear thrust, are in direct opposition to Gnostic principles. Instead of telling of Simon of Cyrene bearing Jesus' cross, the explicit statement is made that Jesus went out bearing his own cross. In view of the fact that some Gnostics asserted that, since a nonphysical being could hardly be crucified, it had actually been Simon of Cyrene who hung on the cross, having been miraculously changed to look like Jesus, this Johannine variation from the Synoptics looks like a deliberate attempt to refute the Gnostic assertion. Striking also is the failure of the noun *gnosis* to appear in the book, although the corresponding verb appears more frequently than in any other part of the New Testament. This looks like deliberate avoidance of a word which was in bad odor among Christians when the book was written, just as *communism* is in bad odor with us today. Similarly, the word for "faith" is completely lacking, though the corresponding verb meaning "to believe," "have faith," "trust," is almost as frequent in the Fourth Gospel as in all the rest of the New Testament.[6] This may also have been a word with an undesirable

[5] Quoted in G. H. C. Macgregor and A. C. Purdy, *Jew and Greek, Tutors unto Christ,* Scribner's, 1936, p. 326.

[6] More accurately, the ratio of occurrences in John to those everywhere else in the New Testament is about 2 to 3.

connotation. Later Gnostics at least contrasted their "knowl-edge" with the inferior "faith" of the common Christians.

PHILO

Perhaps the best evidence that the type of thought found in the Hermetic writings is much older than the writings in which it has come down to us is found in the writings of Philo of Alexandria, who wrote before A.D. 50. But whereas the Hermetic type of religion can be described as Hellenistic with influences from the Old Testament and Judaism, Philo's religion, as has been shown, is Judaism with strong Greek influences. Most of the concepts that John shares with such writers, Philo also shares—though just as for John, so for Philo, they have charac-teristic and important differences. All three move in the same intellectual climate.

That John was acquainted with the works of Philo has often been claimed; but while this is possible it is certainly not proved. Nevertheless, because of their common Jewish roots, John is at many points closer to Philo than to the Hermetic writers. The relationship to the Old Testament is closer for Philo and John, of course. They share a number of symbols in addition to *light,* especially *water* and *the shepherd.* For Philo *faith* includes an element of personal trust and belief in God's revelation, which is related to the Johannine concept rather than the Hermetic. Similar is the emphasis on love. "To live according to God is defined by Moses as loving him."[7] "For both of them, eternal life is to know God—the one true God, as they both say—and for both of them such knowledge is, in part at least, a matter of faith and love. And when Philo contrasts the slavish fear of God as the attitude of those who do not really know him, with the love of God which is the attitude of those who know and are his friends, we are very near indeed to the language of the Fourth

---

[7] Philo, *On the Posterity and Exile of Cain,* 69, F. H. Colson and G. H. Whittaker (trans.), Loeb Classical Library, Harvard University Press, 1929, vol. II, p. 367.

Gospel: 'No longer do I call you servants, for the servant does not know what his master is doing; but I have called you friends, for all that I have heard from my Father I have made known to you.' (John 15:15.) This conception of the knowledge of God, however, is in Philo somewhat uneasily associated with a type of mysticism which finds its goal in pure awareness of absolute being."[8]

Particularly important is Philo's conception of the Logos. If we take the points which Augustine says he found in the "Platonists," almost every one of them can be illustrated from the works of Philo. But striking as are the resemblances to John, the differences are equally striking. For while Philo occasionally personified the Logos, it is never for him a real personal being. And that the Logos could become flesh and dwell among us is far from his thought.

PALESTINIAN JUDAISM

If it is clear that the author of the Fourth Gospel was at home in the type of religious thought reflected in different ways in the Hermetic literature and Philo, it is equally clear that he was also familiar with Judaism—not simply with the content of the Old Testament and some of the technicalities of the rabbinic interpretation of it, but also with some of the same concepts found in the sectarian literature of Qumran.

Central in this interpretation is, of course, the concept of the divine revelation of what is required of man, the Torah or Law. There are some dozen references to the Law in the Fourth Gospel. Now, Torah in Hebrew and *nomos* in Greek may both be translated "law" in English; but the Hebrew and the Greek words (not to mention the English) have, in general, different ranges of connotation. The significant point is that in

---

[8] C. H. Dodd, *The Interpretation of the Fourth Gospel*, Cambridge University Press, 1954, p. 65. (English translation of Dodd's Greek citations supplied.)

this Gospel the Greek word is used with just the connotations of the Hebrew word, without a trace of the other meanings it has in Greek, and which crop out, for example, in the usage of Paul and James, as well as in Philo.

As for technical details, a few may be cited by way of illustration. In the first place, the formula for citing Scripture, "It is written in the Law," is a translation of a rabbinic formula. John 7:22–24 reveals a familiarity with details of the interpretation of the Sabbath law. Again a passage like John 1:17, "the Law was given through Moses, grace and truth came through Jesus Christ," recalls the Midrash on Psalm 25:10: " 'All the paths of the Lord are mercy and truth': By mercy is meant deeds of loving kindness, and by truth is meant the Law of the Lord."[9] Then there is the idea of the Scripture (Torah) as the source of life (cf. John 5:39). Especially important are the references to the Messiah. This is the only book in the New Testament where the Hebrew word *Messiah* is transliterated into Greek and its equivalence with the Greek *Christos* pointed out. In addition to references to the Messiah's royal position and the expectation that he will be of Davidic lineage (also found in the Synoptic Gospels), there are references to the rabbinic doctrine that when the Messiah appears no one will know his origin, and that when he comes he will remain forever.[10]

Recently much has been made of the claim that there are important affinities between the Fourth Gospel and the religion of the community at Qumran. Certainly there are resemblances.

[9] Cf. *The Midrash on Psalms,* trans. by W. G. Braude, Yale University Press, 1959, Ps. 25. The word *chesed,* translated "mercy" (RSV "steadfast love") in later books translated from Hebrew to Greek was frequently rendered *charis,* "grace," the word used in John. Cf. C. H. Dodd, *The Bible and the Greeks,* Hodder & Stoughton, 1935, p. 61.

[10] Taken by themselves, these details hardly prove independent knowledge of rabbinic positions. They may simply be objections raised in the course of controversies in which the author had a part. But the author's participation in controversies involving the technicalities of Jewish theology would be itself significant.

Both believe in the creation of all things by God. Both conceive of the world as divided into the two camps of light and darkness, and see these camps arranged under personal leadership. For Qumran the leaders are the two created spirits or angels of light and darkness (truth and perversion); for St. John, however, the leader of light is the uncreated Word, while the leader of evil is the prince of this world. For Qumran the struggle between the forces is still on an equal plane, although light will shine victoriously at the end; for John light is already conquering darkness. Both the literatures maintain that all men are to be assigned to either of the two camps. Yet throughout the Qumran literature there is a curious mixture of determinism and free will, while John is quite clear that men remain in darkness because they obstinately turn away from light.[11]

Brown also finds significant parallels in references to truth and perversity, emphasis on brotherly love, and the fountain of living waters. Many others have been suggested with more or less plausibility. It seems clear that the author was familiar with such ideas, which may have had a wider currency in first-century Judaism than the later victory of Talmudic Judaism might suggest. There is, however, no evidence that this familiarity was gained by reading the literature of Qumran (which was presumably not available to the general public) or by direct contact with the community.[12] It is to be noted that there is nothing specifically Palestinian about the points Brown mentions.

That the Fourth Gospel, though it undoubtedly shows evidences of contact with Hellenistic religious thought, has deeper roots in Judaism is shown not so much by scattered parallels to rabbinic theology or the doctrine of the Qumran covenanters,

---

[11] R. E. Brown, "The Qumran Scrolls and Johannine Gospel and Epistles" in *The Scrolls and the New Testament*, Krister Stendahl (ed.), Harper, 1957, p. 195. *Arranged* looks like a misprint for *arrayed*.

[12] The suggestion that John the author had been directly or indirectly associated with John the Baptist, who is supposed to have been a renegade from Qumran (it is not generally put quite so bluntly), and that the ideas came through this channel, hardly deserves serious consideration.

as by the fact that the author's thought is profoundly influenced by the Old Testament. Even here, however, as in the case of the other influences, in the end the author uses these materials in his own way. What emerges is something unique, which cannot be entirely explained in terms of any of its predecessors.

THE CONTENT OF THE GOSPEL OF JOHN[13]

The Gospel opens with an introduction which presents the idea of God's Logos, with God from the beginning, agent of creation, the source of the light and power to become God's children. The Logos became flesh and dwelt among us; and through him, and him alone, God has been made known as by an only Son. This prelude presents, in abstract terms, the author's conception of the ultimate nature of him whose story the book tells.

The prologue does not specifically identify the Logos with Jesus, but the statement that only the Son has ever revealed God is followed by a series of testimonies—from John the Baptist, Andrew, Philip, and Nathanael—that Jesus is the Son of God, Messiah, the fulfillment of Scripture, and King of Israel.

The body of the book is devoted to the career of the Logos made flesh, and divides into two large subdivisions which may be called, respectively, the Book of Signs and the Book of the Passion.

The Book of Signs consists of seven episodes which present Jesus under various symbols and in various aspects as the life-giving Word. First, we have a series of new beginnings. The miracle at Cana shows Jesus as the source of a new relation to God, replacing the old Jewish system of purification. In the cleansing of the Temple, he appears in essentially the same role, with the added suggestion that through his death he will super-

---

[13] Here and throughout the discussion of John, I am largely dependent on C. H. Dodd, *The Interpretation of the Fourth Gospel*, Cambridge University Press, 1954. The rival position of Bultmann is accessible in English in the second volume of his *New Testament Theology*.

sede the Temple. These are followed by the discussion with Nicodemus, which presents the initiation into eternal life as a rebirth, and introduces such themes as the "elevation" of the Son of man, God's love for the world, and the coming judgment. The discussion with the woman of Samaria presents the idea of Christ, the living water, as the continuing source of eternal life, and the idea that real worship is not dependent on a specific spot. In the course of the discussion, Jesus explicitly claims to be the Messiah.

The second episode presents Jesus as the life-giving Word in healings of the nobleman's son and of the man at the pool of Bethesda, which show the word of Christ giving life to a child at the point of death and to a man as good as dead. These are followed by a discourse presenting God as perpetually active, and Jesus as doing what God alone can do, especially in giving life and effecting judgment. The challenge to monotheism which this presents is also discussed. Jesus asserts that those whose minds are not closed will be able to see in the life, which his word really gives, the evidence of his origin.

The third episode presents Jesus as the bread of life, growing out of the narrative of the Feeding of the Five Thousand. In veiled terms it is suggested that Christ becomes bread of life to the world through his death. The effect of this is to produce a sharp division between the multitude who are alienated by this, and a small group of followers who know him as having the words of eternal life.

The next episode, the fourth, centers around the Feast of Tabernacles, of which characteristic features were libations of the great altar with water, and the brilliant illumination of the Temple. Jesus offers himself as the life-giving water and the light of the world. Meanwhile, the hostility of the Jewish leaders shows itself in increasing measure. The two are not disconnected, for in the thought of the author, Jesus' death is the means by which he becomes in reality the source of life and light to men.

The theme of judgment by the light is followed up in the fifth episode, which revolves about the healing of a man born blind, and the allegory of the Good Shepherd. The Jewish leaders, claiming to have the light, make plain their utter darkness, and thereby show themselves, in contrast to Christ, the Good Shepherd, to be evil shepherds, such as are denounced in Ezekiel 34.

The series of signs, going hand in hand with the growing tension between Jesus and the Jewish leaders, moves toward a climax in the sixth episode. In the raising of Lazarus, this episode presents the victory of life over death, the victory which Christ gained by his triumph despite the seeming victory of his opponents.

But this still is not the whole story. In the seventh and concluding episode, which tells of the anointing at Bethany, anticipating his death; and the triumphal entry into Jerusalem, proclaiming his sovereignty; there then come Greeks asking to see Jesus. He does not reply directly to their request, but announces that the turning point has come. Now his glorification, which has from the early chapters been connected with his death, can proceed. He explains that his death itself will be the means of life, just as the buried seed is the source of life for many other seeds.

The end is at hand; and this now is the theme for the second large division of the Gospel. This in turn has two subdivisions, the first of which may be called the Farewell Discourse, and the second the Passion Narrative.

At supper[14] alone with his disciples, Jesus washes their feet. Judas goes out to do his dark deed. It is night. To the Eleven, Jesus speaks of the life which is to be realized by the disciples, representing all Christian believers, describing it as his dwelling in them and their dwelling in him, reproducing the divine pattern of mutual indwelling of Father and Son. This is to be

[14] John clearly distinguishes this from the Jewish Passover.

understood in terms of the divine love, existing between Father and Son, exhibited in Christ's self-offering. This love is to be returned by men in trust and obedience to him, and in love to one another.

From this upper room Jesus goes out, to be arrested, tried, denied, scorned, condemned, and crucified. In general, the story follows the same outline as that of the Synoptics, but with certain points emphasized in accordance with the Johannine conception. Thus, he emphasizes the voluntary character of Jesus' sufferings, and that his death at Roman hands by crucifixion typified the "lifting up" by which he would draw all men unto him.

As in the Synoptics, the Crucifixion is followed by the Resurrection; but here, too, John tells the story in his own way. He begins with the story of the empty tomb (the one detail common to all four Gospels), but this is followed by an account of an appearance to Mary Magdalene and an appearance to the disciples gathered in Jerusalem, when he confers on them the Holy Spirit. These have no parallels in the Synoptic Gospels.

The Gospel concludes with another appearance, this time with Thomas present, as he had not been on the former occasion. Being given the signs he demanded, he hails Jesus as Lord and God. With obvious reference to those who did not see the Logos in his physical appearance, Jesus proclaims, "Have you believed because you have seen me? Blessed are those who have not seen and yet believe." It is the author's purpose, he tells us, to recount the signs by which men may believe that Jesus is the Christ, the Son of God, and, believing, have life in his name.

LEADING IDEAS

The Fourth Gospel presents Jesus as the One come from God to bring to men eternal life. Jesus is characterized as Messiah, Logos, Son of God, Son of man. As Messiah, he is the one promised in the Scriptures, the rightful ruler of men's lives. As

Logos, he is the mind of God, the order of the universe "projected into objectivity"; he is God at work, revealing himself, God's thought, and God's power. In calling him Son of God, the author does not have in mind anything like the Nicene doctrine of the Trinity; for, in John, the Son is clearly subordinate to the Father (5:19, 26–27, 30). The relation is one of complete unity of will, of mutual love. He is the judge who determines man's future, though he does so not by holding a trial, but by bringing light, by which men are either attracted or repelled according as their deeds are good or evil. But this light is not just a revelation of the principles of conduct. It is as he is "lifted up" that he draws all men unto him. This union of all men in him brings out the relationship of this concept with the Hellenistic concept of the archetypal man which has appeared in Paul and elsewhere. From this point of view he is called "Son of man."

The eternal life which Jesus brings is not everlasting life as such (though it may include that) but genuine life, life which participates in the spiritual reality which underlies the natural world. To be eternal is to be essentially timeless, like the truths of mathematics, or the principles of beauty and righteousness, which in Platonic terms, at least, are what they are, and would still be the same even if they never found embodiment in concrete cases. But if the concept of the eternal is Greek, the concept of life is Hebrew. Life can express timeless characteristics, but it is itself dynamic, active, striving. It is full, rich, abundant.

One of the striking differences between the Fourth Gospel and the others is the absence of predictions of the cataclysmic second coming of Christ, either to hold a judgment or to set up the kingdom of God. For John, Christ's kingdom is not of this world. John does not postpone to the future the full realization of God's blessings. For this the Gospel of John substitutes the concept of eternal life, life which has the quality of expressing the nature of reality, which may be entered on here and now. In these circumstances the traditional eschatology loses its meaning. Just as the idea of the judgment as an event is replaced by the idea of judgment as response to the light (as some insects fly to a light and others scuttle out of sight, according to their nature), so the promise of a later return of Christ is replaced by the promise and gift of the Holy Spirit. The gift of the Spirit, which is to guide the disciples into the fullness of reality (*not* into "truth" as a set of principles of religion and morality), is the climax of the personal relationship between Jesus and his disciples, rather than a later outpouring of divine power as in Acts. The Spirit will be their advocate before the world.

To have eternal life is to know God. To know God is not to be supplied with information about him, theological or philosophical. You can know a lot about someone without knowing him. Neither is mystical contemplation of him knowing him. As in the Old Testament, to know God is to acknowledge him, to serve him, to obey him, to experience his dealings with men. It is interaction, not just thought.

We come to know God through faith in Christ. This is more than assent to the assertion that Christ is divine, in spite of appearances to the contrary. Faith, in this Gospel, means the ability to recognize and appreciate the divine in Christ. It is not a matter of knowing beforehand what is divine, and then concluding that Christ conforms to this concept. To have faith in Christ means to discover through him what really is divine. To see him so is to see the Father, and to see him in this pregnant sense is to know him and to have eternal life.

Eternal life can be described as a life in union with God. Once again, the language suggests the concepts of Greek mysticism, the merging of the individual in the one divine reality. But this is clearly not what is meant. Just as knowledge of God is not contemplation of him, so union with God is not loss of individuality in him. Not through mystical absorption in God, but through love, is the way to union with him. In Christ, God's love is made manifest; and love is called forth by love. "God so loved the world that he gave his only Son, that whoever believes in him should not perish but have eternal life" (3:16). In Christ, the love of God is brought into history; and through him men may discover and acknowledge the meaning of divinity.

THE FIRST EPISTLE OF JOHN

Actually there is little reason for calling this an Epistle. Though the author frequently refers to the fact that he is writing to them, the book has neither the regular introduction and conclusion nor the tone of a letter. One would guess that originally it was a sermon, perhaps written out for wider circulation. Though its author may not be the author of the Gospel, the two works are certainly closely related. The contrast between light and darkness, the idea that eternal life is to be realized here and now, the emphasis on love as the central demand made on believers, growing out of fellowship with Father and Son, link the so-called Epistle to the Gospel.

Though in some ways the point of view of the Epistle seems nearer to a more primitive type of Christian teaching than is found in the Gospel, its main emphases are clearly determined by the growing threat of Gnostic ideas. Its author is greatly concerned to emphasize the importance of the real humanity of Jesus the Christ, against those who would assert that matter was evil and that the Savior had only the appearance of a human body. Against those who would maintain that religious maturity was not dependent on ethical conduct he says, "Whoever does not do right is not of God" (3:10).

We have already seen, in discussing the second and third Epistles, the divisions that propaganda for such Gnostic ideas was producing. So this book stresses the necessity for love among the brethren. "If anyone says, 'I love God,' and hates his brother, he is a liar; for he who does not love his brother whom he has seen, cannot love God whom he has not seen" (4:20). This obligation is traced back to the nature of God. "God is love," this writer says, and thus brings to expression for the first time in history a far-reaching idea. To understand its meaning is to understand the New Testament.

Suggestions for Further Reading

GENERAL

ATLASES

A good atlas is important. The maps found in some editions of the Bible are almost worthless. There are three good atlases: G. E. Wright and F. V. Filson, *The Westminster Historical Atlas to the Bible*, Revised Edition (Westminster Press, 1956) has excellent maps and good illustrations. The text gives a good sketch of the historical background. Emil G. Kraeling, *Rand-McNally Bible Atlas* (Rand-McNally, 1956), has more extensive text on historical background, many illustrations, and good maps. L. Grollenberg, *Atlas of the Bible*, translated and edited by J. M. H. Reid and H. H. Rowley (Nelson, 1956), is lavishly and beautifully illustrated; the maps are good, with useful explanatory comment printed on them. This, as well as the extensive text, often reflects the conservative position of Catholic Biblical scholarship. A useful study is Denis Baly, *The Geography of the Bible* (Harper, 1957). Nothing takes the place of George Adam Smith's *Historical Geography of the Holy Land* (many editions) in giving the "feel" of Palestine, although many of the author's archeological conclusions are out of date.

BIBLE DICTIONARIES

These books give information about specific words and topics, in alphabetic arrangement. The two comprehensive dictionaries in English are: J. Hastings, *Dictionary of the Bible*, 5 volumes (Scribner's, 1898–1907); and Cheney and Black, *Encyclopedia Biblica* (Macmillan, 1899–1903). These, although indispensable in many respects, are badly out of date in others. They will doubtless be superseded by the *Interpreters' Bible Dictionary* now in process of publication. More recent, though less extensive, are Davis and Gehman, *Westminster Bible Dictionary* (Westminster Press, 1944); and Miller and Miller, *Harper's Bible Dictionary* (Harper, 1952).

For some of the theologically important terms in the New Testament, *Bible Key Words, from Gerhard Kittel's Theologisches Woerterbuch zum Neuen Testament*, vols. I and II (Harper, 1951, 1958) is helpful.

389

Many topics in connection with Judaism are illuminated by the *Jewish Encyclopedia* (Funk, 1901–1907); and the *Universal Jewish Encyclopedia* (Universal Jewish Encyclopedia, Inc., 1939–1944). The latter is more popular in treatment, but accurate and more nearly up to date.

CONCORDANCES

Essential for Bible study is the concordance, listing in alphabetical order under the various words in the Bible all the passages in which a word occurs. This is obviously useful in locating passages when you have forgotten the reference—or for discovering that the supposed passage is not in the Bible—but the real importance of the concordance is that it makes it possible to study the meaning and history of important terms. Since the New Testament was written in Greek, and since a given Greek word of necessity has different English translations according to context, and the same English word is also necessarily used to translate more than one Greek word, this type of study, if it is to be done in English, requires a concordance which shows these differences. For this purpose Strong's *Exhaustive Concordance to the Bible* (Abingdon, 1958) is most useful, giving with each word a number identifying the original word and referring to an appendix showing other translations of the word. Young's *Analytical Concordance to the Bible,* revised edition (Eerdmans, 1955; Funk & Wagnalls, n.d.) groups together the English words translated from each Greek word, but gives no clues to other English words translating a given Greek word. These concordances are based on the King James Version. Nelson's *Complete Concordance of the Revised Standard Version Bible* (Nelson, 1957) is simply a concordance of English words, no attention being paid to the original Greek or Hebrew. Cruden's *Complete Concordance to the Old and New Testaments* (various publishers and dates) is a similar work based on the King James Version.

INTRODUCTIONS

In Bible study, the word *introduction* is commonly used in a technical sense, meaning a book which discusses authorship, date, and literary features. In English the most comprehensive is J. Moffatt,

Introduction to the Literature of the New Testament (Scribner's, 1918). More up to date, yet often dated in its conclusions, is A. H. McNeile, *An Introduction to the Study of the New Testament,* second edition, revised by C. S. C. Williams (Clarendon Press, 1953). M. S. Enslin, *Christian Beginnings* (Harper, 1938), especially Part II, issued in the Torch Book Series as *The Literature of the Christian Movement,* is valuable. Samuel Cartledge, *A Conservative Introduction to the New Testament* (Zondervan, 1957), is conservative in conclusions but not in method, and gives a good statement of opposing positions. Reflecting the positions of form criticism is M. Dibelius, *A Fresh Approach to the New Testament and Early Christian Literature* (Scribner's, 1936). E. J. Goodspeed, *An Introduction to the New Testament* (University of Chicago Press, 1937) reflects his currently fashionable theory of the origin of Ephesians. Clear and readable, less technical than the foregoing books, is E. F. Scott, *The Literature of the New Testament* (Columbia University Press, 1932). More recent than Scott, and reaching quite different conclusions from the present book on many points, is Richard Heard's *An Introduction to the New Testament* (Harper, 1950).

INTRODUCTION

The Canon of the New Testament

Many of the introductions have chapters on the history of the canon. See especially those of McNeile, Enslin, Scott, and Heard, mentioned above. A. von Harnack, *The Origin of the New Testament* (Macmillan, 1925) is indispensable. A brief history is given in A. Souter, *The Text and Canon of the New Testament* (Scribner's, 1925). F. W. Filson, *What Books Belong in the New Testament* (Westminster Press, 1957) considers the rightfulness of the selection actually made.

The Historical Approach

The most useful general discussion of historical methodology is to be found in Louis Gottschalk, *Understanding History, A Primer of Historical Method* (Knopf, 1950). Langlois and Seignobos, *Introduction to the Study of History* (Holt, 1932), and Allen Johnson,

The Historian and Historical Evidence (Scribner's, 1930) have valuable material. Some of the specific problems presented by the application of these methods to the New Testament are discussed in James Moffatt, *The Approach to the New Testament* (Hodder and Stoughton, 1921).

Helpful in dealing with problems of faith are H. E. Fosdick, *The Modern Use of the Bible* (Macmillan, 1924); C. H. Dodd, *The Authority of the Bible* (Harper, 1928), now reprinted in the Torch Book Series; and W. Neil, *The Rediscovery of the Bible* (Harper, 1954).

In considering the problem presented by miracles, Hume's questions are still relevant, in spite of the theologians: "On Miracles," in *Essays,* edited by Green and Grose (London, 1907). For a more popular view, see C. S. Lewis, *Miracles, a preliminary study* (Macmillan, 1947). F. C. Grant, in his *Introduction to New Testament Thought* (Abingdon, 1950), has a good chapter (Chapter VII) on the subject. Alan Richardson defends the historical and religious value of Jesus' miracles in *The Miracle Stories of the Gospels* (SCM Press, 1941). *The Quest of the Historical Jesus* (Black, 1926), by A. Schweitzer, includes a survey of the attempts to rationalize the miracles. The ancient attitude is discussed in *Miracle and Natural Law in Graeco-Roman and Early Christian Thought,* by R. M. Grant (North-Holland, 1952).

TEXT AND TRANSLATION

On the text, see the introductions (except Scott) and the book of Souter mentioned in connection with the canon; also the articles in Volume I and XII of the *Interpreters Bible.* Unfortunately, little progress in this field beyond the merest elements can be made without some knowledge of Greek.

The history of the various English versions is given in H. G. May, *Our English Bible in the Making* (Westminster, 1952).

Useful translations, in addition to the King James Version and the Revised Standard Version are: Twentieth Century, Weymouth, Ballentine, Moffatt, Goodspeed, and Phillips. Published under Catholic auspices are translations by Knox, Spence, Confraternity of Christian Doctrine. The latter is a revision of the Douay Version.

JESUS: BACKGROUND AND SOURCES

The Sources

In general, lives of Jesus (see below) written from the modern historical point of view discuss the sources in some detail. There is a particularly good survey of the extra-canonical sources in D. M. Beck, *Through the Gospels to Jesus* (Harper, 1954). For the Jewish sources, see Klausner, *Jesus of Nazareth* (Macmillan, 1929) and especially M. Goldstein, *Jesus in the Jewish Tradition* (Macmillan, 1950).

The difficult problems presented by Josephus' references are discussed in H. St. J. Thackeray, *Josephus, the Man and the Historian* (Jewish Institute Press, 1929).

The apocryphal Gospels may be found in *The Apocryphal New Testament,* edited by M. R. James (Oxford, 1924). Recently published is *The Gospel of Thomas,* edited by A. Guillamont, *et al.* (Harper, 1959). See also, *The Secret Sayings of Jesus,* by R. M. Grant, with D. N. Freedman (Doubleday, 1960).

In addition to discussions of the Synoptic Gospels in *Lives of Jesus,* see also the introductions and commentaries. Parts II and IV of *The Four Gospels,* by B. H. Streeter (Macmillan, 1925, with many reprintings), are clearly and simply written and still valuable. More recent, with many fresh insights, is F. C. Grant's *The Gospels, Their Origin and Growth* (Harper, 1957).

The Evaluation of the Sources

General questions are considered in C. H. Dodd, *History and the Gospel* (Nisbet, 1952); and E. F. Scott, *The Validity of the Gospel Record* (Scribner's, 1938). Both of these depart, in different ways, from the positions of form criticism (see below).

On the problem of the relation of the Synoptic Gospels and John, the literary relationships are carefully considered by P. Gardner-Smith, *St. John and the Synoptic Gospels* (Cambridge, 1938). W. F. Howard, in *The Fourth Gospel in Recent Criticism,* revised by C. K. Barrett (Epworth Press, 1955), gives a survey of the discussion. In an appendix to his *The Interpretation of the Fourth*

Gospel (Cambridge, 1954) C. H. Dodd offers a judicious discussion of the historical aspect of the Fourth Gospel.

A detailed discussion and comparison of the traditions as found in the various Synoptic Gospels is given by W. E. Bundy in *Jesus and the First Three Gospels* (Harvard, 1955).

The positions of form criticism are presented by M. Dibelius, *The Message of Jesus Christ* (Scribner's, 1939); *A Fresh Approach to the New Testament and Early Christian Literature* (Scribner's, 1936), and *Jesus* (Westminster, 1949); most fully in *From Tradition to Gospel* (Scribner's, 1935). Bultmann, also one of the pioneers in this field, has not been as extensively translated into English. However, *Form Criticism,* edited by F. C. Grant (Willett, 1934), contains a summary of his position in a translation of *The Investigation of the Synoptic Problem.* In general, see also H. J. Cadbury, *The Making of Luke–Acts* S.P.C.K., 1958); and Vincent Taylor, *The Formation of the Gospel Tradition,* 2nd edition (Macmillan, Lond. 1935).

THE JEWISH BACKGROUND

The historical and political situation is described in most lives of Jesus and in R. H. Pfeiffer, *History of New Testament Times, with an introduction to the Apocrypha* (Harper, 1949); and in M. S. Enslin, *Christian Beginnings,* Part I (Harper, 1938). C. Guignebert, *The Jewish World in the Time of Jesus* (Kegan Paul, Trench, and Trubner, 1939) deals with non-Palestinian as well as Palestinian Judaism. Economic conditions are presented in J. Klausner's *Jesus of Nazareth* (Macmillan, 1925). See also F. C. Grant, *The Economic Background of the Gospels* (Oxford, 1926).

Pfeiffer, Enslin, and Guignebert all present the religious aspect of Judaism; but the outstanding work in this area is G. F. Moore, *Judaism,* 3 volumes (Harvard, 1927, 1930). Volume I, pages 110–121, gives a masterly summary of "normative" Judaism. A good summary, based on Moore, is found in G. H. C. Macgregor and A. C. Purdy, *Jew and Greek, Tutors unto Christ* (Scribner's, 1936).

A summary and paraphrase of Talmudic teaching can be found in A. Cohen, *Everyman's Talmud* (Dutton, 1949). Extracts are presented by C. G. Montefiore and H. Loewe, *A Rabbinic Anthology*

(Macmillan, 1938). Wider in scope but less extensive in matter is S. W. Baron and J. L. Blau's *Judaism, Postbiblical and Talmudic Period* (Liberal Arts, 1954). Some similar material forms part of *The New Testament Background* by C. K. Barrett (Macmillan, 1957).

For the Pharisees, L. Finkelstein's book of that title (Jewish Publication Society, 1940) is basic. Material on Sadducees will be found in Bible Dictionaries. The relationship of the Zealots to the nationalistic hopes growing out of the Hasmonean period is discussed in W. R. Farmer's *Maccabees, Zealots and Josephus* (Columbia, 1956). The Essenes, presumably the source of the Dead Sea Scrolls, have been the subjects of numerous volumes, whose value is not always in proportion to their readability. Most useful are the two volumes by Millar Burrows, *The Dead Sea Scrolls* and *More Light on the Dead Sea Scrolls* (Viking, 1955 and 1958, respectively). These include translations of selected texts. A complete translation of the earliest discoveries, somewhat free but generally reliable, can be found in *The Dead Sea Scriptures in English Translation* (Doubleday, 1956) by T. H. Gaster.

The Jewish hopes for the future have been the subject of many discussions. *The Messianic Idea in Israel,* by J. Klausner (Macmillan, 1955), and *He That Cometh* by S. Mowinckel (Abingdon, n.d.) deal with much the same material from radically different points of view. On the subject of the kingdom of God, John Bright's book of that title (Abingdon, n.d.) is excellent. Texts of the Jewish apocalypses are given in English translation by R. H. Charles in *Apocrypha and Pseudepigrapha of the Old Testament* (Oxford, 1913). Excellent translations and commentary for the Old Testament apocrypha are provided in the *Jewish Apocryphal Literature Series* (Harper, various dates, still in course of publication).

JESUS: CAREER & TEACHING

GENERAL

Thomas Kepler's anthology, *Contemporary Thinking about Jesus* (Abingdon, 1943), gives a good introductory survey of some of the important problems and a variety of approaches to them. Among the important comprehensive treatments are M. Goguel, *Life of Jesus* (Macmillan, 1933); and C. Guignebert, *Jesus* (Knopf, 1935). Both are clearly written. Guignebert suffers from excessive scepticism. Goguel is perhaps overacute. Written from a Jewish point of view, but intending to be objective, is J. Klausner's *Jesus of Nazareth* (Macmillan, 1925). H. Branscomb, *The Life and Teachings of Jesus* (Abingdon, 1931) is somewhat dated. *Through the Gospels to Jesus,* by Dwight M. Beck (Harper, 1954) is useful. In his short book, *Jesus* (Westminster, 1949), M. Dibelius gives one of the best treatments. R. Bultmann has dealt with Jesus in *Jesus and the Word* (Scribner's, 1934), and summarizes Jesus' teaching in the first chapter of *New Testament Theology* (Scribner's, 1951). A special effort to present Jesus in his true setting is made in Sherman Johnson's *Jesus in His Homeland* (Scribner's, 1957). *Jesus, What Manner of Man* by Henry J. Cadbury (Macmillan, 1947) is more concerned with how his mind worked, what were his underlying attitudes, etc., than with the specific incidents of his career. How Jesus may have appeared to various groups of his contemporaries is the subject of *The Man from Nazareth,* by H. E. Fosdick (Harper, 1949). John Knox tries in *Jesus, Lord and Christ* (Harper, 1958) to show how the results of the historical approach can be used for theological construction.

SPECIAL TOPICS

Jesus' teaching is considered in S. MacL. Gilmour's *The Gospel Jesus Preached* (Westminster, 1957). More limited in scope, but still very illuminating, is E. C. Colwell, *An Approach to the Teaching of Jesus* (Abingdon, 1947). *The Peril of Modernizing Jesus,* by H. J. Cadbury (Macmillan, 1937) stresses Jewish elements in his teaching and outlook. Very different in method are: D. Daube: *The New Testament and Rabbinic Judaism* (University of London, 1956); and *Rabbinic Literature and Gospel Teaching,* by C. C. Montefiore (Macmillan, 1930). Important treatments of the parables are found in books by C. H. Dodd and J. Jeremias, entitled respectively *The Parables of the Kingdom* (Nisbet, 1953) and *The Parables of Jesus* (Scribner's, 1953). Jesus' attitude toward the Law is judiciously considered in H. Branscomb's *Jesus and the Law of Moses* (R. R.

Smith, 1930). Some of the problems presented by his healings are discussed by S. V. MacCasland, *By the Finger of God* (Macmillan, 1951). On the ethical teaching of Jesus see (beside the general discussions) such books as the following: E. F. Scott, *The Ethical Teachings of Jesus* (Macmillan, 1925). This is clear and well written, as all Scott's books are. *Eschatology and the Ethics of Jesus* by A. N. Wilder, revised edition (Harper, 1954), shows the relation of these two sides of Jesus' teaching. Hans Windisch's *The Sermon on the Mount* (Westminster, 1951) is basic for an understanding of the relevance of Jesus' teaching today.

In Part II of *The Death of Christ* (Abingdon, 1958) John Knox deals with the problem of Jesus' own understanding of his death.

For a history of the study of the life of Jesus in modern times, A. Schweitzer's *Quest of the Historical Jesus* (Black, 1926) is still unsurpassed. Also useful is *The Search for the Real Jesus,* by C. C. McCown (Scribner's, 1940).

THE EARLY FOLLOWERS OF JESUS IN PALESTINE

SOURCES

Problems connected with Acts are dealt with in the commentaries. See also *The Making of Luke–Acts,* by H. J. Cadbury (S.P.C.K., 1958); *Studies in the Acts of the Apostles,* by M. Dibelius (Scribner's, 1956); and the five volumes of *The Beginnings of Christianity; Part I, The Acts of the Apostles,* edited by F. J. Foakes-Jackson and Kirsopp Lake (Macmillan, 1920 to 1933).

BACKGROUND

See the references above under "Judaism." Also H. J. Cadbury, *The Book of Acts in History* (Harper, 1955).

HISTORY: GENERAL

H. Lietzmann, *The Beginning of the Christian Church,* Chapter V (Scribner's, 1949). *The Birth of Christianity,* by M. Goguel (Macmillan, 1954) provides an extended treatment in Part II.

THOUGHT

R. Bultmann's *New Testament Theology* (Scribner's, 1951) vol. I, Chapter II, gives a succint survey. C. H. Dodd's *The Apostolic Preaching* (Harper, 1951) which attempts to show the unity of the central elements in the apostolic message has been very influential. Brilliant but one-sided is K. Lake's *Landmarks of Early Christianity* (Macmillan, 1922).

SPECIAL TOPICS

A wide variety of topics receive careful treatment in Foakes-Jackson and Lake, *Beginnings of Christianity* (see above), particularly in Volume IV, Commentary, and Volume V, Additional Notes. *On the Resurrection of Jesus,* S. V. MacCasland's book of that title (Nelson, 1932) discusses the subject from a historical point of view. Relations between the followers of Jesus and other Jews are well presented in Riddle and Hutson, *New Testament Life and Literature* (University of Chicago, 1946), Chapter IX. The problem of the relationship of the early Church and the Dead Sea Scrolls is discussed in *The Scrolls and the New Testament,* edited by Krister Stendahl (Harper, 1957). M. Simon considers *St. Stephen and the Hellenists* (Longmans, 1958). On early Christian "communism" see O. Cone, *Rich and Poor in the New Testament* (Macmillan, 1902).

THE GRAECO-ROMAN WORLD

GENERAL

The Cambridge Ancient History, especially Vols. VII, X, XI (Macmillan, 1928–1939—a new edition is in process), has much important material on this topic. W. W. Tarn's *Hellenistic Civilization,* third edition, revised by its author and G. T. Griffith (Longmans, 1952) is the standard work. A selection of documents is found in C. K. Barrett, *The New Testament Background* (Macmillan, 1957). For the Roman period, S. Dill: *Roman Society from Nero to Marcus Aurelius* (Macmillan, 1905) is a classic. The three volumes by M. Rostovtzeff on *The Social and Economic History of the Hellenistic World,* second edition, revised by Peter Fraser (Oxford, 1957) is most valuable. The attempt is made by T. R. Glover in *The World of the New Testament* (Macmillan, 1931) to catch the spirit of this world. A valuable collection of texts from inscriptions and papyri is found in A. Deissman, *Light from the Ancient East* (Doran, 1927).

HELLENISTIC RELIGION

The later Greek religion is depicted by M. Nilsson, *Greek Piety* (Oxford, 1948); and in *Personal Religion among the Greeks* by A. J. Festugière (University of California Press, 1954).

HELLENISTIC JUDAISM

There is no adequate treatment of this complex but important subject. Brief essays are found in *The Legacy of Israel*, edited by E. Bevan and C. Singer (Clarendon Press, 1927); H. Loewe, *Judaism and Christianity* (Sheldon Press, 1937) Vol. II, Chapter 2; and by R. Marcus in *The Jews*, second edition, edited by L. Finkelstein (Harper, 1955), vol. II. See also H. A. Wolfson, *Philo* (Harvard, 1948) Chapter I, § iii. Somewhat more comprehensive treatments can be found in R. H. Pfeiffer's *History of New Testament Times* (Harper, 1949), Part I-B; and in *The Jewish World in the Time of Jesus*, by C. Guignebert (Kegan Paul, Trench, and Trubner, 1939). For Philo, Wolfson in the book already mentioned presents Philo as a Jew whose religion is quite unaffected in any essential point by his contacts with Hellenism. In opposition, E. R. Goodenough, *By Light, Light* (Yale, 1935) and *An Introduction to Philo Judaeus* (Yale, 1940) sees him as primarily a Hellenistic mystic.

S. Angus, *Religious Quests of the Graeco-Roman World* (Scribner's, 1929) covers all phases of its topic. G. H. C. Macgregor and A. C. Purdy's *Jew and Greek, Tutors unto Christ* gives a good summary. Well-chosen extracts from ancient sources are provided in *Hellenistic Religions* (Liberal Arts, 1953), and *Ancient Roman Religion* (Liberal Arts, 1957), both edited by F. C. Grant. *The Mystery Religions and Christianity*, by S. Angus (Scribner's, 1925) treats these religions more fully than the book already mentioned. Particularly valuable is F. Cumont, *Oriental Religions in Roman Paganism* (Dover, 1957). For Gnosticism see H. Jonas, *The Gnostic Religion*

(Beacon Press, 1958) and R. M. Grant, *Gnosticism and Early Christianity* (Columbia University Press, 1959). The Nag Hammadi finds are described in *The Jung Codex,* edited by F. L. Cross (Mowbray, 1955). The texts themselves are in process of publication.

Various aspects of the interaction of Christianity and this world are presented by W. R. Ramsey, *The Church in the Roman Empire* (Putnam's, 1893); A. von Harnack, *The Mission and Expansion of Christianity in the First Three Centuries,* second edition (Putnam's, 1908); and R. Bultmann, *Primitive Christianity in its Contemporary Setting* (Meridian Books, 1956).

PAUL

The literature on Paul is enormous. The following books, among many others, will be found helpful.

A wide variety of Pauline problems is presented briefly in T. Kepler's anthology, *Contemporary Thinking about Paul* (Abingdon-Cokesbury, 1950). A brilliant history of modern Pauline studies is found in A. Schweitzer: *Paul and His Interpreters* (Black, 1950).

SOURCES

D. Riddle, *Paul, Man of Conflict* (Cokesbury, 1940) and Knox, *Chapters in a Life of Paul* (Abingdon-Cokesbury, 1950) discuss the relative values of Acts and Paul's own Epistles as sources. Problems of the separate books are discussed in the various commentaries. For the content of Romans, E. F. Scott, *Paul's Epistle to the Romans* (SCM Press, 1947) is a good restatement, not a commentary. On the question of the genuineness of Ephesians, see E. J. Goodspeed's *The Key to Ephesians* (University of Chicago, 1956) and C. L. Mitton's *The Epistle to the Ephesians* (Oxford, 1951). It is most unfortunate that there is no up-to-date presentation in English of the other side.

GENERAL

Paul's career and ideas are presented in A. D. Nock, *St. Paul* (Harper, n.d.); J. Knox, *Chapters in a Life of Paul* (see above); S. Sandmel, *The Genius of Paul* (Farrar, Strauss and Cudahy, 1958), a valuable interpretation by a Jewish scholar.

Other books limit themselves to presenting his thought. Schweitzer's own interpretation is found in his *Mysticism of Paul the Apostle* (Black, 1956). R. Bultmann's *New Testament Theology,* Vol. I, Part II (Scribner's, 1951) takes quite a different line, with more attention to Paul's relation to Hellenistic religion. Stevens' *Pauline Theology* is old but still useful (Scribner's, 1897). C. H. Dodd discusses *The Meaning of Paul for Today* (Allen and Unwin, 1956). William Barclay offers a helpful treatment in *The Mind of Paul* (Harper, 1958). H. F. Rall's *According to Paul* (Scribner's, 1944) gives a good summary and exposition. An outstanding study challenging many current assumptions is found in *Paul and the Salvation of Mankind,* by J. Munk (SCM Press, 1959). Paul's religion rather than his thought is emphasized by J. S. Stewart's *A Man in Christ* (Harper, n.d.).

Enslin's *The Ethics of St. Paul* (Harper, 1930) is the best treatment of that topic.

William Ramsey, *St. Paul the Traveller* (Putnam's, 1896), and H. J. Cadbury, *The Book of Acts in History* (Harper, 1955) deal with the general background.

The problem of Paul's relation to Judaism and Hellenistic religion is variously treated by A. Deissman, *Paul* (Harper, 1957); J. G. Machen, *The Origin of Paul's Religion* (Eerdman's, 1947); W. D. Davies, *Paul and Rabbinic Judaism* second edition (S.P.C.K., 1955); H. H. A. Kennedy, *St. Paul and the Mystery Religions* (Hodder and Stoughton, n.d.). Schweitzer's historical study (see above) revolves about this problem.

The relation of Paul to Jesus is the subject of *The Mind of Christ in Paul,* by F. C. Porter (Scribner's, 1930).

THE CHURCH AND THE LARGER WORLD

PERSECUTION

For the general problem of the relation of the church to the state, see C. J. Cadoux, *The Early Church and the World* (Clark, 1925); R. M. Grant, *The Sword and the Cross* (Macmillan, 1955); and O. Cullman, *The State in the New Testament* (Scribner's, 1956).

In addition to the appropriate volumes in the standard series of commentaries, F. W. Beare, *The First Epistle of Peter,* second edition (Macmillan, 1958) is excellent. In *The Epistle to the Hebrews* (Hodden and Stoughton, 1951), W. Manson presents an original thesis. On Revelation, S. J. Case's volume, *The Revelation of John* (University of Chicago Press, 1919), and E. F. Scott, *The Book of Revelation* (Scribner's, 1940) are useful. W. Ramsay's *The Letters to the Seven Churches* (Armstrong, 1909). Chapters 2 and 3 offer a detailed study of the background of Revelation.

ORGANIZATION

On *The Pastoral Epistles,* B. S. Easton (Scribner's, 1947) offers a clear, sound treatment of the important questions. H. Lietzmann, *The Beginning of the Christian Church* (Scribner's, 1949) treats the problem of organization in its broader context. B. H. Streeter's *The Primitive Church* (Macmillan, 1929) includes the "Apostolic Fathers" in his treatment. A. von Harnack's studies marked an epoch in the treatment of this topic, and his results are presented in *The Constitution and Law of the Church* (Putnam's, 1910). With his name should be coupled that of Edwin Hatch, *The Organization of the Early Christian Churches* (Rivington's, 1882).

BOOKS PRESENTING TEACHING

GENERAL

See R. Bultmann's *New Testament Theology,* vol. II (Scribner's, 1955); and M. Goguel, *The Birth of Christianity* (Macmillan, 1954), part IV.

JAMES

In addition to the usual commentaries in series, J. B. Mayor, *The Epistle of St. James* (Macmillan, 1913), should be mentioned. Though out-of-date in many respects, it is the fullest treatment in English.

SYNOPTIC GOSPELS

The books on these Gospels mentioned above under "Sources" are relevant here. Besides these, *The Synoptic Gospels,* by J. H. Ropes (Harvard, 1934), emphasizes their content, and deserves to be better known.

GOSPEL OF JOHN

A history of the problems is presented in W. F. Howard's *The Fourth Gospel in Recent Criticism,* revised by C. K. Barrett (Epworth Press, 1955). Howard's own conclusions are given in his *Christianity According to St. John* (Westminster, 1946). The role of the Holy Spirit is stressed—perhaps overstressed—in *The Gospel of the Spirit* by E. C. Colwell and E. Titus (Harper, 1953). The outstanding treatment in English is that of C. H. Dodd, *The Interpretation of the Fourth Gospel* (Cambridge, 1954). Students frightened by the array of languages which Dodd utilizes so easily should realize that he usually paraphrases the content of his quotations. The other great work on John, Bultmann's commentary, is not translated into English; but his results are available in his *New Testament Theology* (see above), volume II, part III.

Index of Names and Subjects

Index of Biblical References

417

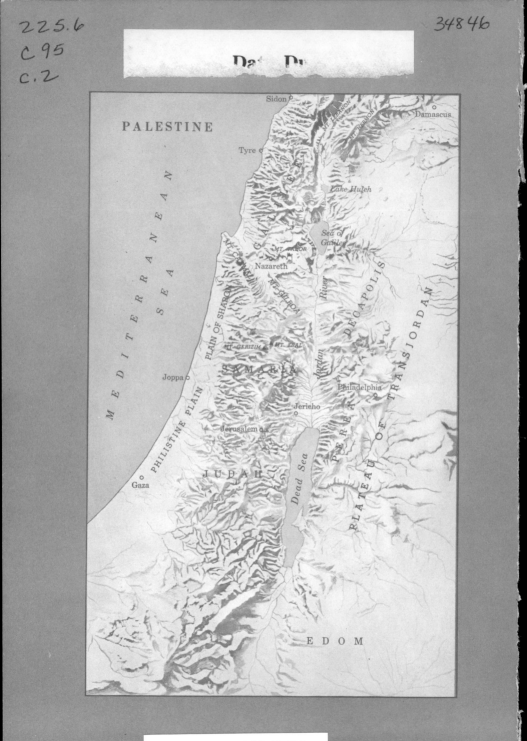